The
Darling Diaries

With Best Wishes

Stan Darling

dec 20/95

The
Darling Diaries
MEMOIRS OF A POLITICAL CAREER

STAN DARLING

with

Beth Slaney

Dundurn Press
Toronto • Oxford

Printed and bound in Canada by Best Book Manufacturers

The publisher wishes to acknowledge the generous assistance and ongoing support of the **Canada Council**, the **Book Publishing Industry Development Program** of the **Department of Canadian Heritage**, the **Ontario Arts Council**, the **Ontario Publishing Centre** of the **Ministry of Citizenship, Culture and Recreation**, and the **Ontario Heritage Foundation**.

Care has been taken to trace the ownership of copyright material used in the text (including the illustrations). The author and publisher welcome any information enabling them to rectify any reference or credit in subsequent editions.

J. Kirk Howard, Publisher

Canadian Cataloguing in Publication Data

Darling, Stan, 1911–
        The Darling diaries: memoirs of a political career.

ISBN 1-55002-253-9

1. Darling, Stan, 1911– 2. Canada – Politics – and government – 1935 – .* 3. Canada. Parliament. House of Commons – Biography. 4. Legislators – Canada – Biography. 5. Politicians – Canada – Biography. I. Slaney, Beth, 1922– . II. Title.

FC631.D37A3 1995   328.71'092   C95-932912-9
F1034.3.D37A3 1995

Dundurn Press Limited
2181 Queen Street East
Suite 301
Toronto, Canada
M4E 1E5

Dundurn Distribution
73 Lime Walk
Headington, Oxford
England
0X3 7AD

Dundurn Press Limited
1823 Maryland Avenue
P.O. Box 1000
Niagara Falls, N.Y.
U.S.A. 14302-1000

Contents

Progressive Conservative Party of Canada

Parti progressiste-conservateur du Canada

Tribute to Stan Darling

I met Stan Darling for the first time in 1984. I knew he was different from the moment he rose to speak at a national meeting of the Progressive Conservative Caucus. He was one of the older members of the Caucus but the issue he raised was the one issue most young people I knew at the time cared about, the environment.

Through the years, we came to admire this exceptional man who seems to have an insatiable appetite for life itself.

In the course of his political career, he has demonstrated how a single person can make a difference for his country and for all the generations that follow.

His personal initiative to fight acid rain marks the beginning of a long and protracted battle with the US government that finally led to the signing of the Clean-Air Act between Canada and the United States in 1991.

We owe this singular achievement in good part to Stan Darling and as Leader of the Progressive Conservative Party of Canada, I will forever remember him as a source of inspiration.

With best wishes,

[signature]

National Headquarters
275 Slater Street, Suite 501
Ottawa, Canada K1P 5H9
Telephone   613 238-6111
Fax   613 238-7429

Bureau national
275, rue Slater, bureau 501
Ottawa, Canada K1P 5H9
Téléphone 613 238-6111
Télécopieur 613 238-7429

Stan and William K. Reilly were presented with gold medals from the Americas Society for distinguished service in the cause of greater Canadian-American friendship and understanding on September 23, 1991 in New York. From left to right: Hon. William K. Reilly, Hon. Jean Charest (then minister of the environment), Stan Darling, and Ambassador George Landau, president of the Americas Society.

PROLOGUE

March 25, 1991 ... I have had to eat my words today, in front of a group of my acid rain peers. I stated some time ago that I would never live to see the day when a formal Acid Rain Control Treaty would be signed. The March 13th signing of the United States/Canada Air Quality Control Treaty which, received a great deal of media coverage, took place in the beautiful, former Reading Room, in the House of Commons, which later became the Progressive Conservative Caucus Room. There were a great many invited guests and the media were in full force.

Prime Minister Brian Mulroney paid tribute to the many people who had worked hard to bring this treaty about. He mentioned our former Washington ambassador, Allan Gotlieb, and the present ambassador, Derek Burney, as well as deputy ministers and other officials. However, he omitted to mention the Acid Rain Committee or any involvement that I had had for the past ten years or more. I was sort of disappointed about this.

Then, as he began to introduce President George Bush, Mr. Mulroney mentioned that there was one Member of Parliament in particular for whose work a special thanks should be made; the Member For Parry Sound/Muskoka, who he called, "Mr. Acid Rain." That certainly made me feel pretty good.

When Mr. Bush started to speak, he looked over to me and said, "Mr. Darling, I want to thank you most sincerely on behalf of the United States and Canada, for the great work you have done." This was certainly one of the highlights of my parliamentary career.

When the President was finished speaking, he walked over to me, shook my hand, and presented me with the gold pen he had used to sign the treaty. You can rest assured that this pen is a treasured momento and was not an inexpensive pen from Kresge's or Woolworth's. It received a lot of publicity across the country with newspaper headlines reading, "President Presents Pen to MP."

THE EARTH SUMMIT

Rio de Janeiro, June 1, 1992 ... The fact that 188 nations are meeting in Rio this week is worth headlines in every newspaper in the world. I arrived from Ottawa yesterday and, believe me, I was surprised and delighted to be asked to represent Canada at Earth Summit 92. Being a Canadian delegate at this conference is a real plum for me. Because of my ten-year involvement with acid rain and the environment I really wanted to attend, but so many others in Ottawa felt the same way, I didn't think I had a chance.

Secretary of State for External Affairs Barbara McDougall, and the minister of state for the environment, Pauline Brouse, were both all set to go to Rio. At the last minute, Prime Minister Mulroney would not approve either McDougall or Brouse. I had mentioned casually to Jean Charest, the minister of the environment, how much I would like to attend the conference and Charest said he would see what he could do. Just a week ago, he asked me if I could go for two weeks as a delegate. Needless to say I was delighted. The Hon. David MacDonald, Chairman of the Standing Committee on the Environment, was also a delegate, as were the NDP representatives Jim Fulton and Lynn Hunter, so we made an interesting Canadian group including Sheila Copps, Brian O'Kurley, Paul Martin, Marlene Catteral and others.

The United Nations had been planning Earth Summit Rio for over two years. Maurice Strong, who was to become Chairman of Ontario Hydro in the future, was United Nations Conference on Environmental Development (UNCED) Secretary-General, for the United Nations, responsible for the overall planning of the conference.

I understand that invitations have been sent out by the UN to heads of state of every country in the world. It must be the largest conference ever held and there will be, I am told, at least 120 of the world's leaders attending, all of whom will, we expect, speak at the plenary sessions during the next two weeks. I hope to hear President George Bush from the U.S., Prime Minister Mulroney, Prime Minister John Major of Great Britain, President Francois Mitterand from France, Chancellor Helmut Kohl from Germany, and many others.

Although it seems to me that the premise of the conference is to discuss worldwide environmental concerns, I expect to hear many other things of equal importance, especially from Third World countries. I assume that they will be in favor of pollution control but the fact that many of them are industrially *not* in a position to be much of a polluter at this time, doesn't stop them from wanting to become polluters with their own industrial bases. They may also feel that money spent to reduce pollution should be paid out by the polluters themselves, those who have caused acid rain pollution in the first place.

June 2 ... I heard today that one of the reasons Rio was picked for the conference is because of the RioCentro which will accommodate over 4,000 delegates at one time. Quite new, it has every appointment imaginable. Security in Rio is very tight, in fact it is out of this world. I've never seen more vigilant police and there are 25,000 soldiers and police guarding the heads of state and the delegates to the convention. Highways all around Rio are policed at every cross-road and there are armed tanks and Bren Gun carriers at the ready everywhere I look. It reminds me of an armed fortress. All those attending the sessions were approved months in advance of the conference, with a very few exceptions. We all want to see as much of Rio as possible but have been warned to not go out alone, and to stay away from the beaches, where roaming gangs are swarming people and causing anxiety and problems. It is easy to see the huge gulf here, between the very rich and the very poor, even though the government has not given us a guided tour of the slums of Rio!

Rio is a city of contrasts – absolute luxury in the upper 2 or 3 per cent, and absolute poverty for the rest. People are living in shacks with nothing and the crime rate is terrible. Street gangs roam everywhere, robbing and beating people. I was just told of two or three people who have been through this in the last little while. One was Lee Clark, MP, a professor at Brandon University in Manitoba, and the parliamentary secretary to Environment Minister Jean Charest, MP. Clark attended an earlier conference where he was robbed in broad daylight. We've all been warned by security to never walk along the beach alone, never take a camera with us, never wear jewelry or a watch. One Swedish diplomat, walking along the beach early in the conference, was threatened with broken beer bottles by a gang. Naturally, he handed over all his valuables and felt lucky to get away with his life.

Maurice Strong opened the first morning's session by stating: "Two years in the making, twenty years in anticipation, this twelve-day United Nations Conference which opens today in Rio de Janeiro, will do so in an atmosphere fraught with urgency and trepidation – but also with an almost surreal sense of exhilaration at the immensity of its task. No place on the planet can remain an island of affluence in a sea of misery. We are either going to save the whole world, or no one can be saved. One part of the world cannot live in an orgy of unrestrained consumption while the rest destroys its environment just to survive."

It occurred to me last night, as I climbed into bed at the Nacional Hotel, that the security is probably much tighter during the Earth Summit than at any other time in Rio's history. Police have put on a special campaign to round-up 15,000 street children, take them out of the city to a sort of concentration camp and keep them there until the summit is over.

Although this is the first such summit ever held, I am told, another one is set for two years from now. I've been trying to take in every speech I can, given by various heads of state and by experts in world environmental matters. Most are talking positively about how much their countries will do to reduce environmental problems. But when it comes down to dollars, there is some reluctance to spend very much. When world aid is discussed, Western countries have a benchmark of how much they will spend – 0.7 per cent of the GNP for Third World Aid, whether it is for food, expertise, or education. The United Nations in New York set this percentage some years ago, and all countries agreed to follow. Although very few, it seems to me, have ever achieved it. Canada is at 0.44 per cent, which is quite a way from the agreed-upon 0.7 per cent but it is still a lot of money. It is also higher than what is presently being spent by the United States, Great Britain, Japan, France or Germany. With the highest record of aid to other countries are the small countries such as Scandinavia, the Netherlands. Some of these are close to the 0.7 per cent, and Holland is above it.

Prime Minister Mulroney pledged that Canada would reach 0.7 by the year 2000 or in six years from now. It is difficult, when the countries which are considered the wealthiest in the world, are experiencing a recession and are struggling to get out of it. But, in the long run, any country can only dig down for the dollars that they can afford to give.

June 3 … I enjoy having other international parliamentarians observe "You are from Canada." As we all wear our security badges, it is easy to see where delegates are from. We Canadians also wear our Maple Leaf pins. So many people say, "What a wonderful country Canada is; Canadians are the most fortunate people in the world." I can't help answering with a few of my own thoughts. Yesterday, I found myself saying to a man from Kenya, "I wish you would come back to Canada with me and tell that to the Canadians. They are always complaining that Canada is not a good place to live."

I'm pleased to see how much other countries look up to Canada and many people from less fortunate countries have a deep reverence for our nation, even though there is 11 per cent unemployment in Canada. I've had conversations with people whose unemployment is much higher than that. Last month in Ottawa, I was dealing with several new Canadian citizens who were trying to get permission for their relatives to come to Canada. They felt that there was no hope for their own country. I've found that immigrants who do come to Canada work very, very hard, often taking jobs we Canadians wouldn't want. Most have two or more jobs, and live with ten other people in a house. And many wind up very successful. We Canadians wonder why!

It is gratifying to see that Mulroney's profile in Rio is among the highest of all senior heads of state. He is certainly one of the most senior. Canada's stature on the world scene is much greater than its population of 27 million people would warrant. We are also the second largest country in the world with great natural resources. We are a great trading nation and eighty per cent of our goods are exported. Canada would be in a very tough position if there were no trading arrangements and yet, the Canadian people, in their stupidity, scream against the Free Trade Agreement; if the agreement were not in place, the United States would have us right by the throat and could do anything they wanted. The latest example is the tribunal that found against the U.S. on the softwood lumber incident. Because of that, they are going to have to pay Canada $500 million in restitution of the duty they assessed Canadian lumber manufacturers.

As well as the Environmental Conference here in Rio, there is a well-publicized conference for private people and organizations and non-governmental organizations (NGOs) with representatives from around the world. Their meetings are all held outdoors on the famous Copacabana Beach. There are tents, little booths, receptions and concerts. It's all very emotional and very visible. All the delegates and participants have paid their own expenses to the conference and many countries, including Canada, have displays there. Our Indian Affairs Ministry has brought materials and displays concerning the environment and how it should be protected. Our native peoples have also brought displays and materials about many of their grievances in Canada.

On June 5th, on a hot, sunny morning, King Carl XVI Gustaf of Sweden, the president of the 1972 conference on the Human Environment in Stockholm, addressed a huge audience of a thousand or more on Copacabana Beach. He was standing on a platform with his back to the shining waters of the bay, and said, "After thousands and thousands of hours of work in preparing documents and negotiating texts and creating the conditions for success, we are now in the middle of the final negotiations. It is a time of uncertainty and confusion regarding the outcome. Words, expressions, and ideas are still floating in the air."

King Gustaf was planting a tree as a good symbol of the need for a long view, as he said, "beyond the lifetime of individuals." And as he said to the president of Brazil, H.E., lir. Fernando Collor, "We express our confidence in the future, in the potential for sustainable development and decent living conditions for all human beings."

It was a very moving experience to be a part of such a huge group.

June 6 … In a New York Times article this morning, journalist Joy Elliott said, "The summit security plans took over a year to devise and involved the mobilization of 25,000 Brazilian military and police all over Rio. Another sixty or so United Nations police work solely inside the RioCentro buildings."

Federal police started searching hotels which were to house foreign representatives before we arrived. They were looking for weapons and were setting up a 24-hour surveillance inside those hotels. Outside the hotels, we all notice the state military police patrolling streets on foot and in cars, making the city what they call, "an island of security." In tunnels and on the main streets, the army is "deployed" on a scheduled basis. We've also heard that there are security posts and checks throughout the city. Navy frigates, carrying combat divers, are patrolling the hotel coast. The bays are closed with special operations planned to deal with interlopers in speedboats. Roads and tunnels will be closed to through traffic from noon on June 11th till the 15th, when motorcades of arriving and departing presidents, prime ministers, princes, sheikhs and kings will be the only travellers. Heads of state, I understand, are allowed to bring their own personal security people in whatever quantity they wish. It seems a long way from Burks Falls, Ontario.

At the moment, our hotel manager says Rio is the most guarded city in the world. But headlines in the Rio paper stated today that the Director-

General of Brazil's federal police, Romeo Tuman said, he had planned the strictest possible security for the heads of state who are packing Earth Summit this week – *but* – he is also counting on "divine intervention" to back up his crack security squads!

Today, we attended Jean Charest's reception at the museum here. The Amway Corporation brought with them one of the largest and most outstanding displays of Innuit carvings and paintings ever shown, with everything from big statues to the most intricately carved figures. Among the familiar faces I've seen at the reception was John Denver, the singer, and I had the pleasure of shaking hands with him. There were over 500 invited guests here and Mr. Charest makes a knowledgeable and charming host.

Many displays on the Copacabana Beach stressed the environment and how it should be protected. There were thousands of people strolling along this beautiful beach, from all over the world.

June 7 … We're hard into the sessions today. It will be interesting to see how many countries actually sign the Biosphere Agreement. It is one of the most important aspects of the conference. Among the countries holding back are, surprisingly, United States, Saudi Arabia, and Iran. They are certainly *the* big oil producers and apparently do not want to recognize any interference with this production. Canada is taking a big interest. We are on the special buses which pick us up at our hotels every morning, by nine o'clock. There are not only the plenary sessions but also various side sessions to attend, which zero in on certain aspects of the environment.

Decisions are being made right, left and centre to sign the Biosphere Agreement before the conference ends, which will outline various improvements needed to eventually solve the pollution problems, worldwide. For example, reductions of acid rain and controls on forest cuttings; but I think this is easier said than done. Canada doesn't look all that great regarding our huge forest industry, where cutting is going on at a great rate, especially in British Columbia. Environmentalists don't want to see one more tree cut down in B.C. It's amazing to me that when the NDP party was in opposition, they were screaming all the time about forests being cut down and devastated. Now that they are in power, they find out that it is always easier to criticize than it is to set policy. There is much bad publicity in British Columbia right now about clear-cutting their forests.

John Crosbie, Canada's outspoken fisheries minister, and his wife Jane, asked me to accompany them to a special botanical garden party. This incredible garden is owned by the world famous botanist, Dr. Bertle Mark. We saw at least 3,000 different plants, flowers and shrubs on display. Our hosts took us on a tour and described all the different species. We were also guests at his reception in his fabulous hilltop home, which was full of artifacts and art from all over the world. Luncheon was served in this beautiful setting. A group of Brazilian natives were selling their handicrafts and we were their best customers. We also enjoyed a display of tribal dancing and music. Dr. Mark's home was high in the hills, among the trees, with a breathtaking view in every direction, overlooking Rio de Janeiro. I thought it was wonderful to be with the owner and to hear his descriptions in his own words.

Between the two hotels where our Canadian delegates are housed, there is a "beautiful" waterway which runs through the gardens to the beach and on to the sea. I just found out today that it is really an open sewer, with raw sewage running between these two superb hotels. The smell, at times, is awful and it seems incredible to me that Brazil is so unthinking and uncaring to show its pollution so obviously to people from other countries. And especially at an international conference on the environment!

Delegates were told that several large shopping centres in Rio are offering special displays for foreign visitors to the summit. The Barra Centre, near RioCentro, is organizing a fruit and flower fair, called Brazil in Nature. Twenty-five bilingual attendants will help foreign customers to appreciate the orchids, camellias, African violets, fiber handicrafts and exotic fruits from the Amazon. As one of the past presidents of the Agricultural Society of Ontario it will be interesting for me to see the flora and fauna of another country. Incidentally, my next-room neighbor at the hotel said that they were amused to note the names of the popular movies being shown down the street from us. They include: Fried Green Tomatoes, The Gladiator, and Bugsy. So much for foreign films!

June 8 ... If and when the Biosphere Treaty is signed by heads of state, the next steps seem to be to make sure that legislation will be brought in, in all our own countries, to carry out these promises. I consider the treaty a "memorandum of intent," to do *something*, whether or not the polluter countries really try to do something positive about these major, and worldwide, problems. Every country is certainly well aware that, because of its industrial growth, something must be done and done soon. Some very positive commitments have already been made, and made publicly. That so many countries are speaking frankly about their problems, is, to me, the major accomplishment of the summit. As I looked around RioCentro today, I realized that every country attending could return home after the conference ends, and agitate for changes.

Sao Paulo … This, the second largest city in the world, seems a long way from Burks Falls. Jean Charest is attending a trade fair here and he asked me to come along too. Each person attending has paid his own way and I was pleased to hand over my $200 airfare. There are twelve of us Canadians on the special chartered plane.

It is amazing to walk into this immense building, housing the fair, and see Canada's huge red and white flag dominating the building. The Royal Canadian Mounted Police are very much in evidence, and tour guides from Canada are dressed in very visible red jackets. There are about twenty different Canadian industrial exhibits to see here, primarily on the environment. Mr. Charest was all set to open the Canadian section of the fair when he suggested that we walk around the hall first to see the various countries' displays. When Mr. Charest was about to cut the ceremonial ribbon to declare Canada's exhibit officially open, he asked that I be the one to cut the ribbon. I was overwhelmed by his generosity as, of course, he didn't have to do this; he just wanted to pay a special tribute to someone who had been involved in the fight to improve the environment for so long. This was certainly another highlight in my life.

Unfortunately, we couldn't stay to see much of Sao Paulo as we had to return immediately to the conference in Rio. We both felt that those companies with such upbeat displays here, would eventually receive a great deal of business from attending the fair. It attracted many thousands of people from all over the world.

Paul Martin, who is a Member of the Opposition, and on the Environment Committee, is one of the most vocal people at the conference.

With our tight schedule, there is very little time to sight-see. But one thing I have to see is the huge, 120-foot Statue of Christ of the Andes before I leave Rio. From pictures in National Geographic and other places, I have been haunted by the statue for years. Today, officials of the summit kindly provided a car and driver for me and Brian O'Kurley to drive to the top of the mountain to see this amazing structure. We were warned that there might be a bit of fog although the sun was shining when we started out. We drove up to the final 330 steps and as we climbed to the top, very slowly I might add, the statue was completely veiled in fog. We decided to climb up anyway. In front of the statue, there was a long ramp. We were standing about one hundred feet in front of the statue and couldn't see a thing but fog. All of a sudden, the fog cleared away and there was this incredible Statue of Christ, moving eerily in and out of the fog in front of me. It was one of the most moving experiences I have ever had. I was able to take some photographs before the fog settled in again.

At Rio Summit, I have listened to and have seen some of the most important people in the world. On June 4, I listened to His Excellency Archbishop Renato R. Martino, head of the Holy See Delegation from the Vatican. He said, "The ultimate purpose of environmental and developmental programs is to enhance the quality of human life, to place creation in the fullest way possible at the service of human family. The ultimate determining factor is the human person." I learned later that these thoughts were first voiced by Pope John Paul II to the United Nations Centre for the Environment in Nairobi on August 18, 1985.

June 9 ... Before breakfast this morning, I received a memo addressed to all members of the Canadian delegation: It said, in part, "There is a possibility that some terrorist organizations may be looking at this very important conference as a way to advance their particular agendas. They could attempt to draw attention to their cause by disrupting the conference or by launching an action against targets in its vicinity. Delegates are advised to be alert to unusual activity or behavior. The safety of the conference is in the hands of the authorities; in this case the Brazilian police and related security bodies, such as Interpol." This, somehow, did not seem out-of-place in the middle of this heavily guarded city. But we will all keep our eyes wide open.

The executive director of the United Nations Population Fund, Nafia Sadik, told us today, "If there are no debates on population at the conference, it is not because there is a lack of awareness over the issue. It is because the South does not want any other issue apart from the environment and development to cloud the Rio agenda. Many delegates here however feel that fundamental issues of development, vis-a-vis the population issue, are vital to the planning of our future."

The most visible television crew here is NHK, the Japanese media giant. Its large crew conducts innumerable interviews of delegates and summit participants every day and records each individual response to every question asked. The director of TV is 61-year-old Tsuneo Fukada, who said that he knew very little about environmental issues before coming to the conference. Top cameraman is 61-year-old Mitsuo Numate. I felt right at home with their crew!

We can't begin to carry around all the press kits, speeches, information packages and hand-outs. Today I received a "Schedule of Parallel Events" from summit organizers which include documentation on the following:

- the women and shelter network, and human settlements workshops;
- a round table on urban and industrial issues;

- the transfer of problems of ecologically and socially sustainable projects within the field of agriculture and agro-forestry;
- gender dimensions of environment and development;
- round table biotechnology;
- green belt movement as it affects the environment, development, women and human rights;
- information and hydroelectric projects; and
- development alternatives with women for a new era (DAWN), our first environment is ourselves.

It occurs to me that there is a difference here between "people" concerned with the environment and "women" concerned with similar problems. It is impossible to attend every workshop and still hear the world leaders, which, to me in any case, is vital.

I expect we will all be charged for overweight luggage on the trip back to Ottawa!

RioCentro, where the main sessions are taking place, is nearly twenty miles from downtown Rio and is 600,000 square meters in size, with three huge halls for big sessions and long corridors, walkways and a warren of offices. Security is the main topic of conversation at the sessions and outside the center there are demonstrations and protesters all around Centro. Police deal with their angry speeches constantly. "We always knew that conditions would be adverse," one UNCED officer understated today. All of this is, of course, well covered by the press.

A spokesman for the daily paper, Earth Summit Times, which covers all the happenings in, around and concerning the summit said today, "In the twenty-seven years I have been directly involved in newspaper affairs, I have never encountered a more dedicated and devoted group of journalists, than those we have assembled for this newspaper in Rio. Under the most trying circumstances, they have labored for twelve to twenty hours a day, sometimes more, to produce a newspaper of quality and relevance." All of us from Canada certainly depend on the Summit Times for an accurate recap of happenings and a summary of upcoming events. I hope the writers are well paid.

Although not in attendance at the conference, Boris Yeltsin is certainly one of the most talked-about figures participating. His address, which was circulated to the conference as a whole, called for a Global Environmental Monitoring System which would include its space components as well. Under the United Nations Environmental Program's Earth Watch program, the UN put together the Global Environmental Monitoring System that today relies on remote sensing from space, together with ground-based data collection. We were told that this informs governments and the public about environmental conditions and trends for many natural resource components of the Biosphere. It also rates loss of arable soil, and such vital aspects of our planet. Even if Boris Yeltsin couldn't get to the conference in person, he has certainly made his point before the Earth Summit delegates and heads of state.

I've heard a lot of talk about the environment since arriving here ten days ago, but no one has impressed me more than Gro Harlem Brundtland, prime minister of Norway, Chair of the World Commission on the Environment and Development. She summed up her remarks by saying, "Faced with these challenges and ever-dwindling natural resources, I see the Rio Earth Summit as a rung of the ladder leading to what will have to come; a better organized world community where we pool our resources as well as our formal sovereignties in order to obtain more real sovereignty and choices for the future, not foreclosing the choices of future generations."

Going down in the elevator to the hotel coffee shop this morning, a delegate said, "Heads of state and government leaders will not end this two-week conference next week; they will make the decisions reached here last and endure." Everyone on the elevator nodded in agreement.

Glancing through the newspaper left on our bus today, I read an article by Walter Russell Mead of the Los Angeles Times who must have been harassed, as some of us are, with the huge piles of research we receive daily. "The political manoeuvring here in Rio is intense. Nobody wants to make any sacrifices to help the environment, and nobody wants to be blamed for the consequences. The result, expressed in thousands of official documents consuming the paper production of whole provinces of Brazilian rain forests, is a mass of hypocritical platitudinizing unmatched in the history of the world."

Having driven around my vast Parry Sound/Muskoka riding in every kind of weather, including the moose season, I thought I'd seen everything but I am delighted to not be driving around Rio. There are many car rental companies near our hotel including Hertz, Avis, Budget, National, Nobre, Unidas and Interlocadora. But few automatic cars are for hire. Even the Brazilian president says that the locally-made cars are "wagons and hopelessly outdated." I think the secret to road survival in Rio is to figure out what the "lunatics" on the road are planning to do and go in the other direction!

I understand the representatives of major countries are quartered at the neighboring Rio Palace Hotel. They include Sweden, Switzerland, Norway, Liechtenstein, Iceland, Finland, Peru, Denmark, Iran, Quatar, and others.

Perhaps never before in our world's history have so many world leaders assembled in one place for a common cause. This is a tribute to growing human maturity. However, the man in the seat beside me on this morning's bus to the conference pointed out that a team of government scientists are currently mapping changes in the earth's surface. The latest satellite imagery pictures suggest that the richest forests of the United States may be in worse shape than the tropical rain forests of South America. I thought about the past ten years of hard work with our American friends in the field of acid rain reduction!

June 10 ... Today's most compelling headline states: "Canada eager to talk fishing." Canada's minister of fisheries and oceans, John Crosbie, told journalists last Saturday, after UNCED's main committee approved the conference resolution, "We are going to be dealing with the states and countries involved, principally the European Community and South Korea, and we are trying to get those problems resolved." John, whom I am happy to call a friend, referred to the problems of overfishing on the high seas. He is keen to start bilateral talks with "the suspected culprits" right away.

In a city where poverty and its pernicious bedfellows, malnutrition, disease and homelessness, occupy too many citizens of South America's largest country, the Brazilian people seem uninterested in UNCED. No, those are not my words, although in many ways I agree with them. They were said recently by Lance Gould, a journalist with the Earth Summit Times. He continues, "Most people here in Brazil seem more upset about their own country's economic hardships than in the environmental hardships outside it. Summit 92 is all marketing to make Brazil look *good*. The highway from the airport is new, but our schools are starved for money. So, Rio has set its table while much of Brazil worries about its next meal. Economically, said the publisher of a Sao Paulo paper, "Brazil is in the Third World and we are slipping into the Fourth."

I've tried to pick up a copy of every talk given by heads of state. Among the highlights so far are:

- A very frank talk by the Hon. Philip Leakey, minister for environment and natural resources, Kenya, who stated, "Kenya firmly believes that prevention is better than cure; and education on environmental issues is the shortest and most effective route in preventing further environmental degradation."
- Scotland's Andy Wightman spoke about his country's devastated forest and suggests the following things must be done immediately: (1) Admit

to the forest crisis in Scotland and other Northern countries. (2) Effectively protect, manage and expand natural forest areas. (3) Introduce land reform to ensure forest protection and management. (4) Reduce consumption of certain wood products. (5) Contribute to international efforts to protect, sustain and restore forest land in Scotland, and worldwide. A tall order, we all agreed, but not out of line with Canada's thinking.

• Jacques Cousteau, spoke movingly about the capacity of our planet to sustain life, and of the confusion between; instruction and education, pleasure and joy, money and morality, tradition and innovation and the individual risk we are imposing on others.

Czechoslovakia, Jordan, the Netherlands, the International Oil Pollution Compensation Fund, the Food and Agriculture Organization of the United Nations, the Emir of the State of Kuwait, the World Food Program, the Union of Myanmar, the Petroleum and Mineral Resources, Kingdom of Saudi Arabia, Ecology and Natural Resources of the Russian Federation, the Federative Republic of Brazil, Ministry of the Environment, State of Israel, the Republic of Estonia, Latvia and Lithuania, the Republic of Nauru, His Majesty the King of Sweden, Her Excellency, Madame Vigdis Finnbogadottir, president of Iceland, the president of the United Republic of Tanzania, H.E. Ali Hassan Mwinyi, were present at these sessions, and many many others. As well, George Bush, John Major, Helmut Kohl, Francois Mitterand, and, of course, Brian Mulroney – they all made major addresses. Some were thoughtful, some were intriguing by what they did *not* say.

Prime Minister Mulroney began his address with these words: "Our generation has seen our planet from space. We know its beauty, and understand its fragility. The reconciliation of economic development and environmental preservation is not only necessary, it is inescapable. We are the leaders."

Mr. Mulroney, who was well received by those attending his session, discussed the debt initiative for the least developed countries, sub-Saharan Africa and Commonwealth Caribbean countries, with forgiveness of loans from Canada totalling in the billions of dollars. In Canada, he said, some months ago, "the Canadian Government provides $115 million per year to the IDRC (International Development Research Centre), and we intend to maintain this contribution. We will also double our contribution to the United Nations Environment Program to $11 million over the next five years. Our government will also participate in a three-year United Nations Development Plan to assist developing countries prepare national sustainable development plans. Canada's Green Plan has been well-received by United Nations agencies and it has been suggested as a model for other countries. With a $2 million contribution from our Green Plan and the $8 million budget of the UNDP project, Canada will make available its expertise gained in developing the Green Plan."

Some officials and delegates listening to Mr. Mulroney said, "Canada seems prepared to put its money where its mouth is."

I'm taking home a copy of the Earth Pledge which states: "Recognizing that people's actions towards nature and each other are the source of growing damage to the environment and resources needed to meet human needs and to ensure survival and development, I pledge to act to the best of my ability to help make the Earth a secure and hospitable home for present and future generations."

Let's face it, George Bush is not the most popular delegate at this conference! One summit reporter likens the U.S. involvement in Earth Summit to, "The Planet versus the president of the United States. As the President talks about initiative on forest protection and developing nations, the rest of the world agrees on a Biodiversity Treaty. The president says it's too expensive and saves his greatest passion for that most critical of environmental issues: who leaked a memo designed to embarrass the Head of the Environmental Protection Agency? So much for deforestation, global warming, the greenhouse effect and the world community."

Another reporter carries right on in the same vein: "Meanwhile, the Earth Summit's success is being jeopardized by the Bush Administration's refusal to sign a convention protecting the diversity of nature because of disagreements and the way they are paid for."

President Bush is certainly the man receiving the most publicity at the summit. Comments I heard today about Bush and the United States were very upsetting. Several people had read an article in the Washington Post, reprinted in the Jornal Do Brasil, that stated in no uncertain terms: "For President Bush and the United States, the United Nation's environmental conference in Rio de Janeiro is turning into a huge fiasco. The Americans have got themselves entirely isolated and are now publicly browbeating small countries such as Austria and Switzerland for supporting positions that embarrass the United States. It's hardly a display of deft diplomacy." On the one hand, critics say, President Bush and his government seem to want a world agreement on forest management to preserve and protect the diversity of life that inhabits them, and to help stabilize the global climate. On the other hand, their administration flatly refuses to have anything to do with the treaties on biodiversity and global warming presented in Rio. But, in all fairness, it is not only President Bush who thinks the treaties are flawed. I have heard much talk that it would transfer money much too loosely and jeopardize established patent rights.

The bottom line? We must consider the terms of life on the planet over the next generation and continue to search for ways to keep the ever-expanding population, who scramble for a better way of life, from making life much worse for everyone in both rich and poor countries alike. Perhaps because I have been around for a few years, I find nothing new in that concern.

June 11 ... I learned today of the Summit Ostrich Prize 1992. It has been presented to three countries during the past couple of days. They were chosen from all participating countries in UNCED, as those countries responsible for the worst performances at the summit. Winners were, the United States of America, Saudi Arabia, and the United Kingdom. The awards were presented by a group of NGOs (non-governmental organizations), Friends of the Earth International, Greenpeace International and several other such groups who search to identify constructive actions in their countries. Finding none, they decided to root-out the worst of a bad bunch. According to a journalist friend in Rio, the NGOs consulted, and all agreed that, the United States' behavior has been the most negative, harmful and irresponsible. The group formed these decisions by recalling that the "United States opposed, blocked and undermined the initiatives on climate change, biodiversity, biotechnology, models of consumption, weapons of mass destruction and the elimination of nuclear wastes."

Saudi Arabia came a close second, for many of the same reasons. The United Kingdom's award was based on the fact that "it has always claimed the role of leader while running after the United States president, George Bush, and for hindering the signing of the Biodiversity Convention, opposing advances on climate research and promoting feeble provisions for furthering sustainable development after the summit." I would be interested to hear what President Bush and Prime Minister Major, among others, say about this dubious "award."

Movie star Jane Fonda and her husband Ted Turner have both been very visible and vocal throughout Summit 92. She was a major attraction, I have been told, in the Global Forum at Flamengo Park, where she spoke to over a thousand people. She has been very critical of the U.S. government and has been quoted as saying, "President Bush may lose votes for not signing the Biodiversity Convention."

Time alone will tell!

The talk around our hotel is that the Rio Conference itself has been important because it marks the point at which just about all the world's governments have acknowledged at least in principle, that they can deal with their deepest environmental concerns only by working together across the borders of the world.

To me, and to many people I have worked with for the past ten years regarding acid rain, this will mean sending resources, money and technology from the rich countries to the poor ones in exchange for more effective conservation and pollution control. However, the terms of that exchange are not clear and they frequently raise more issues than they solve. All in all, the 1992 Earth Summit has been, I think, a dynamic and creative conference, resulting in the creation of the UN Commission on Sustainable Development. Twelve members of the European Community have decided during the conference to sign the Convention on Climate and Biodiversity, and Japan will follow the European countries. The United States is the only major industrialized nation which has refused to sign. The signing countries have also said "yes" to signing the agreement to control emissions of polluting gasses, which are responsible for the greenhouse effect. The convention has called for the reduction of these volumes of emissions by the year 2000 when, it is expected, they will be down to 1990 levels. The European countries are certainly showing the ecological way forward to the developing nations.

The lumber-exporting countries in Southeast Asia, led by Malaysia, have turned down the American proposal, which includes international control of the rain forests and sets limits to reduce the cutting of these forests. While these talks are still going on here, Brazil seems to prefer a declaration of intention on the forest issues, rather than sign an agreement for the safeguarding of the world's resources. Brazilians, however, seem willing, from what I have heard, to accept a modified version of the American proposal. Of course, the bottom line in all these talks is, "Who will pay?"

Rio has planned superb entertainment for the summit delegates. On Sunday, British actor Jeremy Irons will host the Concert for Life, with Placido Domingo, trumpeter Wynton Marsalis and about twenty other top stars, most of which, I sadly admit, I have never heard of. It will be seen by thousands of people "in person," and on three giant screens on the other side of Lagoa, near the Parque de Catacumba, and, of course, around the world by satellite.

It is intriguing to think of my family and friends watching this same program in the Almaguin Highlands, while I am in Rio.

June 12 … There wasn't a dissenting voice today when conference

Chairman Ambassador Tommy Koh of Singapore, bowed to a standing ovation. The main committee finished its work at 6 a.m. yesterday, as Koh had pushed his group with a mixture of force and good humor to clean up as much of the unresolved agenda as possible. I was one of the many who agreed with Angela Harkavy, of the National Wildlife Federation, who said, "The global partnership has been formed, even if some had to be brought in kicking and screaming."

June 13 ... The last word on this incredible two-week summit in Rio de Janeiro has got to be from Secretary-General Maurice Strong. In a moving wrap-up yesterday, he told a packed house that not many specific commitments could be expected but strong and categorical declarations from rich and poor countries were heard, who felt that they were making a tremendous political investment in the Rio Summit Conference. "The world cannot be changed overnight," Strong said. "I am hearing both rich and poor countries saying clearly, that the survival of humanity needed to be debated." And debated it has been!

Our ultimate host, the president of Brazil, H.E. lir. Fernando Collar, summed things up pretty well. "Today, the main goal lying in the minds and hearts of those in Rio is the firm intention to find a better order, with a view to saving life on earth. May God help us."

Although we leave this beautiful city with a great deal to think about, we won't miss the temperatures which today reached well over 90°F!

June 23, Ottawa ... Rio Earth Summit 92 was definitely a step in the right direction. However, there were certainly no earth-shaking announcements from which we Canadians will see immediate benefits to our environment. But let's not kid ourselves – we've got to keep pressuring. With 33,000 delegates, 188 countries, and nearly 120 heads of state present, something good must come out of Earth Summit 92. I left Rio with several strong impressions and understandings: the conference was successful because of the accomplishments achieved by the participating countries, and the number of agreements that were signed.

As well, clear-cutting in Brazilian rain forests will be drastically reduced, and certainly, gains in fighting global warming have been made.

But, perhaps my most important impression was to learn what other nations think of Canada. Our prestige is right at the top of the list. It was an unforgettable experience to be at the summit, as one of a very small, select group, and a real thrill to be a delegate from Canada.

EARLY POLITICAL DAYS
Burks Falls and Ontario

October 27, 1993 ... I was told today in no uncertain terms to start cleaning out my files, so that my long-time secretary in my riding, Ina Trolove, can start boxing things up in order to close down our offices. The election is over, my twenty-one years in Ottawa are over, and the next part of my life is beginning.

In a huge file marked "speeches," I came across one which is undated, but speaks for itself. It begins: "For the past twenty-one years, I have faithfully served my Parry Sound/Muskoka constituents to the best of my ability. During those years, I am proud to say that I was able to garner an unbroken track record of six consecutive election victories, many times when the public opinion polls were running against our party and our government. Overall, I have been in the unique situation of having served over fifty consecutive years in public life – five years as a Burks Falls councillor, twenty-six years as the Reeve of Burks Falls and twenty-one years as your Member of Parliament.

"From where I sit, there is no greater satisfaction than that of being entrusted with a position of public confidence, enabling you to help your fellow citizens overcome obstacles and maybe make their lives just a bit better for the effort." I was asked recently why I had allowed my name to stand for Reeve and then for Member of Parliament, and I think I covered the reason in this speech. I said, "Perhaps there is no more difficult task in a lifetime than that of making a decision to finally call it a day on a way of life and a career that has brought so much personal pleasure and joy. I always fought the good fight to ensure that all areas of Parry Sound/Muskoka received their fair share of federal financial assistance, grants and programs."

It all started in 1941. An old Burks Falls friend, Albert A. Agar, suggested that I run for Municipal Council. He said that he was going to put my name up and he did. In those days, nobody wanted the job, so I won the position by acclamation. Mr. Agar was criticized by some of the prominent business men on the main street, who wanted to know why he recommended me, saying that I would never amount to anything. In any event, I served on council for five years.

In 1945 I ran for reeve and was elected by acclamation. I held that position for twenty-six years, completing my last term in 1972. The salary for councillor then was $26 a year, based on thirteen meetings a year at $2 per meeting. When I became reeve the salary was increased to $39 a year. During all those years, I was only contested in 1966. I was often asked the reason for my success. I replied that people seemed to be satisfied with the way I handled the job. And, I pointed out, my salary was not exactly enticing, and many people did not want the job. After talking with the Toronto Star, which had enquired about my "longevity" in politics, it stated in their headlines next day: "Reeve Attributes Long Service to Low Pay."

For many years I was a member of the Parry Sound Municipal Association, serving three consecutive years as president. They eventually passed a motion that you could serve two years only in succession.

I was also involved in the Ontario Mayor's and Reeve's Association and was honorary treasurer for some years.

I was persuaded to throw my hat in the political ring and run for the PC provincial nomination for the Parry Sound District in 1971. I was unsuccessful and figured that my aspirations for higher political office were finished. But when Federal MP Gordon Aiken was retiring, I was persuaded to consider running in his place. He announced his retirement in December 1971 and it took effect on October 30, 1972, following the federal election.

Around this time I had a visit from Hugh Mackenzie of Huntsville, early in 1972. He was announcing his candidacy for position of MP, in other words, he was contesting the Conservative nomination. After a great deal of small talk with Hugh and the president of the association, Don Harnsworth, and in answer to their little quiet smiles, I said, "I know what is going through your minds, but the answer to your unspoken question, "Am I going to run or not in this riding?" is No. I will admit that I have had a few people ask me, but that's as far as it has gone, so you are off and running with a good head start."

It was not until two weeks before nomination day that I finally decided to throw my hat in the ring. I was getting many phone calls and a great deal of support from Conservatives in the Parry Sound district Aiken had served for fifteen years. The night of the nomination was stormy and icy. We were warned to keep off the roads, but despite this, bus loads of people came in from Parry Sound and other areas. With about 1,000 present in Huntsville, I won by twenty-five votes over Hugh Mackenzie, who has remained a tower of strength and a good friend. He has helped me to get re-elected each time.

I came across a clipping today, from the 1944 North Bay Nugget which really started me remembering. The heading was "CCF elects candidate in Parry Sound." It was dated September 13, Callander. "The CCF Convention was held at Magnetawan to nominate a candidate for the riding of Parry Sound for the next federal election. About 180 people attended. Ninety-nine delegates took part and this was one of the largest crowds to ever attend a convention in Magnetawan. The meeting was a decided success. Those nominated were: Roy P. Smith, MPP for Parry Sound, P.J. Keeling, Callander, the Reeve of Callander and CNR agent there, Stanley Darling of Burks Falls, C.E. Culbert of Burks Falls, Earl Taylor of Parry Sound, Delmer Vondette, Parry Sound and Emerson Bushy of Parry Sound. Two who declined to enter the list after being nominated were Roy Smith and P.J. Keeling. The voting was by single ballot and the results of the third ballot were Taylor 49, Darling 43."

There was a busy political atmosphere in Ontario then. I remember a key person in the early 1940s, John Collingwood Reade, who was well respected in the broadcast and journalism field. Reade was one of the leaders in the Leadership League, formed by Globe and Mail publisher George McCullough. It was formed to prod the government into becoming more aware of and involved with the "common man." I was instrumental in bringing Reade as a guest speaker to Burks Falls.

Jim Coleman, a popular sports writer for the Globe was also a League member, doing speaking engagements far and wide. CCF Leader Edward (Ted) Joliffe also travelled around the province and I accompanied him some of the time.

I also asked Agnes McPhail, the first woman Member of Parliament to come to Burks Falls and we had the pleasure of entertaining her in our home. As well, Dr. James G. Endicott, a United Church minister, was very much a left-wing politician, and was classed a communist because of his views. He was also a Burks Falls guest. He died recently at the age of 90.

At that time, Roy Smith won the provincial election of 1943 by about 740 votes over Fred Johnstone of Sundridge, the Johnstone family were not too happy with me at the time.

All this was good experience for what was to become my life work. I was a member of many provincial organizations as Reeve of Burks Falls, from the Ontario Good Roads Association to the Ontario Mayor's and Reeve's

Association, where I was honorary treasurer for years, and in the end, vice-president. After I entered Parliament, of course, I became ineligible to become president.

Some people accused me of being "very vocal," and perhaps I didn't mind speaking out when I was convinced that I was right. I recall one meeting at the Ontario Science Centre in Toronto. Ab Campbell was Metro Chairman, the Mayor of Toronto was William Dennison. He was bemoaning the fact that Toronto was not getting its fair share of tax money from the provinces. I stood up, took a handkerchief out of my pocket, wiped my eyes and said, "The words of the Mayor of Toronto really bring tears to my eyes, as Toronto is hard done by. Every time I come to Toronto, there are new skyscrapers going up all the time while in the village of Burks Falls, if there is so much as a new backhouse built, we are delighted." After the meeting, the Mayor said to Mr. Campbell, "Ab, you are not going to associate with this awful fellow after what he has just said about Toronto are you?"

Looking through some photographs this morning I came across one taken in 1957. I was president of the Georgian Bay Development Association at that time. The General Manager was Neville Keefe, and he arranged with those in charge of the upcoming Canadian visit of Queen Elizabeth and Prince Philip to have them come to our area for a brief visit. The Royal train came from Washago arriving at the Parry Sound station. The guests were presented to Her Majesty and Prince Philip. Mona and I were platform guests and many people said, "How come the Reeve of Burks Falls is able to meet the Queen when so many prominent people are not included?"

Mona was quite concerned about what she should wear but I had told her to stop worrying – everyone would be looking at the Queen. However, this did not go over very well with Mona.

I had the chance to talk with Prince Philip. He asked if my job with the Georgian Bay Development Association was full-time. I replied, "Since there is no salary attached to it, I do have another job, in the insurance and real estate business." Prince Philip then asked about the local economy. I replied that tourism was the most important industry and the Prince then asked how long the season lasted each year. Meaning to say, two months, I inadvertently replied, "Two weeks." I then corrected that statement and mentioned that the season ran from the 24th of May till Labor Day, but with the peak season being the last week of July and the first week of August – a very short season. In his forthright way, Prince Philip replied, as he turned to talk with another guest, "Yes, but they make a bloody killing."

In repeating this to tourist people, they all seemed to take a dim view of the Prince's remarks.

Following our brief informal talk, there was a motorcade to the government wharf where the Royal yacht HMS *Britannia* was anchored offshore as she was too big to tie up at the dock.

At about this time, there were five development associations in Ontario. Toronto wanted to get into the association but we would have no part of Toronto. An umbrella association was then formed called the Ontario Organization of Regional Development Associations. Presidents were elected annually and included: Charlie Griffen of Barrie; Mayor Les Cook of Barrie; Gordon Mallion of Tottenham, Willard Kinzie of Barrie. Eventually I was elected president, with the next annual meeting taking place in Burks Falls.

The Burks Falls Council worked very hard to bring in new industry and business, without much success initially.

When I was reeve, in the early years, the nearest liquor store was in Huntsville and the town businessmen were interested in attracting one for Burks Falls. After much government lobbying, a site in South River on Highway 11 was chosen. It was the home town of the incumbent member of the provincial parliament, Allister Johnston. A few years later the Department of Agriculture decided to also locate a sales barn and government stock yards in the same village. Needless to say, I told him that this was not fair to other villages. We were being by-passed by several such projects.

The one thing we wanted to be assured of was that Highway 11 would continue to go through our village, and the village by-pass did not come about until I was no longer reeve.

Burks Falls had set its heart on a liquor store and after much wheeling and dealing, spearheaded by Herb Hunter, who operated the variety store, and a petition being circulated, there were only two businessmen who had not signed it. One was John Fell, who operated Hotel Central, and the other was Reeve Stan Darling.

With Ted Boyes, I took the petition to Toronto and saw the General Manager of the Liquor Control Board who said they would approve a store for Burks Falls but could not find funds to build it. Should we be able to build it, the Liquor Control Board would rent it from us. As Ted Boyes was a contractor, we formed a partnership then and there to build it. With an excellent property close to the main street, we put together a holding company and started to work. When work was under way, the United Church minister, Reverend Russell May, took exception, went to the village office and said he would start a petition against the liquor store. I pointed out that the person spearheading the petition was the chairman of the board of stweards of his church. He was quite surprised to hear this.

I said go ahead with your petition, but who will sign it? Every businessman in town, but two, had already signed the one to have the liquor store located here. He looked over our signed petition, and the next Sunday preached a sermon on the evils of alcohol, and that was the last we ever heard about it.

Burks Falls was a very busy place those days and among many other projects we built the Burks Falls High School in the early 1950s. We built a new 225,000 gallon water tower with a cost of over $25,000. We installed water and sewers to property. In 1948, we built the Red Cross Hospital with a council grant of $15,000 toward the cost of $225,000. Burks Falls was chosen over other villages because we had municipal water, cheap hydro and a high school. During its many years of service, the hospital delivered over 4,000 babies, including my three grandsons.

We built various buildings to house the Agricultural Society, which are still in use today and I became president of the Ontario Association of Agricultural Societies in 1957.

The one year that I was president, the convention was held in Toronto at the King Edward Hotel. The Mayor of Toronto was always invited and that year it was Nathan Phillips, known far and wide as the Knife and Fork Mayor. No matter what guests were served at the dinners he attended, Mayor Phillips always received roast beef. I mentioned to him that we had something in common. "We have both been serving our municipal governments for over 15 years but with a big difference in our remuneration." I said, "Your Worship received $15,000 a year as Mayor; you also received honorariums as a member of the police commission, the hydro commission etc. while I received the princely amount of $39 per year." Mayor Phillips looked me over, and smiled, saying, "Well, you are probably not worth a damn cent more."

Not all the projects undertaken by the council went through smoothly. The replacement of our old 39,000 gallon water tower is a fine example. Mr. G.D. Martin, president of Thompson Heyland, approached us with an offer. If he could receive a suitable fire insurance rate, to install sprinklers in his plant, he would require a storage tank which held at least 75,000 gallons of water. It would have to be heated during the winter and I discussed this with him. He agreed that it would be appropriate for his firm and the municipality to cooperate. We eventually had a new stand pipe installed. The cost of the new tank was $21,000 with the money borrowed at 7 per cent. The interest was over a twenty year period, which came to the cost of the tank itself. The council made an agreement with the company whereby the company would pay the town $1,000 a year for 20 years, so we ended up with a new water tank at half price with a 225,000 gallon capacity. Both parties were happy.

Dr. A.W. Partridge of Burks Falls owned property which bordered the southern boundary of Burks Falls limits. He also owned property which had been a tannery. This property had a deep ninety-four-foot well with plenty of water but of poor quality. He requested of the council permission to install water to his Armour township property and agreed to pay the costs. I asked him to agree to let the village have the rights to this well in case there was ever an emergency shortage of water. He asked what, if any, emergency I was thinking of. I replied that, should the village need water for *any* urgent reason.

The council drew up an agreement and had it registered. Years later, when Burks Falls was approached by the Department of Highways, wanting to by-pass the village, they purchased the property with the well on it. The Department of Highways officials met with the council and when I viewed their new plan, and the rights of way that they had marked out, I exclaimed in horror, "We will lose our emergency water supply if you go that way!" Councillor Harve Fowler spoke up saying, "I know nothing of this agreement." I gave him a kick under the table, and he said no more. The end result was that the village received $15,000 compensation for the water rights. This was another good financial deal for the village.

During these productive years, Burks Falls received its electrical supplies from Knight Brothers Limited, but they had a limited generating capacity. No one could have an electric stove or heater, just lights. The rate was ten cents a kilowatt hour, with a discount resulting in a net of eight cents. The village council started negotiations with Ontario Hydro and a Public Utilities Commission was set up. I was the first chairman, because, as reeve, I had the most experience in this area. I held this post for two years, 1948 and 1949.

We had unlimited power and the price 3 1/2¢ was less than half what it had been, another great step in improving the life of Burks Falls. Turning the power on for the first time was Robert Saunders, chairman of Ontario Hydro, at a special village ceremony. There was a considerable delay before Mr. Saunders arrived. When he did arrive, he said, "Mr. Darling, no doubt you will hear tomorrow what caused my delay. It was the signing of the St. Lawrence Seaway Authority when Ontario Hydro will join in with the development of hydro power, together with the Seaway." When the moment came to officially turn on power for Burks Falls, Mr. Saunders looked at a young boy standing beside me and asked who he was. I replied that it was my eldest son, John. Mr. Saunders said, "Well, Mr. Reeve, how would it be if we asked John to turn on the power?" And so John was the one who officially turned on the new power system for the village of Burks Falls.

While I was Reeve of Burks Falls, we entered into negotiations with both the provincial and federal governments to obtain grants to install sewers. Special grants were going to be withdrawn soon and we needed immediate approval which we received. However, the sewers were not connected and operating until after I had become a Member of the House of Commons. The Canadian National Railway decided during these years, to close down the Burks Falls station. Council once again obtained approval from the federal governing body to leave it open for a while. We all felt mighty good about that.

These were busy, productive years. My two sons Peter and John were born, my insurance and real estate business was prospering, and all in all it was a fine time.

EARLY POLITICAL DAYS
Burks Falls and Ontario

Following my election in the riding of Parry Sound/Muskoka on October 30, 1972, I prepared myself to go to Ottawa. I knew my life was going to be very different from anything I had known in the past. Mona wasn't interested in living in Ottawa permanently, preferring to come down for special events. She still had her home, family, friends and activities in Burks Falls and I could understand that.

I tried out various hotels in Ottawa but didn't like them too well, and when finding that the rates at the Chateau Laurier were only $2 a day more than other hotels, decided to make that my home. However, I still had to check out each Friday and drive back to Burks Falls. To make life easier, I kept many of my clothes in my office on Parliament Hill. The daily rate at the Chateau in those days was $16.

I found that it was costing me more to live in Ottawa than most MPs, as I was there five days a week, I left Burks Falls after Sunday morning church for the drive back to Ottawa. I wanted to be bright and early in my office on Monday. I usually left the House after Question Period on Friday afternoons unless there was something special to remain for.

My first visit to the Parliament Buildings was a great thrill and brought a lump to my throat as I walked up towards the buildings. I looked specifically at the Peace Tower, as I had seen so many pictures of it. Although I had been a visitor there in the past, this was something special.

When I took the Oath of Allegiance and signed the book on my first official visit to the House of Commons, I was also very moved. The Clerk of the House of Commons at that time was Alistair Fraser.

After contacting the Party Whip, I was assigned an office. If I remember correctly, the Party Whip then was Tom Bell, a New Brunswick MP. He was followed by Bob McKinley.

My office was Room 541 in the main Parliament buildings. I had a private office and a secretary, and half an office which I shared with another MP; our secretaries were situated there. Next door was MP Pat Nowlan, a very distinguished MP from the Annapolis Valley. He had followed in the footsteps of his illustrious father, George Nowlan, MP, who was a minister of national revenue in the Diefenbaker government. Pat and I got along very well. The only problems was that he was a great cigar smoker, with his fumes filtering into my office, which didn't please me too well.

During these early months, the House of Commons sat in the evenings every Monday, Tuesday and Thursday and I made a point to be present on most occasions.

I always had dinner at our common table in the dining room which held twelve or more, for the evening meal, and then went into the House. As the dining room was also open for breakfast, several of us would gather each morning to discuss topics of the day. One of the "faithfuls" was Angus McLean, the former minister of fisheries in the Diefenbaker government. He later resigned to become leader of the PC Party in Prince Edward Island, and then Premier of P.E.I. An outstanding gentleman, he was also a blueberry farmer, a World War II hero, and an officer in the RCAF.

I often took part in committee meetings in the evenings. I have always been interested in learning new things. I would say to myself as I walked through the halls of the House, how lucky I was to serve for so long a time – twenty-one years eventually – as a Member of Parliament.

Winter 1973 … I became a member of the Standing Committee on Indian Affairs, and Jean Chretien is minister of Indian affairs and northern development. Our critic of Indian affairs is Flora MacDonald. I am also sitting on the Department of Regional and Economic Development, a committee which provides funding for economic areas which are very low growth, such as the Maritime provinces and rural parts of Canada.

I hope in the future to have more input into setting up funding for my own riding and other parts of Northern Ontario. So many of the areas are badly in need of grants and funding.

It is interesting to get to know so many MPs on a first name basis, on both sides of the House. Perhaps it is because I spend so many long hours here each day. I must admit that my hours are beginning to pay off. Because I am a member of so many committees I frequently have the chance to travel to other parts of the world as a delegate. I am particularly interested in the Canada/U.S. Parliamentary Association such as acid rain committees where I hope to become a spokesman.

Another organization, is the Commonwealth Parliamentary Association, a fifty-country group, more or less, which were former members of the British Empire. I am also a member of the Standing Committee of National Defence and will, I assume, become involved with NATO and the North Atlantic Assembly. Meetings are held in Europe, and in North America.

Spring, 1973 ... One of the bonuses of being a member of so many committees is that I now have the opportunity to host visitors from my riding and show them around Ottawa. Frequently we have lunch or dinner in the Parliamentary Dining Room, and I also try to have them meet the prime minister, when he is available, or a Cabinet minister.

I must admit that most visitors are impressed with the Parliament Buildings and are always invited to the gallery during Question Period. They are frequently photographed with the prime minister, who is most gracious about this, and the photos are quite often seen in their local papers.

April 1973 ... I was asked today how many hours a week I put in for my job. Very few people have any idea how much time is involved in being an MP. I start off by eight o'clock or earlier each morning, and, if I am lucky, I can crawl into my bed by eleven at night.

I attended a dinner one night recently, I think for NATO, in Room 602. My colleague, Dr. Bruce Halliday, was sitting beside me, with about a dozen guests present. One Liberal Senator whose name was Hamilton, suffered a heart attack at the table and died right there. It was a great shock to all of us.

As Members of Parliament, we are fortunate to have the services and facilities of the National Defence Medical Centre, where outstanding doctors look after members of the armed forces, Members of Parliament and Senators.

I keep promising myself to have a tour of Ottawa but so far there has not been enough time. Next week, I always say.

I attend a great many receptions at the various Embassies around town. All MPs receive a formal invitation from the ambassadors of the countries involved and it is fascinating to meet with them and learn about their cultures and countries.

Business has kept me in Ottawa a great deal this spring and I always make a point of attending services in Christ Church Cathedral, which is close to the Parliament Buildings and my apartment.

May 1973 … One of my grandsons asked me what the opening of Parliament is like, he was writing an essay, I think. Well, the new Parliament which opened in January 1973, opened with great fanfare. The Speech from the Throne, given by the Governor General Jules Leger, was impressive. I was surprised and somewhat frustrated when the Members of Parliament met in the House of Commons and then paraded to the Senate for the Throne Speech. Our wives and members of the diplomatic corps had special seats there, but Members of the House of Commons had to stand at the end of the Senate Chambers, behind the brass rail. It was difficult to see and hear. Mona told me afterward how much she had enjoyed it all. She was sitting beside a charming young lady who introduced herself as Maureen McTeer, the research assistant for a young Member of Parliament from Alberta, Joe Clark.

As a new and naive Member, I was under the impression that it was necessary to be in the House of Commons when proceedings began, and to be there throughout. I found out that many members didn't agree with this. These days, the House opens at 2 p.m. and begins with Question Period which runs till 3 p.m. We adjourn for two hours for dinner at 6 p.m. and return from 8 p.m. till 10 p.m. and often later.

But on Wednesdays we do not sit beyond 6 p.m. unless there is an emergency. On Friday we adjourn at 5 p.m. We spend the mornings in our offices, and often at committee meetings. We were all asked, after being elected, what projects we would like to participate in.

I am surprised how many Members leave the House immediately following Question Period. When I do leave the House, I spend some time in the lobby making phone calls and discussing various pieces of legislation with my colleagues. There is also an opposition lobby for Members of the Opposition.

I was interested to learn that the Official Opposition always has an early morning meeting to discuss plans for Question Period, which is more or less arranged. Six or seven questions are allocated to the Leader of the Opposition and Senior MPs, who are critics of the various ministries. I enjoy Question Period, so it is no hardship to attend. I was surprised, to say the least, when a colleague, and a former Attorney General in Ontario said he felt that Question Period was a waste of time and that anyone who sat through it hadn't anything better to do!

September 1973 … I think that there are some real characters in our party, some of them very senior members. Jack Horner from Alberta, Pat Nowlan from Nova Scotia, Gordon Fairweather from New Brunswick (a former Attorney General, if memory serves me), who was called a Red Tory; he was also head of the Human Rights or a similar group and served with great distinction. They all have interesting personalities.

A group of us sit in the fourth or fifth row, at the end of the Chamber nearest the Speaker and my closest seat-mate, is Joe Clark. I told him today, in no uncertain terms, that he was being very impolite to the Prime Minister because he was always heckling him and pointing his finger at him with great rage and in a critical manner.

(After many years in the House, I noticed in a diary entry that when Joe Clark became prime minister, he lectured us all on correct decorum in the House. I agreed with him but pointed out that he was one of the worst offenders when he first came into the House, recounting his words. Prime Minister Clark said to me with a smile, "I didn't do that did I, Stan? Do as I say, not as I do!")

For a long time my seat-mate has been Paul Dick, not the greatest attender in the House. I criticized him today, asking where he had been. He said, "I have to make a living, Stan, and my law offices are in Ottawa."

Another colleague, Tom Cossitt, is a unique Member of Parliament and had been president of the Liberal Association for the riding of Leeds/Grenville. Not only does he dislike Pierre Trudeau, he seems to have a special hate fixation against him, always interrupting the Prime Minister in a real rage. I'm afraid I kid him, and tell him to "cool it, Tom."

When the controversial swimming pool was built indoors at 24 Sussex Drive everyone wondered how it had been funded, supposedly by friends of Mr. Trudeau and the Liberal Party. Tom showed a personal dislike of the pool, the money being spent on it and the whole project. He constantly heckled Mr. Trudeau about it and when the pool was almost finished, and someone in the House had asked Mr. Trudeau about it, he said he was making special arrangements for the Honorable Member from Leeds/Grenville to be the first person to use the pool. However, Mr. Trudeau continued, that would be before the water was put into the pool!

I had often wondered what I would say in my maiden speech in the House. I could speak on any piece of legislation, and could spend some part of the speech extolling the virtues of my riding, which, of course I did!

I was telling my sons Peter and John about the speech last weekend and stated to them that during my comments I pointed out that I was not too thrilled with some of my fellow Members who constantly interrupted and heckled the Prime Minister during his speeches. I felt that as prime minister of Canada, he should be given every courtesy and when he was finished, should there be areas that needed questioning or "heckling," then that was the time to do it and it would be quite in order.

Later, in the Lobby, one of our distinguished Members criticized me very strongly and said it was not my position to congratulate or extol the prime minister. My colleague's name was Eldon Wooliams, Member for Calgary North and first elected in 1957. He had hoped, I was told later, to receive an important Cabinet post in the 1979 election when the PC Party took power and Joe Clark became prime minister. He was so hurt to be overlooked that he did not run in 1980, a great loss to Parliament.

For anyone who thinks our sessions are dull, I recall one time when several of our Members stormed the Speaker's Chair and were very irate at some ruling. There was quite an uproar which was finally resolved. Tom Cossitt was one of the Members deeply involved in the fracas. I have warned him time and again that his anger was not good for him, and in the fullness of time, this proved to be true. He died a young man.

November 1974 ... I can't help being critical of the small attendance in the House during debates. For Parliament to function, there must be a quorum of twenty Members and it is often difficult to do this as the Members frequently fall below twenty. When the Opposition is in an ugly mood and wants to embarrass the government, they call for a quorum, and if there aren't sufficient numbers, they adjourn for the day. With 260 Members supposedly in the House, there should always be a quorum.

My diary tells me that when Erik Neilsen was House Leader, there had to be a quorum before the Speaker could call the House to order, and before we could have the opening prayer. I frequently had to return to the Lobby and ask some of the Members there to get into the House. Erik used to say, "Don't worry about it, Stan, it's up to the government to see that there are sufficient numbers in the House, and that they are there on time." Some years later I recall saying when we were the government, "Our chickens have come home to roost, and why should we now cooperate with the Opposition any more than you cooperated with us."

Winter 1975 ... I enjoy sessions when heads of state visit the House of Commons. I often have the pleasure of meeting and talking with them after. There is usually a small reception in the Railway Committee rooms after their address, and many invitations come our way from embassies. There are, I think, about 140. They are, for the most part, large, luxurious and pretentious, and among the most luxurious are the American, French, Japanese and the German embassies and the British High Commission Residence.

Another great thrill in Ottawa is the Changing of the Guard on Parliament Hill. It takes place in the summer months, and I always think of the Changing of the Guard at Buckingham Palace in London. I think the ceremony in Ottawa is more impressive, with more soldiers participating and, of course, the military band to which they march.

I recalled a conversation I had, as a boy, with my uncle, Lt.-Col. E. Scarlett of the 91st Highlanders in Hamilton, Ontario. It later became the Argyle and Sutherland Highlanders. My uncle said, "The military band is one of the greatest curses there is, my boy. The music is so stirring it gets people all worked up and excited and they want to join the army and go to war." I have that feeling every time I see the Changing of the Guards on Parliament Hill.

This week we have been debating a housing bill and as a junior Member, I was one of the last to speak and the House sat until 5 p.m. on Friday. A young MP, Dean Whiteway of Winnipeg, said he was leaving then for his home riding and would be leaving by 7 p.m. and in bed by 10:30. It was a cold, blustery winter night, and I started out for the long drive through Algonquin Park to Burks Falls, five or more hours away. The snow was coming down and the wind was blowing, a real blizzard, and there were a great many accidents along the way. All I could think of those last few hours was Dean Whiteway, safely home in Winnipeg, curled up in his own bed. And there I was, fighting to get through a blizzard to spend a couple of days in my riding, and with my family.

One night, a friend was driving me home and I was dozing away in the front seat. I woke up suddenly to find headlights glaring right at me and thought there was going to be a head-on crash. My driver had gone off the slippery road, into a deep snow-bank, and the snow reflected back our head-lights. I had a winter carnival to open in Huntsville that night, and so I got out to hitch-hike. I was lucky enough to get a ride with a logging truck, right into Huntsville. I learned later that my friend was able to get out of the ditch with the help of another motorist passing by. I didn't take many winter drives to and from Ottawa through the years without seeing a great many car accidents and I always thanked God when I returned safely.

SORTING OUT THE POST OFFICE

Emsdale, 1992 ... I've been through some tough gatherings in my time, but last night's meeting in Emsdale was just about the toughest. It has been announced by the postal authorities that the Emsdale Post Office, south of Burks Falls, and in my home riding, will be closed. In my largely rural area, the post office is often the centre and the meeting place of the village and township, and residents do not take kindly to changes. I have tried everything I possibly can try to keep this post office from being closed down. I've been to committee meetings, discussed it with the president of Canada Post and told everyone of influence about my family's history in the area and how my head is on the block if it closes down. But many of the angry residents accused me of not being concerned and seem to be holding me responsible for the closure.

Canada Post is on an austerity kick and they feel that it would cost less to have the stamps sold and mail picked up in a corner of a store in the village rather than to pay for the upkeep of the post office. The post office will now be in the Credit Union in Emsdale and open for longer hours than the old post office. In the long run, people will get better service than before, and one of the executives of the credit union will act as post master. This is certainly the trend in postal services and there are still a great many postal outlets in general stores around the country. When the post office closed in Port Sydney recently, there was no uproar and the opening of the service in a nearby store seems to be working out well. The trend is that when a post master retires or dies, then the service will be changed. Rural delivery routes are still going as strong as before and because of an increase in population – such as in Huntsville, Bracebridge and Gravenhurst – post offices were running out of mail boxes and wall space for mail sorting. The answer seems to be to establish outside boxes in groups, in nearby areas, so that the morning courier could deliver large quantities of mail for the area all at one time.

The big complaint about outside boxes is, of course the difficulty for older people, or those who find it difficult to get around, to get down to the boxes, especially in bad weather and snow. The Post Office has given each community thirty days to come up with a petition as to why their post office should not be closed. As the government appoints a person to run the Post Office Authority, it is not possible for a Member of Parliament to interfere in this process. I feel strongly that the post office should remain as the one contact that the government has with small towns, but the post office is somehow not able to put this vital service on a paying basis. The figures that I read are that they lose up to $100 million year after year and they are trying to wipe out this deficit by reorganizing. Courier services are putting a dint into postal delivery profits, there is no doubt about it. I know my insurance company has its own courier services because of the limitation of the post office to give us good, reliable service. All of this has triggered a lot of memories about the post office in Burks Falls when I was reeve.

Ottawa, 1974 ... Walter Dinsdale was the head of the Post Office Committee for our party when I first served on the committee. He had been the minister of Indian affairs in the Diefenbaker government and we held regular meetings to look into complaints. The biggest headache these days is the postal union, one of the most unpopular unions in Canada. They choose the most awkward times to strike, usually just before an important holiday like Christmas. The present head of the union is an "imported" Scotsman named Joe Davidson who is agitating for his union, making outrageous demands of the postal authorities. I understand a strike has been discussed to take place just before Christmas and when Mr. Davidson was interviewed by the newspapers, he was asked why he wanted to inconvenience the public at that time. I will never forget his response. "To hell with the public," he said, and this response followed him to his grave. He eventually retired on a good pension, and returned to Scotland.

Toronto, 1989 ... We are visiting various post office terminals in the area. The biggest post office in Canada is called the Gateway, in Mississauga. It's the size of three football fields. A second huge sorting plant near Woodbine Racetrack in the east end of Toronto is also fully automated. As usual, I spoke up and asked to see the one area that our committee had not been shown. The post office guides asked me what I was talking about and I replied, "I'm looking for the place where certain workers in hobnailed boots and with hammers abuse the parcels and smash them up pretty well." They did not find my remarks very amusing. However, I had in mind something that had happened to me a short time before.

A friend sent me a lovely Christmas cake in a cake tin for a gift. When it arrived, it was completely squashed, packaging tin and all. How this could happen, considering that it was even in a tin, was a wonder to me. At that time the Post Master General was a Liberal, and a very good friend of mine, the Hon. J.J. Blais. I got up in the House of Commons and showed the Christmas cake which I had brought along and reported on the accident to it. There were a good many chuckles over this incident and it was reported in all the papers.

When I first started out in the insurance business in Burks Falls our postage rate was 6¢ and the mail was delivered promptly. I would take my insurance policies for mailing each day to the CN station for the 12:20 train at night, hand the parcel of letters to the night agent who gave the mail to the man on the train's mail car. The mail would be would be sorted on the way to Toronto, and delivered in Toronto the next morning. For letters needing a quick reply, I would receive these the following day. When the mails stopped being sorted on the trains everything started to deteriorate. Train service was also being withdrawn because, we were told, people were not patronising passenger trains as much as they had. In most centres at this time there were two mail deliveries a day. The morning train brought mail at 6 a.m. and the mail was sorted and in our boxes by 9 a.m. The afternoon train arrived around 3:30, and our afternoon mail was also prompt.

The postal services today are, in my estimation, chaos! Perhaps because the post office is no longer operated by the government and there is no longer a postmaster general. The change came about in the early 1980s, in the Trudeau government because one year the post office lost $600 million. Legislation made it a crown corporation, with a board of directors and an ultimatum to put it on a paying basis within five years. The first postal chairman was a tall, aristocratic man, the former chairman of the TTC, Michael Warren. His salary was around $150,000 a year. Postal rates were increased, small post offices were closed down and this was a great blow, as many post offices were the only direct link that people had with each other.

Queen Victoria promised to provide her subjects with a penny mail delivered to every part of the British Isles. We have come a long way since then, but I feel that every taxpayer should be guaranteed good mail service wherever they live.

When I was on the Post Office Committee we decided to find out what kinds of services were available in other countries. We visited Great Britain and Germany. The Post Office system in Great Britain at that time was making millions of pounds profit and the difference in operations with Canada's was very slight. Mail and telephone systems and the radio were all handled through the Post Office. So each department helped the other to adjust any loss that might occur and staffing was also more efficient. Mail was delivered overnight. Germany also had a very efficient postal service and their own mail cars on the railway. Their mail was delivered with a next day turnaround. At that time they were talking about the new electronic mail which would soon be available with delivery within twenty-four hours. Well, the fax machine has made a big difference these days, and now, of course, Internet and other computerized deliveries. But in my estimation whether it is the U.S., Canada, or any other country, mail delivery and postal services will always be controversial, and as postal services increase in cost, a bone of contention.

CAPITAL PUNISHMENT

Someone asked me the other day if I had ever felt like killing someone. Well, I can't say I have, and I can't say I haven't, but I recalled one incident some years ago on Parliament Hill which brought me mighty close.

Her Majesty, Queen Elizabeth II, had signed the Charter of Rights, or the Bill of Rights, in, I believe, 1981. I can still see Prime Minister Pierre Trudeau there, and Andre Oulette, who officiated as well. Mona and I were sitting a short distance from the ceremonial table. It reminded me that a few years before, a huge crowd on Parliament Hill made up of disgruntled farmers from Quebec, who were angry at the Liberal government, had come to complain. The minister of agriculture was the Hon. Eugene Whelan. I was standing on the steps under the Peace Tower talking to Mr. Whelan, when the farmers started throwing wet balls of milk powder at us. I was sprayed with one and had to have my suit dry-cleaned. I remember that I had a very special pen in my suit pocket and forgot to remove it before cleaning. I never did get it back. All in all, a very unhappy event.

During the years I was a backbencher, there were at least three debates on capital punishment. I made my position clear right from the start, I am in favor of capital punishment for first degree murder, which includes cold-blooded gangster killings, murders in bank robberies and, of course, rape killings. Through my parliamentary years we have learned of some particularly gruesome and hideous murders which brought a lot of mail to Ottawa, as well as a great many newspaper articles.

Ottawa 1976 … I heard Mr. Trudeau and others debating the capital punishment issue these last few days. The prime minister is against capital punishment, and our vote concerning this vital issue is close. I had the chance to speak today and outline my argument in favor of it. I said that once the issue was aired and discussed and voted on I felt certain the vote would favor it. I remarked that I was worried that Prime Minister Trudeau in his eagerness to sway others to his opinion, might use a rubber hose on some Members of Parliament in an effort to get them to change their minds. I also mentioned that he might make tempting offers of appointments, trips and other perks with the same results in mind. I think that the French Canadians are very strong for law and order. Well when the vote came, it was very close with only six votes difference.

Well, surprisingly, some of my colleagues took exception to my remarks about Mr. Trudeau using a rubber hose. Some demanded that the Speaker have me withdraw my remarks and if memory serves me, it was my long-time friend in my environmental work, the Hon. Charles Caccia. The Speaker was Charles Turner, a Liberal MP from London, and, incidentally a retentionist who voted for the return of capital punishment.

The Speaker smiled at me and said, "I must ask the Honorable Member from Parry Sound/Muskoka to withdraw his remarks." That is the only time in twenty-one years I had to withdraw any remarks I made in the House of Commons.

May 13, 1976 ... The Bracebridge Herald Gazette reported today that "MP remains firm on capital punishment." They reported that I said, among other things, that "The responsibility of the Cabinet ministers should not be to the well-being and comfort of those convicted of violent crimes, but their responsibility is to those millions of law-abiding Canadians who must wonder at times if there is really anyone on their side." Statistics bear out my concern. Violent crime in Canada increased 90 per cent in the ten-year period from 1965 to 1974. In 1965 there were 243 murders in Canada and in 1975, 545. The murder rate in this period doubled from 1.2 per 100,000 population to 2.4.

I said in my speech to the House, "The Solicitor-General and the minister of justice are constantly talking about peace and security and I wonder for whom. It is my view that this bill, if passed, will provide peace and security only for the criminal element and murderers – I am talking about cold-blooded and premeditated murder, the Mafia-type killing – the killing of victims during armed robbery and rape, and of course the killing of police and guards."

I favor a more humane method of capital punishment than hanging, but Canada is not ready for total abolition – the chief reason being the growing crime rate, combined with the government's present way of dealing with crime.

Despite the fact that thirty-eight policemen and jail guards have been murdered in cold blood in the same ten-year period, no convicted murderer has been executed. There are seven and eight times that number of attempted murders. I find the tedious arguments of social workers and do-gooders of every conceivable stripe developing into a sort of pattern. These people are the first on the scene when a person is charged with a serious crime such as violent assault and especially a brutal murder, before the innocent victim has had a decent burial and before the accused can be brought to trial. We are told that the accused is not to blame for the crime – that society is to blame and the accused murderer is just as much the victim as the person who was murdered.

When a long prison sentence is imposed on a convicted murderer, we hear that it is too inhumane – keeping a human being caged up for up to thirty years. This sends social workers and a couple of Cabinet ministers into a frenzy. And so we have things like weekend passes, supervised and unsupervised leave, time off for good behavior, and of course, early parole. What happened to the poor victim?

May 1976, Ottawa … Over breakfast today in the Dining Room, some of my colleagues and I got into a hot argument over capital punishment. Needless to say over my wholewheat toast and tea, I sounded off in no uncertain terms. "It is doubtful that violent criminals are treated more gently anywhere else in the world," I said. "The plain fact is that there is a deterrent effect in imposing severe penalties for severe crimes and this not being done here."

I certainly voted against the 1973 bill which extended a partial ban on death penalty. A bill being introduced by Solicitor-General Warren Allmand would impose a minimum jail term of twenty-five years for murderers of working police and prison guards and parole would be possible in fifteen years.

In going over my notes I see that Lloyd Francis (a Liberal minister from Ottawa West) and parliamentary secretary to Treasury Board President Jean Chretien, said he favored the death penalty. The twenty-eight members of the Cabinet, will, I expect, back the bill as a group, but Mr. Allmand and Prime Minister Trudeau have promised a free vote for Liberal parliamentary secretaries, and backbenchers.

October 1975 … The Oakville Journal printed a letter today signed by G.F. Martin which stated that the Philbrook Report "Survey Results" indicates that "63.8 per cent of your constituents were for capital punishment." The statement has been made that an innocent person might be executed. Are we then to penalize the whole population on a premise that could probably never come true? I believe that "guilt beyond a reasonable doubt" in addition to which there are twelve people to concur in the decision, should be sufficient. There are other means of capital punishment if hanging proves abhorrent to some people.

Someone left a circled paragraph from a May 1976 newspaper article on my desk this morning, with the part circled in red ink stating "Attacking the noose (in capital punishment), Darling also attacked the news media in general. 'The news commentators when reporting on this bill to abolish capital punishment, depict a sinister noose on the screen,' Darling said, 'It might be an idea for some of them to put the noose around their own neck.' He said TV commentators should show murdered victims on the screen instead, or in newspapers instead, it would be a pretty gruesome scene."

I don't take back one word I said!

I think that 75 per cent of my constituents feel that capital punishment should be retained in one form or another. I have received five letters from people who think it should be abolished, but over 300 letters from people who are in favor of capital punishment. I think a national referendum on the matter is in order.

There are many debates taking place in the House, and a great number of petitions with names running into the hundreds of thousands presented to Parliament.

In July, 1976, Eldon M. Woolliams from Calgary North said, "I support the amendment to Bill C-84 which would substitute life imprisonment and a period of twenty-five years before parole, for first-degree murder. With incredible statistics available regarding escalating crime, what protection do guards, police officers and others have. A case recently shocked me when a person being escorted from one jail to another asked to go to the bathroom, where he obtained a gun, and then killed the police officer when he was being escorted from one institution to another. I am shocked to think of the situation in which we are placing police officers, guards and correctional officers. I point out the number who have lost their lives, without adequate compensation for their families who suffer because of either the first or second murder these people commit. I asked the Solicitor General, if this bill should pass on third reading, to conduct an honest and responsible review in an effort to see that the families of the police officers, guards, and correctional officers who are victims, are compensated for the death of the provider." This was certainly another point of view.

During a hot debate in July, 1976 I stated, "Speaking on an amendment regarding high treason, I was subjected to heckling by the Honorable Member. I was trying to state that, instead of concentrating on hanging, the bill should concentrate on the death penalty because many retentionists are violently opposed to the archaic and gruesome form of capital punishment adopted in this country. We believe that a criminal who has been found guilty of first-degree murder without any extenuating circumstances which would lead the jury to advocate mercy, should be removed from society as painlessly and as quickly as possible. I have stated categorically that a drug could be administered, a needle could be given, and that would be the end of it. But no, from the prime minister, Mr. Trudeau, down, we keep hearing about hanging, hanging, and hanging.

Despite a great deal of heckling and many interruptions with admonishments from Mr. Charles Turner, the Acting Speaker, I said, "I apologize Mr. Speaker. They certainly cannot sell me that bill of goods, the entire Cabinet deep down in their conscience, every damn one of them, is an abolitionist."

(There were sounds of Oh Oh, in the background as I made this statement) I continued in my usual shy manner, "Nor can they sell me the idea that all the parliamentary assistants are also abolitionists. So far as *our* leader is concerned, he is not voting the way the great majority of us are, but he is doing it on his own, and with a low profile and has made his position known. But he is not using a big stick as the Prime Minister has."

(In the background I heard a lot of heckling including, "because he hasn't got one.")

After some pretty hot questioning I stated, "There has been no constraint from *our* leader on how we should vote. It is a free vote in Parliament, no question about it. We saw a so-called free vote here the other day. When the Prime Minister stood up, he stood alone and all at once he raised his hands and his Cabinet rose as one, So that is a free vote."

In the middle of all this "discussion" the Acting Speaker said, "Order please. I would like to quote Standing Order 35, which reads as follows: 'No member shall speak disrespectfully of Her Majesty, nor any of the Royal Family, nor of His Excellency or the person administering the Government of Canada; nor use any offensive words against either House, or against any member thereof.'"

I replied, "Thank you very much, Mr. Speaker. Now if I could get back to my brief remarks ..."

The Acting Speaker said "I suggest that the Honorable Member should withdraw those last remarks." I replied that I would certainly withdraw my remarks and I heard someone in the background say, "What a darling." I continued: "Let me qualify that. Some Honorable Members who are looking with a very hungry eye at the front benches, might have second thoughts, if you know what I mean. If the Honorable Member for Lachine/Lakeshore (Mr. Blaker) will keep quiet for a few moments, and let me finish my remarks, I want to go, along with seventeen of my honorable colleagues on this side, to view the Olympic site and see where much of our money is going. We will be leaving at four o'clock. Is that all right?"

And then we were onto another topic altogether.

In 1981 with the capital punishment issue still raging, I wrote in my Parry Sound/Muskoka report for June: "The issue of capital punishment, although seemingly one of death, actually concerns life. The report of a murder triggers several responsive chords. We become terribly angered. We experience a sense of shared grief and in proximity we feel momentary fear. And we feel helpless which requires assurance from authority. We need to know that anyone who murders another is considered to have committed the ultimate crime and is subject, without question, to the ultimate punishment. We do not need, nor want, options. Those who murder don't offer their victims an option.

"At the beginning of this year I described to this House the tragic deaths of two men in my riding – Chester Blackmore and Ontario Provincial Police Constable Rick Verdecchia. Statistically, the deaths of these men would be classified as murders number one and two for 1981. Would the numbers one and two begin to describe the night of horror when they were shot dead and a third man, another OPP officer, seriously wounded?

"Chester Blackmore and Constable Verdecchia were far more than numbers when they were alive.

"I refuse to accept that designation for them in death."

On January 12th I gave this address to the House saying, "Madame Speaker, under the provisions of Standing Order 43, I rise on a matter of extreme urgency. All Canadians were stunned to learn of the horrendous murders which were committed New Year's night in the communities of Emsdale and Huntsville and the wounding of a constable from Orillia. Canadians from one end of the country to the other are shouting loudly and clearly, "Bring back the death penalty." Public opinion polls clearly establish that Canadians favor the death penalty. In light of this I move, seconded by the Honorable Member of Simcoe North (Mr. Lewis) that the government refer the question of the return of capital punishment to the Standing Committee on Justice and Legal Affairs and that the committee report back to Parliament without delay so that a really free vote can be taken."

Madame Speaker said "For the presentation, this motion requires the unanimous consent of the House. Is there unanimous consent?" Some Members said, "agreed," some members said "no."

We were back where we started!

While we were getting nowhere with our debates in the House, the media was covering the issue with such headlines as: "MP says all Canada wants the noose back" (Globe and Mail); "Free vote on noose demanded" (Ottawa Citizen); "The value of Human Life" (Bracebridge Examiner) "Policemen bury colleague – Darling wants noose back" (North Bay Nugget); and the Sunday Sun said, "Shocked, angry residents demand, 'Bring back the noose.'"

February 1981, Ottawa ... I was asked during an interview today, for my reasons why we continue to debate for capital punishment. My answer is the same as it has been all my life: "There are certain individuals who do not deserve to live; cold premeditated murderers. Ninety-eight per cent of those charged with murder would never receive the death penalty because so many crimes are of passion, from drunken brawls and family 'more-than-squabbles.' Where wives were arrested for murdering their husbands, a check should be made as to why the wife waited so long and what she had had to put up with. Gangster killings, where a bank is robbed with the killer carrying a machine gun and kills anyone in the way, is something else again. These are the things I must consider."

In 1972 I voted against the bill to extend the partial ban on the death penalty. I was and am in favor of the death penalty for the willful murder of prison guards and policemen in the operation of their duties. In every sentence I understand the sentences of the murderers were commuted to prison sentences.

During the later eighties I carried on a brisk correspondence with people all over the country about capital punishment. One I recall was the Simcoe Presbytery, United Church of Canada. Their first letter to me stated, among other things, "That capital punishment is contrary to the spirit and teaching of Christ."

That our criminal justice system should provide realistic and appropriate sentences for crimes of violence.

That violent videos, films and television programming, and coverage by the media of violent events, and that advertising and sales of war toys for our children should all be banned.

I received many such letters. By 1986 the controversy still continued. Christie Blatchford of the Toronto Sun, wrote after the murder of Alison

Parrott, age 11, "No punishment is enough. In the wake of the murder of Alison Parrott, 11, I wish I could believe in capital punishment. I wish I could believe in the punishment value of the death penalty. I wish I could stop thinking about what will happen if the police make an arrest in the murder; about lawyers and police arguing about whether under the law such a person is sane and able to understand the horror of his act."

An editorial in the Toronto Sun, dated July 29, 1986, didn't mince words: "The death penalty now." "Bleeding hearts lecture us about compassion on days of sorrow like this when capital punishment is an inevitable topic. Let's talk instead of vengeance.

"It may not be fashionable for liberals but it's in the hearts and minds of Torontonians as they contemplate the criminal madness of recent days.

"In Toronto, the city shudders as the nude body of a little girl is discovered. What a cold, calculated end to the promising life of 11-year-old Alison Parrott. In Montreal the third policeman this year is blown away. Yet Prime Minister Brian Mulroney continues to welsh on that election promise of a free vote on capital punishment. We demand a vote now. We insist on action, not excuses and stalling.

"The last vote was flawed. The abolitionists squeaked to a victory after Pierre Trudeau dictated his Cabinet votes. The three leaders are still against the death penalty but the country isn't. Shouldn't our voices be heard?

"Every poll shows that most people want would-be killers to fear for their lives. Even many of those opposed to state execution for child murderers, cop killers and terrorists want them locked up and the key thrown away.

"Fat chance of that when the Canadian system specializes in freeing criminals. Our criminals must fear our laws. We need fewer days of sorrow. We demand the death penalty now."

The Ottawa Citizen printed a poll showing that, in any age group, Canadian citizens favor the death penalty.

And the Globe and Mail stated: "Grim lesson? Decrease in murders seen after publicized executions."

The Hon. John Crosbie stated that law enforcement officials in St. John's, Newfoundland, will weigh the pros and cons of capital punishment, although they know that he believes himself to be an abolitionist. But MP Bill Domm, who is the son of a United Church minister, who has fought against capital punishment all his life now says that, "watching violent criminals going back on the streets committing more crimes has changed my mind. Execution is a reasonable form of justice."

John Harney in the May 17, 1986, Ottawa Citizen stated Bill Domm's bill to reinstate capital punishment has been rejected by the parliamentary committee that selects the private Member's bills to be debated. Harney said, "The argument for capital punishment is, somehow the guilty must pay capitally for the most capital of crimes. But this argument invokes the kind of moral universe we want to live in. We are all condemned to that choice. I choose to live in a society which shows its abhorrence for the taking of life by refusing to take it itself."

And in the April 17 1986 Vancouver Sun, columnist Jack Clarke concluded his column with these words, "We've had our debate on the death penalty. We've decided as a civilized society that the state shouldn't commit the same crime it has outlawed for its citizens the taking of life. We don't need another debate."

In November 1992, I stated in a letter to my constituents: "The Department of Justice has invited a public consultation on the Young Offenders Act across Canada. You and your fellow Canadians will have until November 15th to respond to the call for views. Groups working with youth and interested individuals are encouraged to obtain a copy of the consultation paper which outlines the nature and extent of youth crime and explains how the Young Offenders Act currently works. Violent and repeat offenders are the focus of growing public concern. The paper places particular emphasis on young people who commit violent crimes or who have come into contact with the law on several occasions. I am working with the federal government to ensure that everyone in my riding with a concern about youth crime has the opportunity to participate in the consultation process."

The debate concerning capital punishment still rages in mid-1995 and will, I have no doubt, continue for long after I am here to give my views.

THE OLYMPIC LOTTERY

Ottawa, 1976 … Things are heating up to publicize and make money for the Montreal Olympics. When I served on the Special Committee of the Olympic Lottery, ministers in charge were, the Hon. Andre Oullette, minister of consumer and corporate affairs and post master general; and the Hon. Bud Drury, president of the Treasury Board; the legislation to make the Olympic Lottery possible was their responsibility. I sat on this committee.

Leading our Party on the committee was Otto Jelinek. Spokesman for the NDP was John Paul Harney who endeavored to have the committee agree on having the Olympic coin made as a medallion and not as a coin of the realm. They very nearly sold this idea to Otto Jelinek. However, I raised a great deal of opposition to it and informed them in no uncertain terms that it must be the coin of the realm if we were going to sell a sufficient number to make it all worth while.

I questioned Mr. Ouelette regarding the amount of money they expected to raise. Their target for the Olympic stamps was $10 million, for the Olympic coins about $100 million. And for the Olympic lottery around $30 million. I said, "I think Mr. Minister that you are way off base. Do you think you can raise $30 million dollars on the lottery? Do you think you can raise $100 million on the lottery?"

Mr. Ouellette said, "Mr. Darling, don't you think we can raise $30 million on the lottery?"

I replied, "No, you will raise $100 million, but you'll never sell $100 million in coins and $10 million in stamps."

I felt strongly that they would not come near these figures on the sale of coins and stamps, but the Canadian people were showing the popularity of gambling on lotteries with many government approved lotteries across

Canada, and, of course, the Irish Sweepstakes lottery taking millions of dollars out of Canada every year. I guess we will never know for sure whether that money ever got to Ireland or not. But in my estimation, the sale of coins and stamps, no matter what the cause, is far from a sure thing. I said I recall Mayor Jean Drapeau of Montreal who visited Ottawa about this time saying, "Of course, gentlemen, it is just as possible for a man to have a baby as for the Olympics to lose money."

I then gave them my estimated predictions and, in the fullness of time, it was proved to be correct. Committee proceedings, which are always recorded, bear out what I had said. In the long run, I think, they raised about $100 million on the lottery and other items. The Olympic Stadium reached the astronomical cost of around $800 million and, Montreal is, I imagine, still paying off its Olympic debt after all these years.

MAYOR DRAPEAU AND
THE HOUSING COMMITTEE

In the early 1970s, after I had gotten my feet wet in Ottawa, I was a member of a special Housing Committee under the Chairmanship of Eldon Wooliams of Calgary. There were eight or nine members of the Committee and Mr. Wooliams had contacted the Mayor of several large cities in Canada to tell them that the Committee would like to visit their cities to view their social housing programs.

Well, we received no response from Vancouver, and Winnipeg and Toronto weren't too welcoming, but Mayor Drapeau of Montreal welcomed our group with open arms. We were headquartered in the Queen Elizabeth Hotel and had an official car and driver to take us around Montreal, through the various areas where old tenement houses some over 150 years old and in terrible condition, were being renovated as social housing.

I recall one that was in the area of St. Henri which was the slums section of Montreal. The houses we saw had no running water, or bathroom facilities and were terrible eyesores. The city was doing a remarkable job of renovation, and making the houses available as low income housing. After our tours, Mayor Drapeau hosted a special farewell dinner for us at the municipally owned restaurant, on the Isle de Ste. Helene. The Helene de Champlain is reputed to have the most excellent wine cellar of any restaurant in North America. We had a delicious meal and I recall talking with Mayor Drapeau before dinner. I said, "Your Worship, we have something in common. I have served thirty-one years in municipal government before being elected to the House of Commons. I was mayor or reeve for twenty-six years in the village of Burks Falls." I asked Mayor Drapeau about their sewage problems and mentioned that our group had heard that 80 per cent of all Montreal sewage was dumped raw into the St. Lawrence River. Well, Mayor Drapeau looked at me and said, "It's a lie, Mr. Darling, it is 100 per cent."

I was shocked by his words and looked aghast. Mayor Drapeau then said, "You know Mr. Darling, the St. Lawrence is a very fast-flowing river."

I couldn't help wondering how the many municipal cities downstream from Montreal felt about the effect of such overwhelming pollution. Mayor Drapeau just shook his head when I asked him about this.

Although this incredible pollution continued for some years, I know that Montreal has now spent millions of dollars to improve their sewage system and establish modern treatment plants.

Mayor Jean Drapeau was an interesting mayor and certainly did a great deal for his city.

CANADA'S SYMBOL, THE BEAVER

Ottawa, 1977 … My friend Shawn O'Sullivan* and I, talked today about one of Canada's symbols, the Beaver. In my riding there is a very well-known trapper named Ralph Bice. He asked me a few weeks ago if I knew that the Canadian beaver was not an official emblem of Canada.

Needless to say, I thought he was joking but Ralph is a pretty serious man and he told me that I had better check it out. I found out that Ralph was right, that it is not recognized as an official emblem. So I started to prepare a private bill which would have the beaver declared Canada's official emblem, or at least one of them.

About this time, in the State of New York, there was a great deal of talk about declaring the beaver as a symbol for New York State. Needless to say, this created a bit of furor in Canada. Shawn O'Sullivan took up the cause for the Canadian beaver and prepared a bill which he asked me to talk over with him.

He was pretty anxious to have his bill go through, and we decided in conversation that I should drop my proposed bill for the same purpose. We agreed that Shawn's bill would be presented to the House of Commons. And so, the beaver become the emblem of Canada, thanks to Shawn O'Sullivan and Ralph Bice and with a nudge or two from me. I have no idea what New York State did about their beaver bill.

---

* A Member of Parliament for Hamilton/Wentworth and when a youth was an assistant to Mr. Diefenbaker.

ACID RAIN

J uly 4, 1992 ... Everyone is in favor of cleaning up acid rain – until they have to find the money to pay for it. I came home from the Rio Earth Summit in June with my head full of facts and figures which I will never forget. For instance:

- more than one billion of our fellow human beings now live in acute poverty, which breeds environmental degradation. Their survival forces them to plunder their environment and unless we are prepared to help alleviate Third World poverty, our entire planet will be at risk;
- acid rain can reduce the yield and marketability of important crops;
- metals are leached from the ground and from corroded water supply systems by acid rain;
- reducing the sulphur-dioxide and sulfates that cause acid rain would lessen significant health risks, and improve viability;
- acid rain damages buildings, property, crops and our health;
- sulphur and nitrogen oxides are the main causes of acid rain;
- there is currently an annual transfer of $10 billion to $125 billion from rich to poor countries to help eradicate cheap and dirty fuels, inefficient technology and population strains; and
- no targets or timetables have yet been set by any countries for reducing the emission of greenhouse gases. The twelve countries who ratified the Rio Agreement included Canada. We are all committed to controlling the emissions in our own countries, but when? The treaty signed dealing with emissions, has a built-in flexibility allowing for stronger measures, if the threat of global warming becomes any more serious.

Ottawa, March 23, 1983 ... The effects of acid rain are now appearing throughout the United States and Canada. The loss of fish from thousands of lakes and streams is the most obvious effect. But acid rain is taking its toll in other ways as well. It is leaching nutrients from forest soils while releasing toxic metals from the ground. Buildings and monuments are being eroded. Public health is in danger. The U.S. National Academy of Sciences estimates that $5 billion or more in damage is done every year by acid rain in the Eastern United States alone, while in Canada, the National Research Council has placed a minimum figure of $350 to $500 million on annual damage to buildings and property. Federal officials estimate that the sector of the Canadian economy potentially at risk from acid rain in Eastern Canada alone represents slightly more than 8 per cent of the total Canadian Gross National Product.

The cause of acid rain is pollution from the combustion of coal and other fossil fuels. In 1980, more than 50 million tons of sulphur and nitrogen oxides were released over North America. In Canada, the level of sulphur-dioxide emissions in 1980 represented 7.5 per cent net over 1955 emissions.

Acid rain has already caused extensive damage to lakes and streams across United States and Canada to the point where fish can no longer live. The National Academy of Sciences warned in 1981 that unless acid rain was controlled the number of affected lakes would double by 1990.

In Ontario, more than 14,000 lakes and ponds have already succumbed to acid rain. The Ontario government estimates that another 48,000 are threatened with extinction. But the effects of acid rain on forests could be far more extensive and irreversible than the damage to lakes and streams. Forests in Eastern United States, Canada and Europe, are suffering from stunted growth and die-back, and the evidence that acid rain is causing forest damage is accumulating at a rapid rate.

A Member of Parliament from Vancouver South, John Fraser, gave a monumental address recently, stating: "Acid rain is perhaps the most serious unaddressed environmental problem on the North American continent today, causing damage conservatively estimated by the Eastern United States alone at $5 billion per year."

That is a sobering statement and I can only imagine the progression of our acid rain problem as the years go by.

April 16, 1980 ... I learned today that a committee was set up to study the problems of acid rain, as nobody in this area was doing anything about it. I have been getting a lot of flak for a few years now from resort owners in the Parry Sound/Muskoka riding I represent, They are crying the blues because tourists are not coming here as frequently as they used to. The reasons given me are that fishing is not nearly as good as it has been in years past, the fish are dying off, and not eatable, and of course, they blame it all on acidified lakes and rivers. When my constituents started really going after me about this, I started looking into it and studying it seriously, for our party. I approached the party by saying that I wanted to sit on this committee because my riding is the greatest tourist riding in Canada. We are being badly hurt. As well, I can't walk down any street in my riding without being buttonholed by someone complaining that nothing is being done about the growing acid rain problem.

So, I was appointed to the committee on acid rain and that was the start of it!

I realize that it will be many years before a final American/ Canadian acid rain treaty will ever be signed between our two countries but I won't give up, to make a poor pun, I'll just keep going on until a steady rain soaks in!

In early 1983 the acid rain committee was headed by Chairman Ron Irwin, Liberal MP from Sault Ste. Marie. He arranged a meeting for the committee to visit Europe and meet Parliamentarians in Sweden. Sweden, I understand has more documentation on acid rain damage than any other country in the world, with statistics which go back one hundred years. They have also spent a great deal of money reducing their acid rain problems. Evidently Europe's worst polluter is Great Britain.

October 23 ... Today I spread the gospel on acid rain, as a Member of the Commonwealth Parliamentary Association at their annual meeting. I pointed out in no uncertain terms that we are fortunate in Canada to have only one border and only two countries involved. We hope to work something out to solve our acid rain problems. But I can see what a monumental problem Europe has, where some countries are very pollution conscious and spend a great deal of money to reduce acid rain. I think Belgium and the Netherlands are on the short list, but many others appear to be more interested in production and apparently haven't much interest in, or money to spend on, acid rain reduction.

The big polluters in Europe are Poland, Bulgaria, Czechoslovakia, East and West Germany.

Recently, our sub-committee talked with officials and professors of the University of London. They gave us a new slant on Great Britain's battle against air pollution. They said that Great Britain has progressed greatly in recent years in reducing its pollution. The majority of their energy used to be produced by coal; this is no longer the case. In fact, in the city of London, coal is prohibited entirely from being used as a heating fuel. Our fact-finding mission to some of Europe's best and worst acid rain countries was worth the long hours and endless meetings. We came back to Canada with a much clearer picture of the culprits and those seriously committed to cleaning up their act.

In a conversation on the plane coming back from London I agreed with the statement made by a member of our fact-finding group that Third World countries are in favor of pollution control. But the fact that many of them are not industrially in a position to do much polluting must also be faced. I don't know how many times I have stated in the past years that the Group of Seven Countries, and those who have benefited through the Industrial Revolution to become big exporters, are really the ones to help the Third World countries make sure their new factories are environmentally sound.

In China, for example, with over one billion people, officials are planning to upgrade their economy by using coal as the base for electrical energy. With its huge coal deposits, this seems to be the way they intend to go. Their immense new hydro development project, the Three Gorges Development, will flood prime land requiring about one million people to be moved out and relocated, before flooding can begin.

Needless to say, most environmentalists are dead set against this. But China, a sovereign state, does not listen to weeping and wailing of its populace. China may be concerned about environmental problems, but I imagine that though they do not have the money to upgrade pollution control technology, they would welcome technical and financial help.

November 13 … Congressman Thomas Lukin of Cincinnati, informed me today in no uncertain terms that we are coming down to the United States to try to scare members of the congress and the U.S. public, so that we can sell them our excess power from Ontario Hydro and Quebec Hydro for their utilities, which, for the most part, are using coal and oil to produce energy. I had to remind myself that Ohio is against the Canadian position because it is one of the greatest polluters in the U.S. with many giant, coal-fired utilities, and steel mills.

Mr. Lukin said: "Mr. Darling, you and your colleagues come down here preaching at us but what have you done in Canada? What controls have you put on your utilities and plants?" I had to reply, none. He went on, "What controls has Canada put on automobile emissions and how many scrubbers do you have on your utility plants in Canada?" Again, my answer had to be that we have done nothing. Mr. Lukin replied that there were over one hundred American scrubbers on the Eastern Seaboard alone, and how come we were in the United States preaching at them?

October 1983 … Environment Minister Charles Caccia, charged yesterday that the U.S. has "isolated" itself from the world community by rejecting a commitment to make a specific reduction in sulphur dioxide emissions by 1993. Turkey was the only other country to specifically reject the agreement signed at the close of a three-day conference. Eighteen of the thirty-five countries and international agencies at the conference have committed themselves to a minimum 30 per cent cut in acid rain causing sulphur dioxide emissions by 1993. William Ruckelshaus, head of the U.S. Environmental Protection Agency and leader of the American delegation said later, "There could be bilateral discussion with Canada at some future time, on the issue."

The Canadian Embassy in Washington continues to be most helpful. They arrange with our Canadian contingent to meet with congress members and such heavyweights as the Coal Institute and some giant utilities. Needless to say, none of them want to spend an extra dollar so they constantly downgrade what damage SO_2 (sulphur dioxide) is doing to the air, One very influential Democrat, Senator Patrick Moynahan from New York, is very much on the side of acid rain reduction, Three other champions of our cause are New York Congressman, James Scheurr, Senator George Mitchell, who is probably the third ranking official in the United States, next to the president and the vice president (he is also Majority Leader in the Senate) and Democratic Congressman, Gerry Sikorski from Minnesota.

June 27 … With summer cottages in the news, I remind myself that an incredible amount of damage is still being done to our lakes and rivers by acid rain. It has acidified a great many lakes and killed marine growth extensively. There is, of course, not only acid rain to be concerned about, but also acid snow.

My riding, Parry Sound/Muskoka, stretches within fifty miles of Sudbury with every bit of Inco's sulphur dioxide heading straight from that 1,215-foot smokestack into my riding.

On a recent visit to Inco, in Sudbury, the vice-president, Walter Curluke, said that it would cost over $400 million to renovate their plant and that this was not affordable. The alternative, Mr. Carluke said, would be to shut down this giant plant with a loss of over 12,000 jobs, which would be a very serious blow to Sudbury. Coal presently being used by Inco is, for the most part, imported from Pennsylvania.

When the Inco plant was closed down by a seven-month labor strike, and then for a further six months by economic conditions, scientists found that the lakes acidity had not decreased despite the fact that emissions were not being produced. Because prevailing winds blow to the north and east, a great majority of the acid rain we must deal with, comes from the middle United States. Although Canada is far from lily-white, it is really our neighbors to the south, primarily New York State, Ohio, Pennsylvania, where Inco buys most of its coal, and Illinois, who are the main polluters. They create havoc with the Eastern Seaboard States such as Vermont, Maine and Massachusetts, and, of course, Canada, Although Canada must clean up its own act, and immediately, we must also realize that much damage being done, especially to our maple trees, may never be corrected, at least not in our lifetime. Acid rain is also seriously damaging historic buildings, and is creating health problems for seniors, and those with asthma, bronchitis, tuberculosis, and emphysema.

June 12 … Colleen Campbell, a Liberal MP in the Trudeau government, is from Nova Scotia. She mentioned a friend of hers, Professor Tom Barnes, from the University of Southern California, who teaches at Berkley. He not only teaches Canadian history but has Canadian ties, through his mother's people in Nova Scotia. He asked Colleen to speak at the University and she has invited me to go along too. She had to have a Progressive Conservative Member with her, in order to get permission to attend.

We spoke with many senior students, teaching students and guests while at Berkley, about acid rain problems in Canada. They showed a great deal of interest.

While we were touring California, we had some amazing experiences including a fascinating tour of Chinatown in San Francisco, and a tour of the incredible Redwood forests, something I will never forget. The Department of the Environment in Canada had produced a film recently, showing damage caused by acid rain. Colleen took a copy with her, as she planned to show it to Berkley students. However, it was stolen from her luggage at the airport by, we think, a baggage man. Perhaps he thought he was stealing a porno film. He would certainly be shocked when he eventually looked at what he had stolen, but we were sorry not to have the film to show our friends at the various gatherings.

Spring, 1984 ... The Canadian government has listed a great many acid rain project details which include:

- $1.5 million will go towards an acid rain communications campaign to convince American tourists that the U.S. should act against American sources of acid rain;
- an agreement has been reached to fight acid rain in seven provinces. This is the most intensive environmental program ever developed to combat acid rain. The goal? To reduce SO_2 emissions by 50 per cent by 1994;
- more than 90 per cent of the $500 million annual cost to control SO_2 will be borne by Canadian industry and provincial utilities. The federal government has committed more than $300 million to assist the provinces in this regard, with 750 million as direct assistance to private industry;
- Ontario Hydro will install ten scrubbers, with a total cost of the scrubber program around $2.5 billion, a program which will scrub virtually all Ontario Hydro's U.S. coal-fired stations;
- the New Brunswick government indicates that it will also require scrubbers to be installed at the Belledune Power Plant;
- an Action Committee on Western-Canadian Low-Sulphur Coal chaired by Deputy PM Don Mazankowski will encourage Ontario industry to use Western-Canadian coal, which creates less pollution;
- Prince Edward Island, New Brunswick and Nova Scotia are participating in three pilot projects, worth $50 million, to develop cleaner and more efficient methods of using coal;
- Falconbridge plans to spend up to $38 million to cut sulphur dioxide emissions and Algoma Steel continues to meet its emission limit by keeping production at 50 per cent of its iron sintering plant capacity.

Washington ... If this wasn't so serious it would be funny. Many of the contributors to President Reagan's campaign maintain that acid rain is caused by ashes from Mount St. Helen, and also from duck droppings on the lakes! I must admit that, during his two terms of office, President Reagan has not done very much, if anything, about the acid rain problems confronting our countries, although he did make a later visit to Ottawa where he addressed the joint Senate and the House of Commons. However, prior to Reagan's arrival in our capital, I pointed out to the Prime Minister in no uncertain terms that he had better lay it on the line and make damn sure that Reagan said something about acid rain in his speech.

The prime minister pointed out to *me* that I am not known in the House for my bashfulness. When I heard that President Reagan would be making a state visit to Quebec City on March 17, 1985, I immediately contacted Don Mazankowski, the minister of transport, to tell him, in no uncertain terms, that we would have to do something positive and suggested that, as a starter, we must be prepared to bring in restrictions and reductions in automobile pollution. Don promised me that this would be done. However, I kept at him to follow up with some real action, but nothing seemed to be taking place. He assured me that legislation was "being prepared" and a memorandum of intent would be issued before President Reagan came to Canada in March.

March 6, 1985 ... A red-letter day in our history. The Canadian acid rain legislation was announced today, exceeding my wishes in its content. It included:

- pollution emission controls on all automobiles and light trucks; and
- a fund of $150 million to be set up to be used by industry for SO_2 emission control, to be applied to the giant smelters such as Inco, Falconbridge and Noranda, as well as the Inco plant in Manitoba and the Hudson Bay mining and smelting plants. Our committee, of course, has visited all these smelters at various times.

In 1986 when Reagan was in Ottawa, the subject of acid rain in his speech went largely unsaid. But just as he was finishing he specifically mentioned Canada's acid rain problems and the differences between the two countries. He made a promise that something would be done, which, of course, delighted me. I had the pleasure of meeting Mr. Reagan after his talk, and the Prime Minister stated to Mr. Reagan that "Mr. Darling is actually Mr. Acid Rain, and one of the prime movers and workers to reduce acid rain coming from the United States."

The president turned to me and said, "Well, we must do something about it."

But that was as far as it has gone with Mr. Reagan.

Several weeks later, in a conversation with the under-secretary of state in Washington, I said that President Reagan had mentioned acid rain in Ottawa and had made a commitment to do something about it. The under-secretary paused for a very long time, obviously trying to give me an honest but diplomatic answer: "That, Mr. Darling, was not in the President's prepared address, and he shouldn't have said it."

November 1 … At luncheon in the cafeteria today I pointed out to several others at my table that President Reagan is not the greatest environmental president and he seems to be listening more to the lobbyists who are financial contributors to his party than to the acid rain champions.

I was reminded sharply by my American visitor next to me that Prime Minister Trudeau was also not very interested in the acid rain problem, and according to information he had received, Mr. Trudeau hardly ever mentioned it at meetings with his counterpart in the U.S. And so, we agreed, the tradition of indifference, or perhaps caution, has gone back a long way. This does not make our work any easier.

When Mr. Reagan and Mr. Mulroney met for their acid rain talks last year, they both appointed special representatives to meet and come up with recommendations to solve the acid rain problems. Canada's choice was former Ontario Premier Bill Davis, with Drew Lewis, an environmental specialist and a friend of President Reagan's, chosen for the U.S.

After a considerable number of meetings, visits to polluted areas and much research, Davis and Lewis produced a report, a full-color brochure, a short while ago. It outlined the problems as they exist, but said nothing new in the way of controlling the damage now or in the future. Bill Davis, whom I have known for years, told me after the report was made public: "Stan, you won't be too happy with this report but it was the best we could come up with, which would be acceptable to the President." This was further proof to me that Reagan was not interested in the environment.

The Hon. Tom McMillan, minister of the environment, and Manitoba's environment minister, Gerard Lecuyer, signed an agreement today to reduce the province's sulphur dioxide emissions by 25 per cent by 1994.

During the mid– to late–1980s, newspapers, radio and television carried a great deal of information, and much mis-information, about the acid rain problems in our two countries. For example, in 1984, Peter Godspeed of the Toronto Star headlined an article with "Acid Rain Relief 46 Years Away U.S. Study Says." His article began, "A child born today may be 46 years old before there is any significant decrease in the air pollution that causes acid rain, a United States government Task Force warns. Emissions of nitrogen oxide and sulphur dioxide, the main components of acid rain, will increase steadily until the turn of the century and beyond, unless governments enact stricter air-pollution controls." "Canada," he continued, "has been pressing the United States for nearly five years to undertake a massive pollution control program to cut acid rain emissions by at least half over the next ten years." But, so far, Mr. Godspeed reported, the Task Force hasn't spent any money studying specific pollution control programs – and it does-n't intend to until at least 1985.

In April 1984, Sandra Postel reported in the St. Petersburg Times, "Faced with alarming new evidence of forest damage in the Eastern United States, the Reagan administration now concedes that air pollutants may be a threat to forests."

Peter Godspeed continued his series of articles on June 21, 1984: "The noxious soup of air pollutants linked to acid rain may be killing as many as 50,000 people a year in Canada and the United States, a U.S. congression-al report released today says."

And the next day, Globe and Mail writer William Johnson headlined his story with "Cut Acid Rain By Half, Mulroney Asks Reagan." His article said, "Brian Mulroney told Ronald Reagan yesterday that the U.S. president could capture the imagination of all Canadians if he would agree to reduce acid rain by half over the next decade." The article continued, "What he proposed for the United States – a reduction of 50 per cent of all acid rain emissions – is precisely what the Canadian government has promised its people."

In June 1984, a "busy acid rain news month," Toronto Star headlines blared, "U.S. Canada acid rain war flares anew over Munich pact." The Toronto Star's Stephen Handelman stated in an article datelined "Munich ... The acid rain war between the United States and Canada has flared up again, following a U.S. refusal to go along with a key international agree-ment on air pollution."

The Southam news chain reported, "Washington ... A key U.S. gov-ernment study, used to show acid rain is not an urgent problem, is being rewritten because some conclusions are wrong. The admission of serious flaws in the September Interim Assessment on Acid Rain Deposition took place Wednesday at a congressional subcommittee hearing but was eclipsed by Prime Minister Brian Mulroney's appeal to Congress for acid rain action."

And in January 1988, Michael Keating of the Globe and Mail stated, "In what is described as a toughly worded letter, federal environment min-ister Tom McMillan has told his U.S. counterpart, Lee Thomas, that a major U.S. acid rain report is wrong and misleading."

And, in the meantime, I was getting hell from my constituents and from the North Bay Nugget's Bill Radunsky, who headlined his May 30, 1984, article, "MOE out to prove acid rain killing Parry Sound trees." The Nugget reported on studies which were proving that acid rain does cause damage to vegetation in nature, and that maple trees in the Dwight-

Huntsville-Sundridge areas are dying off at more than double the normal rate, threatening future syrup production there. As well, another Nugget article pointed out that "Canso bombers are air-dropping lime onto Trout Lake in an effort to reverse the effects of acid rain which is threatening the area's population."

Is it any wonder I am working so hard on the various acid rain committees?

When I first visited the U.S., in the early 1980s, acid rain was one of their best-kept secrets, with the media knowing little or nothing and caring less. At most a dozen members of the U.S. Congress were even sympathetic or interested in "Canada's" problem of acid rain, and many are still absolutely ignorant and opposed to what Canada is trying to do.

October 1987 … I am involved in many Parliamentary Association meetings now, with other countries. One of the most important in my view is the Canada/U.S. Parliamentary Association. We hold meetings every year alternating between Canada and the U.S. Because of my ongoing involvement with acid rain problems, I am chosen as a delegate to a good many of these meetings. I am, therefore, able to speak with some authority on the damage being done to Canada by acid rain heading north from the U.S. This information helps get the message across to many of my U.S. counterparts in the House of Representatives and the U.S. Senate.

September 25 … Washington. Throwing aside my usual shyness, I spoke with our American acid rain colleagues today. I really let them have it. I said, "If you don't give a damn about Canada, you should at least be thinking about your own country and your own lakes and rivers. You are the greatest flag-waving nation on earth, with monuments for everything, and many magnificent historic buildings which have been seriously damaged by acid rain. Some of your finest buildings are in dire need of extensive repairs because of this." I think the message has finally gotten through and we expect to meet on more productive terms in the future!

October … When we were talking at breakfast in the cafeteria this morning about the need for timetables and schedules regarding acid rain control, I recalled a conversation a while ago with Charles Caccia, Liberal environment critic. Mr. Caccia said, "The Americans are obsessed with the costs of controlling acid rain, when they should pay more attention to the cost of *not* controlling it. It will cost more to do nothing than to do something." I certainly agree with that.

June 1987 ... I was invited today, by the consul general in Dallas, Christopher Pearson, to visit him and speak with a university group. Mr. Pearson was formerly government leader in Yukon. He said that he would make arrangements with the Southern Methodist University to have me talk to their group and then tour Dallas, including the place where President John F. Kennedy was assassinated. I was also to see South Fork, the famous ranch which was used in the television series (which I call a soap opera) Dallas. I was. shocked to see the size of the ranch house which looked so pretentious on television but was not large at all. The swimming pool, where many of the scenes took place, was a small, ordinary pool. The camera certainly plays tricks.

During my talk to the Texas group I said, "The Canadian parliamentary Special Committee on Acid Rain, of which I am chairman, visited Capitol Hill earlier this week to deliver a message. We told several senators, congressmen, citizens' action groups and coal lobbyists that Canada can ill-afford much more environmental abuse from acid rain precipitation. It came as no surprise to us that many of them agreed with us wholeheartedly while others looked upon us with glazed eyes and deaf ears. The powerful coal lobby in the U.S. is protecting the best interests of those regions it represents, but it is doing so at the expense of every man, woman and child on this continent."

I recalled that Majority House Leader William Byrd of West Virginia, a coal-producing state, made great promises but despite the assurances that he is a strong supporter of acid rain reduction and pollution control, he has made sure that no legislation has ever gotten before the Senate.

I also mentioned that a total of 14,000 lakes and rivers in Ontario had been damaged, some of them irreparably, by acid rain. The shock on their faces made me add, "I must point out to you that, in Texas, you do not have too many lakes or rivers. They are at a premium. But in my own province of Ontario, despite the fact that there are so many damaged or absolutely dead lakes, Ontario has a total of 800,000 lakes, and Quebec has one million. Canada is indeed fortunate to be a country with the most fresh water in the world." There was some disbelief about my facts, I thought!

Ontario's biggest polluters are still Inco and Ontario Hydro, with Noranda still number one in Quebec. Inco has recently spent $400 million of its own money to upgrade its Sudbury plant and has reduced emissions significantly. But back in its heyday of nickel production, when Inco was producing 90 per cent of the world's nickel, emissions were 7,000 tons of SO_2 daily, seven days a week, and three shifts a day, with 22,000 employees.

[It is interesting to note that things would change dramatically by 1992, with the work-force at less than 9,000 and just as much nickel being produced, but in an automated way. As well, SO_2 emissions were greatly reduced by 1992 and had gone down from 3,000 tons a day to 1,900 tons a day. Inco's goal, I am told, is under 900 tons a day. This large decrease is partially explained by world competition in major nickle production by such countries as Chile and Russia.]

There was an environmental meeting in Vancouver recently that members of our acid rain committees were not invited to attend. However, we were granted permission to sit in on the sessions as "observers." Bob Wenman, MP Fraser Valley, arranged for Mona and me, and others in our group, to attend a tour of the famous Carmanah Forest on Vancouver Island where trees reach the great height of 330 feet or more. Because of "my age," I was told, we could not tramp in with the rest of the group, but were given the privilege of being helicoptered in. The machine circled over these incredible trees and the ancient forest so that we could have a bird's-eye view, and then came down in a breathtaking swoop into the centre of a fast-moving but shallow river. We were then carried from the helicopter to the shore. It was interesting to see, at first hand, what all the discussions were about regarding rain forests, clear-cutting and many of the sensitive issues regarding B.C. lumbering.

June 1990 ... The Hon. John Fraser, PC, QC, MP, Speaker of the House of Commons, and the Hon. David MacDonald, PC, MP, chairman of the Standing Committee on the Environment, signed a letter printed on recycled paper in a brochure called "Greening the Hill." To quote, "Canada is becoming a nation of environmentalists. From all provinces and all walks of life, we are banding together to save and conserve our natural heritage."

"Canada's 295 Members of Parliament have accepted full responsibility for providing leadership not only in their own communities, but also at their place of work, Parliament Hill," the letter continued.

"Greening the Hill" is a comprehensive program designed to eliminate environmentally harmful products and methods and replace them with appropriate alternatives founded on the "4Rs" of environmental protection: Reduce, Reuse, Recycle, and Re-think. The program involves the five buildings in the House of Commons complex and the working environment for more than 3,500 people. Among the projects tackled are:

- no smoking allowed anywhere within any of the Parliamentary Buildings;
- groundskeepers will use environmentally friendly products only;
- an alternative to road salt as a de-icer will be sought;

- photocopies will be made on both sides of the paper and inter-office mail will be delivered in re-usable envelopes;
- the canteen will eliminate the use of disposable packaging; and
- trucks, buses and cars will be converted, where possible, to natural gas.

And many more well-thought-out ideas.

I wish them well.

During my twelve years as a member of many acid rain committees both in Canada and the United States, I became involved with many important American and Canadian organizations. But perhaps the most important one was the Canadian Coalition on Acid Rain, whose president was Jeff Shearer, a Toronto businessman. The organization included an interesting and influential group of members, many with summer homes in Muskoka. They were worried about the condition of the lakes in their area, a number of which had been damaged by acid rain. The coalition arranged meetings and banquets in Toronto, one of which I attended, at the Royal York Hotel. The guest speaker was U.S. Senator Ted Kennedy, with whom I talked at the head table and after the meeting as well.

November 19 ... A second thank-you banquet for the workers on the acid rain committee was held at Casa Loma and I was also pleased to attend that gathering. There were special T-shirts with names of the contributors, and my name was included. In the crowd was U.S. Senator Dan Durrenburger, the Republican senator from Minnesota, who was guest speaker.

The coalition was also celebrating the signing into law of amendments to the U.S. Clean Air Act, by President George Bush, and the successful completion of the coalition's ten-year lobbying campaign to see the acid rain control program in place in both the U.S. and Canada.

At the gathering, House of Commons Speaker John Fraser and I were recognized as being two of the twenty-nine individuals in Canada and the U.S. who have played a key role over the last decade in the fight for acid rain controls.

While many groups have been involved in efforts to curb acid rain threats, no group is more deserving of recognition than the Canadian Coalition on Acid Rain. Of particular note are the coalition's dynamic co-ordinators, Adele Hurley and Michael Perley. Their intense and tireless lobbying of the political and economic leadership on both sides of the border contributed greatly to the November 15th historic signing. By making acid rain a mainstream issue, they also assisted in preparing the public to understand and accept other air pollution threats such as toxic rain, depletion of ozone layers and global warming.

I have heard people say that nothing can be done to protect the environment or reverse its degradation, but I believe those opinions to be greatly misplaced and certainly mistaken. What we have achieved to date with acid rain control is testimony to the power of people to change the course of destructive trends, if there is both a desire and a will.

Scientists believe that the positive actions of the two governments should be enough to protect all but extremely sensitive areas from further damage, and allow areas already damaged to slowly recover. Glancing through some reports from Ottawa last night, in my Burks Falls riding office on Ontario Street, I noticed one from November 28, 1990, where I had stated, "November 15, 1990 may very well go down in history as a major turning point in the ongoing fight for a healthier environment. After ten years of intensive lobbying of the U.S. government by Canada, President George Bush finally signed into law the revised U.S. Clean Air Act."

While the act tackles the sources of many airborne pollutants with tough regulations, it is the act's acid rain abatement provisions that have the most significance for Canada.

The United States is now firmly committed to reducing its acid rain-causing emissions by 50 per cent by the year 2000. Furthermore, the revised act lays a solid foundation for the finalization of a comprehensive transboundary acid rain treaty between Canada and the U.S.

January 1991 ... I read the finished product of an interview I gave a newspaper writer a few weeks ago and do not regret my words: "I am galled by Canadians who whine about what a terrible place Canada is. We have 20 per cent of all the fresh water in the world. Canada is five thousand miles wide, with only 27 million people. Holland, on the other hand, has a population of about 4,000 people to the square mile, whereas in Canada, there are about four to five people to the square mile."

In India, I have been told, an estimated one million people would like to emigrate to Canada. Canada's population is not increasing by natural propagation, so the only way we can grow is to bring in immigrants. Presently, we welcome about 225,000 immigrants each year.

How many of us realize how fortunate we are to live in this wonderful country?

On Wednesday, March 13, 1991, I stated in the House: "Today, our two great nations concluded a formal Canada/U.S. Air Quality Agreement of historical proportions. With the signatures of President George Bush and the Rt. Hon. Brian Mulroney, prime minister of Canada, firmly affixed to the document, a major precedent was set in undoing some of the damage man has inflicted on the environment.

"Beyond a doubt, the fight against acid rain in our two countries has been long and hard but Prime Minister Mulroney is to be commended. By placing acid rain high on his personal agenda, we are here today reaping the fruits of his efforts.

"As well, we must not fail to commend Speaker John Fraser, for the great job he has done as an environmentalist and a former minister of the environment.

"In talking with some members of the press following the signing ceremony, I recalled that we had lobbied for acid rain controls because it was such a huge issue in my riding, where trees have been damaged and heightened acid rain levels in lakes and rivers have reduced growth of new fish.

"When we first went down to Washington years ago, in the early 1980s, the political people we met just looked at us as if to say, 'What the hell are you guys doing here?' They thought we were down there to sell surplus Ontario and Quebec hydro energy. However, we have come a long way since then.

"Under the agreement, the U.S. will:

- cut sulphur dioxide emissions in half from 1980 levels by the year 2000;
- cut nitrogen oxide emissions by two million tonnes annually; and
- impose a permanent cap on acid rain emissions after the year 2000.

"Canada has agreed to:

- cut sulphur dioxide emissions in the seven Eastern provinces to 50 per cent of 1980 levels by 1994; and
- by 1994, bring the three Western provinces into a control program and establish a permanent national cap on sulphur dioxide emissions at 3.2 million tonnes annually by the year 2000.

"Both our countries are committed to:

- refer disputes about implementation of the Accord to an independent third party;
- continue scientific monitoring to determine whether measures are adequate; and
- establish permanent machinery to deal with other air-quality issues and acid rain problems."

When Mr. Mulroney became prime minister in 1984, I said to him that acid rain was the "sleeper issue," and if he wanted to be on the side of the angels he would place it high on his list of priorities. Perhaps he didn't listen to me too well at first, but he certainly made up for it in later years.

It is interesting to note that both Liberals and New Democrats slammed the agreement, with the Liberal Environment Critic Paul Martin saying, "If it is not enforceable, the agreement is no more than a photo opportunity for the Tories."

Jim Fulton, NDP critic said, "Let's not pop the champagne corks yet."

Time alone will tell.

I was pleased to see an article in the Bracebridge Examiner yesterday which closed with the statement, "Some backbenchers can actually change the world for the better, like our Stan."

High praise indeed.

April 4 ... Despite the signing of the treaty, I am well aware that the job of curbing acid rain is just beginning. It will be necessary to check on both levels of government in Canada as well as our American friends, to make sure that steps are being taken, and money approved, to continue the reduction of acid rain in both our countries.

April 7 ... The Acid Rain Committee continues its vital work, with meetings and discussions almost every day. Out of this, a new sub-committee has been formed. I have been appointed chairman.

New York, Sept. 23, 1993 ... The minister of the environment, Jean Charest, was presented today with the Gold Medal for Distinguished Service in the cause of Greater Canadian/American Friendship and Understanding. Mr. Charest immediately placed the Gold Medal on its long ribbon around my neck, saying that it rightly belonged to me in recognition of my long and untiring efforts towards solving Canada's acid rain problems.

What an honor to receive such an award from Jean Charest. It was one of the most important and moving moments in my life to be so honored in such a distinguished company. And by a man who I am honored to call a friend.

The medal was presented by the Society of the Americas, and a duplicate was presented to William Reilly, the United States director of the Environmental Protection Agency.

The bottom line to my acid rain "career" is a headline in a magazine Nature's Pleas, which said, "Mr. Acid Rain Retires After 21 Years." I have been retired from office since October this year, 1993.

The article in the magazine stated, "During the latter part of 1989, several months after Project Preservation began to publish Nature's Pleas, an article about our organization in the North Bay Nugget spurred Parry Sound/Muskoka Tory MP Stan Darling to write us for more information. Sending a small package off to this man, we did not even begin to imagine what a wonderful member, friend and supporter that Mr. Darling would become in the following years. Without his guidance and legwork, our project would never have survived a potentially dangerous money problem four years ago. No month would go by without something in the mail from Stan, be it a package on acid rain or the most recent House of Commons debate on the greenhouse effect. He most definitely is a model member of our group."

Well, needless to say, I had to reply to that article and I said, "For about twelve years I sat as a Member of a number of Parliamentary acid rain committees and had the privilege of chairing two of them. Nothing made those hard, slugging, frustrating years more worthwhile than the signing of the Air Quality Accord by President Bush and Prime Minister Mulroney, on March 13, 1991. Frankly, there can be no greater reward than knowing your efforts in their own small way, have contributed to making the environment a little healthier, not only now, but for future generations."

That pretty well sums up my thoughts about my work in acid rain.

Update on acid rain, Burks Falls, 1995 ... From information sent to me by the Ministry of the Environment's Dr. Bob Slater, an assistant deputy minister, I was able to bring myself up-to-date on our acid rain, clean air program, since I left Parliament in October 1993.

The acid rain program mandate was to limit the wet sulphate deposition to no more than twenty kilograms per hectare, per year, in the eastern provinces of Canada. This was defined as the acceptable level for protection of moderately sensitive aquatic systems. The eastern provinces met their individual SO_2 targets in 1994. In 1994, the federal government began a "greening government program," which would look at reducing emissions from federal facilities. The federal government also began working to develop a new National Strategy on Acidifying Emission post-year-2000. In a status report on Canadian and U.S. acid rain science programs, Canada is ahead of schedule. Health Canada continues to research the health effects of sulphates in Saint John, New Brunswick, the city of 100,000 which has the most acidic air in Canada.

Lake survey data shows increasing nitrate concentrations in a number of Ontario and Quebec lakes and streams which over the long term may undermine ecological benefits derived from SO_2 control. Aquatic ecosystems can be adversely affected by chronic acidification and by short-term decreases in pH that occur during snowmelts and rainstorms.

There is an increase in the number of Quebec lakes considered to be acidic, compared to 1992.

Although goals are being met, many ecosystems are still being damaged, with lakes and streams continuing to be acidified. Health effects are a growing concern. Even after all currently planned emissions reductions in both the U.S. and Canada are in place, some regions are expected to receive acid deposits in excess of critical loads for sulphur currently defined for aquatic ecosystems.

The emerging concern is that nitrogen deposition, which scientists predict may overtake sulphur as the major acidifying agent, needs critical attention, and scientists are turning their attention to developing critical loads for nitrogen.

In short, the acid rain problem has not been solved. The eastern Canada Acid Rain Program has been a good first step, but more needs to be done. Federal and provincial governments have begun working with stakeholders to develop a new national strategy on acidifying emissions for post-2000 to protect acid-sensitive areas, human health, and visibility in Canada, expected to be completed by 1997 and take effect when the present program expires in the year 2000.

GUN CONTROL

January 1973, Ottawa … I've come down to Ottawa for the first time in the House of Commons without any great expectations that I am going to set the world on fire. I'm here for the prime purpose of representing the people of Parry Sound/Muskoka and to help them out with their problems. Being in the Opposition, I know that our party has no direct input or influence on legislation and it would be easy to become cynical. I don't want to just sit back and criticize everything the government is doing, but to be honest, I can't believe that the government will put through every bit of its legislation in Canada's best interests. But when our party is in power, I will be a member of the team. If the team is going to produce anything worthwhile, we will have to work together as a team. Our Caucus will sit every Wednesday that Parliament is sitting. We can say what we want and I expect to voice my opinion whenever I can. The Cabinet, I am told, will go over all suggestions and make the policy decisions after that.

Of course, no matter who is governing Canada, at the time of an election, if the people don't feel that party is governing well, they tell them in no uncertain terms. But the amount of legislation that is held up, for one reason or another and in many different ways, is a disgrace.

Ottawa 1988 … The riding of Parry Sound/Muskoka is a noted hunting and fishing area. Sportsmen have a very strong, vociferous voice and they are banded together under the title Muskoka/Parry Sound Hunt Camp Association. Their president is Jack Newton of Huntsville, and they say that at this time they represent 10,000 hunters in this area. Many members just visit this area for hunting, but this association and similar groups across Canada have a single purpose: to fight any legislation that would make gun ownership more restrictive or would prohibit certain types of guns, such as machine guns. The association has threatened government to carry out a political campaign to defeat the present government unless the gun control bill is withdrawn or greatly diluted.

This association does not seem to be aware that the Canadian public, at large, is very worried. They want much stricter gun laws. I have met with the association at their annual meetings for several years now. I have also arranged for knowledgeable speakers to attend their meetings to answer questions and bring them up-to-date on what the government is trying to do. I've also tried to point out what the majority of Canadian citizens are demanding of its government, much stricter gun control laws.

Coming from a rural area, I am aware that there is a different outlook in these areas than there is in a large city. I am also aware that the majority of citizens are in the larger cities and have a good reason to demand tighter control. A recent vote showed that over 50 per cent of the women in Canada would ban all types of firearms if they had their way. I wonder what the sportsmen would say to that? Incidentally, there are more women voters in Canada than there are men!

Ottawa 1992 ... Well, the bill for gun control has finally come to the House of Commons for the third reading. There were less than fifteen Members who voted against the bill. It was brought into effect under the minister of justice, the Hon. Kim Campbell.

Well, the sportsmen's groups are setting up political action groups and are out to get Campbell, and to defeat the Conservative government because of the negative bill.

At lunch today in the dining room, one of our Members pointed out how short-sighted this action would be. "They don't take into consideration," he said, "that even if the Progressive Conservatives were defeated and are replaced by the NDP or the Liberals, there would be a very good chance that stricter legislation would be enacted." But I am really getting a lot of negative comments from some of the hunters in my riding.

November 7, 1991 ... The Globe and Mail, which is fast to jump on the news controversy bandwagon, had an article in today's paper which was headlined "Campbell says gun bill uniquely Canadian. Country has own firearms culture." Graham Fraser of the parliamentary bureau wrote that Justice Minister Kim Campbell said yesterday that the gun control legislation expected to be passed today is a reflection of a unique Canadian culture.

"Canada has its own firearms culture," she said. "We have many, many law-abiding Canadians who own firearms and that is a very important part of our cultural traditions. We also have a culture that is non-violent, concerned about public safety and has respect for public security."

She said that Bill C-17, which was endorsed at the report stage yesterday in the House of Commons by a vote of 172 to 13, reasserts this. However, Liberal MP Russell MacLellan echoed Ms. Campbell, saying Canadians are proud of their culture. "Our culture here is not dependent on firearms as it is south of the border," he said. "In 1980, 1,400 Canadians died from firearms, 1,100 of those in suicides, while in the States, 34,000 died from firearms."

He also expressed regret that the legislation was not stronger. Suzanne Laplante-Edwards, whose daughter, Anne-Marie, was one of the fourteen women murdered by Marc Lepine in Montreal in December of 1989, told reporters that the bill is a "first step and they were satisfied that progress was being made."

In the Muskoka Advance, on April 26, 1992, I wrote, "The new regulations will improve public safety by reducing the possibility of the theft and accidental misuse of guns. They cover the size of cartridge magazines, set out requirements for collectors, and the storage and transportation of firearms."

The North Bay Nugget said in 1991, "New bill on gun controls will make buying harder." But the Huntsville Forester on September 23, 1992, stated, "Hunt camps had best gear up for the new regulations in gun control legislation." Ev Van Duuren wrote, "Hunt camp groups may want to spend some time boning up on the new gun control legislation this deer season. How hunters keep guns and ammunition in camp will almost certainly change in 1993." New regulations required that when hunters come into camp after a day in the field they must disable their rifles (put in a trigger lock or remove the bolt, etc.), and store ammunition in a separate and locked place. And the Huntsville Herald's Doug Brenner stated on November 18, 1992, "There is considerable controversy in Muskoka this summer over the federal government's new legislation to prohibit certain types of firearms and ensure the safe storage of firearms."

Letters sent to me in June 1993 from the Ontario Handgun Association and on August 2nd of the same year from the Coalition for Gun Control take opposing views. Executive Manager Larry Whitmore of the Ontario Handgun Association concluded his three-page letter about the legislation with these words: "There is already too much law, too much control and too much bureaucracy directed only at the legitimate gun owner." While Heidi Rathjen, executive director of the Coalition for Gun Control stated: "Although the passage of Bill C-17 in December 1991 is an important step in the right direction, much remains to be done. We still register dogs, but not rifles and shotguns. It's still easier to buy ammunition than cigarettes. Assault weapons like the Russian-made AK-47 are still legally bought and sold in Canada." Although I am no longer a Member of Parliament, I still get questions about firearms and gun controls. I don't see this as an issue that will soon go away and as someone said to me today, "I don't see the robbers and hardened criminals applying to anyone for a permit to carry a gun before they commit a crime."

PRAYER BREAKFASTS

February 4, Washington, D.C. … My invitation to the National Prayer Breakfast in Washington, D.C., stated: "Members of the United States Senate and the House of Representatives request the pleasure of your company at the 31st Annual National Prayer Breakfast with the President of the United States and Mrs. Clinton, and other national leaders in the executive, judicial and legislative branches of our government."

The enclosed schedule of events included an international luncheon with congressional leaders and members of the diplomatic community, the U.S. Senate and the House of Representatives. As well, there will be a great many private dinners all around Washington for specially invited guests. Mr. and Mrs. Al Gore – the vice president and his wife – are also taking part in both the breakfast meetings and other events. Over 140 nations from around the world will be represented.

At my place at the breakfast this morning was a small folder listing some of the noteworthy remarks made at previous Prayer Breakfasts by former U.S. presidents, which I find interesting.

Ronald Reagan said, "Fellowships have begun to spring up through the Capitol. They exist now in all three branches of the Government and they have spread throughout the capitals of the world, to parliaments and congresses far away."

George Bush remarked: "Some wonderful things have resulted from these private and off-the-record informal meetings. Many people attending have received personal help in ways that are impossible to disclose without violating the confidentiality of the meetings. The greatest thing, however, is the close friendship established with God, our families and with each other."

Harry Truman said, "I ask only to be a good and faithful servant of my Lord and my people."

Amen to all of them.

When the haunting song "Amazing Grace" was sung, there wasn't a dry eye in the breakfast room. I sang as lustily as anyone the words, "Amazing Grace, how sweet the sound / That saved a wretch like me, I once was lost, but now am found / Was blind, but now I see."

February 5 ... At a gathering tonight, I heard the words spoken by Catherine Kulman, who said, "We lie in a crisis of hope. To see the invisible, believe the incredible and do the impossible." Interestingly, the psalm read at the Prayer Breakfast the day before was number 24, "There is hope for every nation that recognizes God."

I've never attended a Prayer Breakfast without learning something important to me. Senator David L. Boren of the United States Senate Prayer Group, who hails from Oklahoma, said some years ago, "Titles we wear are temporary. We all pray, not that God is on our side but that we are on God's side. I believe that those words are attributed to Abraham Lincoln. He also said that 'titles are not ours but a trust from God. He will give us strength only if we will let Him.'"

Incidentally, I overheard a remark today in the dining room of the Washington Hilton, where the breakfasts are held, which gave me a chuckle: "President Reagan spoke briefly one year at the Prayer Breakfast, concluding his remarks by saying, 'Moses was chosen by God at the age of 80 and lived to the age of 175.' We all wondered if Mr. Reagan was trying to tell us something ... "

February 6 ... Ronald Reagan is still talked about and quoted despite the fact that he has not been president for some time now. At one breakfast at which he officiated, he said, "I want to put prayer back into our schools. God, the source of our knowledge, has been expelled from the classroom."

It is still a hot issue here in Washington, and in Canada as well.

I have done quite a bit of research into the Prayer Breakfasts since joining them over sixteen years ago. They are, perhaps, one of the most important, vital and growing groups in the world. In 1942, members of the United States Senate and the House of Representatives began to meet privately on an off-the-record basis to talk, think and pray together each week. This has continued for the past fifty or more years. In 1953, members of the Congress invited President Eisenhower to join them for a fellowship breakfast in the spirit of Christ. The statement made by Mr. Eisenhower still rings in my mind, "My job is a very lonely one." The fellowship of his friends, and possibly of some political enemies too, must have meant a great deal to him at that time. The National Prayer Breakfast was born out of the warmth and spirit of that first meeting.

The grey eminence behind the worldwide Prayer Breakfasts is Douglas Coe of Washington, D.C. He oversees this great movement in a quiet way and shuns publicity of any kind. Despite this, several presidents have paid tribute to his great achievements in his field.

March 3, Ottawa … Shortly after I was elected to the House of Commons, Alf Hales of Guelph, Ontario, who was one of the senior Members of Parliament, asked me to attend a Prayer Breakfast with him on the following morning. Not one to pass up a free meal, I said, "Sure, I'm not doing anything at that time." Alf said we would be joining with a group who met each Wednesday morning. It had given itself the name "Parliamentary Prayer Group." Well, I raised my eyebrows and thought that this was an unusual happening in Parliament.

We gathered together at 8 a.m. and most of us had already spent an hour or so in our offices, getting ready for the day. A senator read the scripture he had chosen, made his comments on what he had read, and then the group made their own comments as well. It was very interesting. Some speakers mentioned how they had gotten into politics in the first place, and how it had affected their lives. Some of the remarks were quite personal and revealing. Well, I have been an active member of this group longer than any other member, but I have not been involved since my retirement from politics in October. I was asked several years ago to assume the job of treasurer, which I didn't mind accepting until I found out that part of the job was contacting business leaders, politicians and other political people to request donations to sponsor the National Prayer Breakfast, held each February or March in Room 200, the Confederation Room in the West Block of the Parliament Buildings.

The annual breakfasts in Ottawa are quite formal, with a keynote speaker and all members of the diplomatic corps invited. Head table is made up of the Speaker of the House of Commons, the Speaker of the Senate, the prime minister, if he is available, the leader of the Opposition, and the NDP. The chief justice of the Supreme Court of Canada attends and music is provided, quite often, by the RCMP Band. It is impressive and enjoyable. Needless to say, invitations are at a premium with the main room filled to capacity and other guests in a special overflow room. Those not in the main salon come into that room after breakfast to listen to the keynote speaker.

People are often surprised that the speakers are not all ministers, clergy or priests, although one exception was Shawn O'Sullivan, an outstanding speaker, who was a former Member of Parliament, and was then a priest.

February 15 … The first year I was invited to the National Prayer Breakfast in Washington was a thrill. The president and his wife always attend and the Breakfasts have been taking place, in one form or another, since 1942. Transportation to Washington for our Canadian contingent is usually provided by the government, and we always stay at the Washington Hilton (the Members pay their own expenses). This massive hotel has a ballroom large enough to seat the over 3,500 guests who usually attend this once-a-year breakfast event.

At the last one I attended there were representatives from about 150 countries, which I find surprising, considering the expense and travel time involved. In 1993, when I attended, The Reverend Billy Graham was the speaker, and his dynamic address was based on Psalm 23, "The Lord Is My Shepherd."

In early years, I was allowed to take my camera and I have been able to get some unique photos with notable persons but this has now been banned. One year, I sat near Bishop Fulton Sheen and had the pleasure of talking with him briefly. I had always enjoyed watching his television broadcasts and had sent away for his sermons. It was interesting to meet this fascinating, renowned man and tell him how the "man from a little village of Burks Falls" had enjoyed his words and his wisdom.

Special seminars are often held following the Breakfast meetings, and the food, music and entertainment for the entire affair are always excellent, often outstanding. One thing I enjoy is the annual visit to Capitol Hill in Washington, where a luncheon is hosted by the United States Senate Prayer Group and the House of Representatives Prayer Group. I now know the Capitol quite well, and over the years haven't missed many of these special events

March 5, Ottawa … Today I acted as head usher at the Prayer Breakfast in Ottawa. We ushered all the guests to their tables in the main salon, the Confederation Room. The table hosts were already in place to greet their guests and make them welcome. Almost everyone arriving had a table reservation but there were some who found themselves able to attend only at the last minute. As they had no Admit cards, they were assigned to the overflow room – 208 – which adjoins the Confederation Room. We have tried to simplify seating by an arrangement of green cards, for members of the diplomatic corps, blue cards for we parliamentarians and white cards for all others. Jack B. Murta, MP, who has chaired the breakfasts for some years now, is very organized.

I can recall one breakfast, when the then leader of the Opposition in Canada read the scripture, and the words, which were already familiar to me, are engraved on my heart forever: "Neither shall he multiply wives for himself, nor shall he greatly increase silver and gold for himself, and he may learn to fear the Lord his God by carefully observing all the words of this law and these statutes."

This is excellent advice for us all.

On April 19, in Nova Scotia, Dr. Jim Perkins gave a fine address at the University of Nova Scotia Prayer Breakfast. He said, "Those who are caught in the maelstrom of political activity may long for the isolation of the life of meditation and prayer. But there is no one way to serve – political involvement is one way; monastic reflection is one way. Practical ministry is one way. Individually, they are valuable but incomplete. Together they form a force for goodness, which may yet serve to humanize the world and bring to God's children the experience of freedom, justice and peace."

Senator Mark Hatfield's executive assistant said, "If you want to respect laws and sausages, you should not watch either of them being made!"

May 17, Ottawa ... In checking over a memorandum from the Congress of the United States which came my way in today's mail, I notice that Lawton Chiles, of Florida, who signed the memo, states in no uncertain terms: "The Fellowship Breakfast which began many years ago with the leaders of our country, has now become a worldwide family event. There are people coming to Washington from over 150 nations, from every State in the Union, and from hundreds of cities, from every background and every cross-section of our society."

My own understanding is this: After attending the breakfasts for almost twenty years, I think they are so important because a group of friends and family, bound together in Jesus Christ, are gathered together for no other reason than fellowship and reflection.

As well, it transcends every ethnic, language, social and economic background. It is, apparently, made possible only because of our common love, respect and regard for Christ, and for each other. This, I think, is the bond which makes the primary impact, not necessarily the talks and the meetings.

May 27, Ottawa ... Looking through my Prayer Breakfast files today, my secretary pointed out a memo which had been enclosed in the recent invitation to Washington. It quoted the 18th century American political leader, Andrew Oliver, as saying, "Politics is the most hazardous of all professions.

There is not another in which a man can hope to do so much good to his fellow creatures; neither is there any in which, by a mere loss of nerve, he may do such widespread harm; nor is there another in which he may so easily lose his own soul. With all the temptation and the degradation that besets it, politics is still the noblest career any one can choose."

I intend to work that quotation into an upcoming speech as soon as I can.

May 18 ... It is just ten years since I joined the Prayer Breakfasts in Ottawa. I wrote a note to Father Shawn O'Sullivan today to tell him about the special Mass conducted on his behalf. Father Bob Ogle was assisted by Stan Hudecki, MP. I hope Shawn realizes how many of his former colleagues in the House are concerned about him and are praying for his recovery. I also sent him a copy of the notice which had been sent to all members about the special Mass.

June 3 ... At luncheon in the Cafeteria today a group of devotees of the Ottawa Prayer Breakfasts were trying to list their favorite keynote speaker from the breakfasts. At least half of those present said that Shawn O'Sullivan had been the outstanding speaker in the years they had been attending. Shawn was a former Member of Parliament, for about five years until he decided to resign his seat in Parliament and study for the priesthood. He became a very famous young priest, but, sadly, contracted leukemia. A few months before his death, we had arranged to have him speak at our national breakfast. His address was humorous and sad at the same time, and is a never-to-be-forgotten event.

Shawn was elected in 1972, the youngest person ever to be elected to the House of Commons. He was just twenty. Shawn represented the riding of Hamilton Wentworth and his father was the general manager of the Royal Connaught Hotel in Hamilton. Shawn had been involved in politics since he was 12 and had met John Diefenbaker at that age. He went on to become one of Mr. Diefenbaker's assistants in Ottawa.

I was privileged to receive an invitation to attend Shawn's ordination as a priest at St. Michael's Cathedral in Toronto. I was surprised to see such a big crowd of notable public figures attending as I entered the cathederal. I assumed there would be a dozen or so priests ordained at the same time. However, it turned out to be a blessed occasion, with Shawn O'Sullivan ordained all alone.

[Sadly, I also attended Shawn's funeral in St. Michael's some years later. We were close and dear friends, jointly involved in one piece of legislation which was to officially designate the beaver as Canada's official emblem.]

One of my friends at lunch today reminded me of a prayer written by the former secretary general of the United Nations Dag Hammarskjold in 1961, which went something like this: "Give us a pure heart, a humble heart, that we may follow Thee with self-denial, steadfastness and courage and meet Thee in silence."

This was read at the breakfast by the Hon. George Shultz, secretary of state, in Washington, at the last Prayer Breakfast.

June 7 ... Bill Emerson, who is the American chairman of the Congressional Executive Committee in Washington, sent a memo along today to all of us faithfuls, which said, in part, "This past year has brought all of us challenges, some with joy, and some with great difficulties. It is evident that Divine help, guidance and more strength are as much needed today as at any time since the beginning of the National Prayer Breakfasts in 1942. In both House and Senate groups, some informal rules have evolved. The Members meet in the spirit of peace and Christ. All members are welcome, regardless of their political or religious affiliations. Sincere seekers as well as the deeply devoted, all on a common journey to understand the place of faith in their lives, and to discover how to love God and one's fellow man.

"The members will not publicize the meetings, nor will they use them for any kind of political gain. The meetings are off-the-record. No one will repeat what is said. And, above all, members can talk about any and all personal problems on which they need guidance, any sadness for which they need prayers." I expect that this philosophy is what keeps the Prayer Breakfasts strong and is, in essence, a wonderful philosophy for any of us to live by.

July 14, Ottawa ... I tried to make a list today of some of the important and newsworthy people I remember attending a Prayer Breakfast in Washington or Ottawa. At one meeting I recall President Jimmy Carter; His Excellency Jake Warren, Canada's ambassador to the United States; the Hon. Paul Hellyer; Sir Ted Leather, governor of Bermuda; Chief of Staff, U.S. Air Force General Lew Allen, Jr.; senators from Arkansas, New Mexico, North Carolina, Alabama, Colorado, the ambassador of Kenya; an important contingent from Germany; the Hon. Ed Broadbent, leader of the NDP; the Rt. Hon. John Turner; the Chief Justice of Canada; the Hon. John Fraser, Speaker of the House of Commons; and many other notable men and women.

September 12 ... We were saddened to hear of Bill Bussiere's illness today.

He's in Queensway Carleton Hospital in Nepean, with gallstones and hernia. His successful surgery was on Friday and all of us at the Prayer Breakfast arranged to send flowers and get-well wishes and cards.

September 18 … We received a letter of thanks today from Father Shawn O'Sullivan in Seattle. He was thanking us for the "astounding enclosure" he received from his Ottawa friends. He said we had relieved a great burden from his shoulders by sending him our cheque for $11,205, from ninety-six of his friends in Ottawa, to help with medical expenses. The list of donors reads like a Who's Who list. Interestingly, he mentions in his letter that he is writing his thank-you note on "The Chief's birthday." He and Mr. Diefenbaker were very close.

September 27 … I just finished writing a note to Pat Ellis, who is senior vice-president of the Bank of Montreal, Atlantic Provinces Division. He sent me some tapes of the Washington Prayer Breakfast when the guest speaker was a fellow Acadian, Dr. Jim Perkin, president of Acadian University. He thought I might enjoy hearing them and I did.

September 25 … The Prayer Breakfasts are enjoying a very sizeable reputation. Today, I had a letter from the Right Reverend Bishop Christopher, Servian Orthodox, Diocese of Eastern United States and Canada. He lives in Edgeworth, Pennsylvania. I enjoyed meeting the bishop at the Washington Prayer Breakfast recently, and was pleased to extend to him an invitation to attend the March 24th breakfast in Ottawa. Dr. Billy Graham gave the benediction and I was struck once again at his commanding, superb presence.

A book I was reading last night quoted Dwight D. Eisenhower as saying, "The Prayer Breakfasts are working precisely because they are private. In some of the most troubled parts of the world, political figures who are old enemies are meeting with each other in a spirit of peace and brotherhood."

At one Prayer Breakfast in the United States, we were treated to a talk by Roosevelt Greer, better known, perhaps, as Rosie Greer. He was a strong supporter of Bobby Kennedy when he became a candidate for the presidency, as so many people were. He was devastated by Kennedy's death.

One year, Sir Richard Harrison was the keynote speaker and there was a large delegation from Germany attending, including the governor of Badwurtemburg. Jean Wulilee, MP of the Korean Conference, stated at that time that his country of Korea had been invaded by foreigners and by three different foreign powers, three hundred times. The Washington Post had a salute to Ronald Reagan today, who, it said, was the oldest man to ever enter the race for the presidency. It was during his 71st birthday year.

October 14 ... Ottawa. One of the most important aspects of the Prayer Breakfasts is the inspiring speeches we hear. I never leave any of the breakfasts without a notebook full of ideas and quotes. But perhaps the most important factor in the ever-growing interest in the breakfasts is that individuals in every nation are trying to live quiet, Godly lives and pray for the leaders of their countries. They join with others who hold these same convictions.

I know that in Ottawa, every Wednesday morning, a group of very concerned and, often, dedicated politicians meet and spend a brief time together with the power of the spirit of God moving us. Sometimes, the pressure of our schedules and the pressure to perform an act of political courage in the face of contrary public opinion makes us vulnerable. But so many of the people with whom I meet have, surprisingly perhaps, devoted their lives to trying to make a difference.

The breakfasts in Ottawa and, I suspect, elsewhere as well further serve as a quiet demonstration that men and women in positions of responsibility place a very high priority on the spiritual values.

March 9, 1989 ... Ottawa ... This is a date that will be imprinted in my memory forever. Father Shawn Patrick O'Sullivan was a great man. He died today and will be mourned around the world. A wonderful, informed and humorous speaker, he addressed a Prayer Breakfast in Ottawa on March 28, 1985. He opened his remarks by saying, "The reason that I am a priest today is all Paul Hellyer's idea. In his office, one day, I turned to Paul for advice, as I often did. Paul is the most decent man I know. When I talked to him about my future, Paul said, 'Shawn, with your name I think you would be better off becoming a priest.' And for me, the name 'politician' means a badge of honor."

A last recollection of Shawn that always comes to mind when I attend any Prayer Breakfast was his ability to mimic famous characters. One day, when the bells were ringing in the corridors of the House, we were all standing around in the Chamber, and Shawn went down to Mr. Diefenbaker's seat and started to mimic him and to give a speech which was quite humorous. A few of us gathered around him and he did not notice that Mr. Diefenbaker had come into the Chamber very quietly and had walked down to stand right behind Shawn. He kept right on mimicking the Chief, and, of course, we all started to roar with laughter. Shawn thought it was because he was so funny and just kept right on with his "speech." Finally, he sensed that something was not right and he looked behind him to see the Chief standing quietly by. Shawn just as quietly sneaked out to the back of the House and didn't say another word. Neither did the Chief.

We all wondered if he had been amused.

Yes, the Prayer Breakfasts have earned a very special place in my heart. For most of us, the hour on Wednesday mornings is an oasis of replenishment of the spirit. We have the opportunity to form supporting and sustaining friendships that go beyond discipline and doctrine. We share, in the most vulnerable way, our sorrows, our fears and our joys with each other. There are just two basic rules for our weekly gatherings: park your partisanship at the door, and leave inside what is said inside.

Most of us who have served our countries believe that the image of Parliament is changing for the better. There is the beginning of more civility and respect among the Members.

Paul prayed for us long ago with these words: "Never have grudges against others, or lose your temper, or raise your voice to anybody, or call each other names, or allow any sort of spitefulness. Be friends with one another, and kind; forgive each other as readily as God forgave you in Christ."

If only we could all live by those words, worldwide.

HEALTH CARE

Ottawa, October 1986 ... In a discussion over lunch in the dining room today I was asked my thoughts about our health care program and it reminded me of a Canada/U.S. Parliamentary Association meeting I attended. Held here in Canada, it was attended by a large contingent of American delegates who were anxious to know how the Canadian system worked. The Americans, at this time, have nothing comparable for their citizens. There were a variety of experts in the field who had asked to come well prepared to talk about setting up our system and how it worked, some from the Ontario Hospital Plan and from National Health and Welfare, among others. There was a good exchange of queries and answers. A member of the House of Representatives from Texas stood up and said, "Gentlemen, we have a very excellent hospital and health care system in the United States and we certainly don't need Canada to tell us what we are supposed to be doing."

Needless to say, our group took great exception to this remark. A man from our health care system said, "Frankly sir, we don't care what you do or don't do. But we were asked to provide you with this information and it was our pleasure to do so."

It's ironic to realize that the U.S. is going to move toward a much better plan than they currently have in place, one which will provide both hospital and medical coverage for at least 35 million people who presently have no hospital or medical coverage whatever. Senator Edward Kennedy, who has very high praise indeed for our Canadian health plan, stated that he would hope that the United States would be able to adopt such a plan. However, I doubt very much that the U.S. will go that far at the present time.

POLITICAL TRAVELS

Cyprus, 1993 … It is nineteen years since I was in Cyprus for any length of time. I am here for the Thirty-ninth Commonwealth Parliamentary Conference. Our members started arriving at the end of August, with meetings starting on the first of September. The opening ceremonies will take place in the International Conference Centre in Nicosia. The plenary sessions, the General Assembly, the Small Countries Conference and Executive Committee meetings will all be held at the Le Meridien Hotel in nearby Limassol. The secretary general is Art Donahue, QC, a Canadian and a former Speaker of the Nova Scotia Legislature. His father was a former senator. Their permanent headquarters is in the Old Palace Yard, Palace of Westminster, London.

There is a full schedule of events planned here and I expect that our Canadian contingent will work very hard. We have all been issued with our identification badges; we have registered, received an accumulation of documentation, speeches, news releases, brochures and so on.

Beirut, 1974 … After the Commonwealth fact-finding tour of Cyprus had finished, we were offered the chance to go home, "the long way," and visit Lebanon and Jerusalem. We were told that if we were going to visit both countries then we should see Beirut first. If we went to Jerusalem first, and our passports had already been stamped with destination Jerusalem, the Immigration people in Beirut would take a very dim view of the situation.

Beirut is a fabulous city and our hotel, the Inter Continental, is one of the most magnificent in the world. Mona is in seventh heaven, as there are Turkish servants, wearing beautiful costumes, walking around the lobby twenty-four hours a day, with delicious Turkish coffee for the guests. She came back from one of the exotic bazaars this afternoon, and told me that after haggling with some of the merchants, she was offered gold for $36 an ounce, which she turned down. When I think of what the price of gold will be in a few years, I could have exploded!

Balbek, Monday, September 13 ... This is one of the oldest cities in the world, with huge Roman columns and many ancient ruins. It is very impressive. Mona is stopping along the way, bartering with the merchants.

Beirut, September 14 ... We went to a nightclub last night, just outside of the city. It is one of the highlights of the trip. I think it was the most fantastic show I have ever seen. After dinner, the show started, with a long runway down the centre of the room for the performers. Although there were some very beautiful and talented dancers with incredible costumes, what impressed me most was the Arabian horsemen, racing all around the stage in precision. There were also elephants on the stage doing a variety of tricks. It was a pageant that I will never forget.
Jerusalem ... We are at the beautiful Inter Continental Hotel, looking right down on the old city of Jerusalem and on the roof of the famous Mosque, Dome of the Rock. We saw many of the Holy sites yesterday, some marvelous old churches, and were impressed by the Dome on the Rock, particularly with its shining gold roof. We removed our shoes and left them at the entrance, and walked all around the Mosque to see its ancient inscriptions and objects of art, centuries old.

One of the most beautiful sites we have seen is the famous Inn of the Good Samaritan on the way to Jericho. The owner is Arabic and has a fantastic array of souvenirs for sale. I bought an ancient costume, and when Mona was taken around to the back to have her costume fitted, she almost blew a fuse, she thought the man was getting amorous!

September 17 ... Mona was a bit tired from all our travels today and so I went out to the Dead Sea on my own. I walked down to the shore of this historic place and thought of all the things I had read in the Bible as a child, and the history connected with the Dead Sea and Jericho and Jerusalem. I was driven up to the mountain today where the Bible states that Christ was tempted by the Devil to throw himself off the mountain. However, he refused to be tempted.

Mona and I are so pleased that we decided to take the extra time and money to see this incredible part of the world. We have called it a second honeymoon.

Cyprus, 1974 ... "The Republic of Cyprus was invaded by Turkey, a country with the largest army in NATO. Thirty-seven per cent of the republic is now occupied and about 180,000 Greek Cypriots were forcibly expelled and are now refugees in their own country. 1,619 Greek Cypriots are missing since the invasion and the fate of eight American citizens is unknown."

So reads a brochure put out by Cypriot citizens which was part of our press material when we arrived today.

I am part of a Canadian delegation led by the Hon. Donald MacDonald (known as "Thumper"!) which is reviewing our Canadian troops in Cyprus prior to the hostilities. It is both interesting and frightening to see troops lined up on either side of the ten-foot-wide "green line." On one side are very fierce and very large Turkish soldiers and on the other the much smaller, but nonetheless fierce, Greek soldiers.

We are staying at the famous Ledra Palace Hotel, which is very close to the officers quarters. Troops here are in the command of Brigadier General Clay Beatty. Prior to his command here, the commander was Brigadier General Ted Leslie. He is the son of five-star General Andrew McNaughton. Mr. Leslie changed his name some time ago so that he could inherit an estate from an aunt who wanted her name to be carried on. Mr. Leslie ran against me in the 1974 election and, I understand, was promised by Pierre Trudeau, then the prime minister of Canada, that, should he win the riding, he would become minister of national defence.

Today, we had a tour of various historic buildings and we are aware of a great deal of animosity by the Greeks. One story we heard today was of a Greek businessman who had a very large warehouse full of automobiles and bicycles. It was impossible for him at that time to remove the cars and bikes, as the roadway in front of his warehouse belonged to the Turks.

The Turkish commander told the businessman that he could remove his stock providing he gave the commander a new car, but the Greek businessman was too furious to agree and so he kept the bikes and cars stored in the warehouse for a good number of years. He just refused to pay up. It seemed to me that it was not a good idea to cut off his nose to spite his face, as my mother used to say.

Cyprus is at the northeastern end of the Mediterranean, with an area of 9,251 square kilometres. In 1974 the population is around 700,000 of which approximately 81.6 per cent are Greek Cypriots. This includes Maronites, Armenians, Latins and others, with 18.4 per cent Turkish Cypriots.

Monday, September 6 ... The Inaugural Ceremony of the Thirty-ninth Commonwealth Conference is to take place today at 10 a.m. in Nicosia. Guest of honor is Vice-Patron of the association, His Excellency, the president of the Republic of Cyprus, Mr. Glafcos Clerides. We were surprised to find out that our hotel in Nicosia is sixty-nine kilometres from Larnaka Airport, and the session in Limassol are another eleven kilometres from here.

September 8 … There is a big celebration set for today. It is the anniversary of the UN. There have also been the elections of the chairman of the Executive Committee and other officials. The Canadian ambassador in Athens is John J. Noble, whose political career started in 1966 in Ottawa. He and his wife, Linda, have been very visible and helpful here.

Canada has participated in UNFICYP from the beginning in 1964. After twenty-nine years, however, the Canadian government has decided to withdraw from Cyprus because of the slow progress in negotiations and because of the great demands elsewhere for Canadian peacekeepers.

The last Canadian soldiers are scheduled to leave Cyprus this September and the Rt. Hon. Joe Clark has been appointed the UN secretary general's special representative for Cyprus as of May 1993.

September 8 … In a discussion over coffee today, our group stated in no uncertain terms that Canada's interest in Cyprus continues to be entirely humanitarian. We have always favored a peaceful, negotiated settlement of disputes over territory. Canada fully supports the UN in its good offices role, although we are neutral in the inter-communal dispute. We do, however, acknowledge the legitimacy of the TRNC leadership as the voice of the Turkish community in negotiations.

Cyprus became independent from Britain in 1960, and in 1974 Greece instigated a military coup against Makarios, and installed an extreme nationalist as president. While the UN has sponsored through the years a series of inter-communal talks, both sides have ostensibly accepted the principle of a federal solution. However, the UN has a quite different interpretation of what this means.

In 1992, there was $20 million or more in trade between Canada and Cyprus. Cyprus does not receive Canadian financial aid. However, the two countries have concluded bilateral dual taxation and social security agreements.

Canada is represented in Cyprus by an honorary consul, Michael Ioannides, who is responsible to Mr. Norman Spector, high commissioner of Canada for Cyprus. He resides in Tel Aviv.

We are interested in comparing data of the two countries, and I was surprised to learn that their unemployment rate this year is 3 per cent and their inflation runs at 5.6 per cent. There are only 708,000 people on the entire island of Cyprus and their governments run for five years. The next election for president is in 1998 and for legislators in 1996.

I wish I had had more time to do some sight-seeing and shopping here. There are some fine historic and beautiful churches and monasteries in the area and some great restaurants. Several members of our party have managed to buy some lovely silver jewelry and also some embroidered linens. When we were first in Cyprus in 1974, Mona shopped around for a beautiful leather handbag and the prices were great.

All in all, I think Canada has done all it can in the Cyprus disputes and it is time we moved on

[D-Day Anniversary] April 1979, Gravenhurst ... I am attending a Lions Convention here, talking with long-time friend, John Taylor. John is a past district governor, from Alliston, Ontario. He was also a former Deputy Mayor of Alliston.

John told me about a wonderful trip that he would be taking in early June. He was going to France to participate in the thirty-fifth anniversary of D-Day. John had been a tank sergeant with the Sherbrooke Fusiliers and he would be visiting some of the locations where he had fought in World War II. I told him, "John, I'll really look forward to hearing about your trip when you get back."

May, 1979 ... The Trudeau government has been defeated. Joe Clark is the new prime minister of Canada. Our party is in power for the first time since I was elected in 1972. It certainly is the beginning of a very important time in my life.

June 1, Ottawa ... Bill Kempling phoned me today. He is the government whip. He wanted to know if I could leave immediately for France! When I asked him what this was all about he said, "Stan, we would like you to leave immediately for France to represent the government of Canada at the Normandy D-Day anniversary."

I replied that I could not understand why I was being asked. I had never been in the armed forces because of my health, and certainly had not been overseas for them.

Well, my ego was deflated when Bill said, "Frankly, Stan, we can't get anyone else to do it. All the other members of the party say they want to stay close to the phone at home to see if they will be appointed to the Cabinet!"

Well, how could I refuse?

I understand that the PC delegate who was to have gone is Bill Knowles of Simcoe. He was a long-time Member of Parliament and the veterans affairs critic. However, Bill decided not to run in the last election. Other delegation members were former minister of national defence, the Hon. Giles Lamontagne, Senator Duff Roblin and Senator Jack Godfrey.

We flew from Mirabel Airport in Montreal to Paris, with Air France, and by bus to Deauville. We were designated as "The Ambassador's Party" but we saw little or nothing of him.

Following a briefing, the delegation departed for various battleground sites and visited Bayeux, where we gathered together with the ambassador for the lighting of the flame. Omaha Beach was very impressive with its huge U.S. cemetary. Thousands upon thousands of U.S. graves were lined up in rows, with a magnificent memorial, built like a Greek temple, overlooking it all. Guest of honor was General Omar Bradley, who attended in his wheelchair. He is the only living five-star general and a very popular person. He spoke briefly and laid a wreath at the temple steps.

The largest Canadian cemetary was at Beny-Sur-Mer, where a wreath was laid by the Canadian ambassador, Marcel Dupuy. Similar ceremonies took place at various other Canadian cemetaries during this week, while speakers included Brigadier General Ben Cunningham of Kingston, Major General Charles Belzile, the Commanding General at Lahr, Germany, and others. At each town in Normandy, a special ceremony called Vin D'Honneur was offered by the mayor of the town. The one which interested me most was at the Bayeux Cemetary, where I had the honor of representing the government of Canada. I laid a wreath and spoke to the group gathered there. We then visited the City Hall, where I was presented with a medallion by the mayor, which depicted the Bayeux Cathederal and the famous William the Conqueror tapestry displayed there.

At each memorial, French officers read out the names of Canadians killed in that town or city. Following the solemn reading of these names, officers would say, "mort de France." A plaque was unveiled at Vimoutiers and the wreath was laid there by Air Marshal Dunlap.

We were invited to the Hotel de Ville, where I again spoke on behalf of my government. A major from the permanent forces in Lahr interpreted my remarks and translated them into French.

June 5, Normandy … Today a group of us returned to tour the beaches where such fierce fighting took place. I also visited the castle of William the Conqueror, saw two historic museums, one of fine arts and the other of ancient historical artifacts and relics of the Normandy battles.

Deauville … This is a world-famous seaside resort and we dined here at one of its many beautiful restaurants tonight. Some of our group took their chances at the Casino but I was accompanied by two padres, General Parkhouse, Colonel Travis and the Honorable Archdeacon James Wyttles of the Anglican Church, and so I minded my manners!

After a sumptuous buffet dinner, we couldn't find a taxi to take us back to the hotel and so, after walking twenty or thirty blocks and getting rather tired, we encountered a police car, which was, at that moment, arresting two teenagers for some misdemeanor. In my halting French, I explained to the policemen our predicament. They asked us to be patient and wait for a few minutes until they were finished, which we did, and then they drove us back to our hotel.

June 10 ... I was visiting one famous battle scene today, it was called Hellfire Corner. And lo and behold, I ran into my old friend from Alliston, John Taylor, who had told me about this trip two months ago. He was as surprised to see me as I was to see him and we just stood there staring at each other. We certainly had a lot to talk about to each other.

I also met and talked with Canadian war correspondent who was in this very area on D-Day, Ross Munroe. Munroe was until his recent retirement the publisher of the Montreal Gazette.

In the Canadian cemetary at Bayeux, I learned today that not only are many Canadian soldiers buried here but also quite a few British soldiers. As well, in one corner German soldiers are also buried. At that time, the German troops were in retreat and could not stop to bury their dead. The Canadians made arrangements to have their dead buried there too.

Many graves are marked with "Deutsch Soldat." Some have the original names of the soldiers marked on them, but many are not identified and there are many veterans standing, bareheaded, in front of the graves. They are, no doubt, relatives and comrades of long standing. Some gravestones have very tender epitaphs on them which brought tears to their eyes. It is heartbreaking to read the ages on the headstones but most seem to have been in their late teens or very early twenties.

June 11, Paris ... The weather is terrible today, the first bad day we have had since arriving here. We are at the Holiday Inn at Orly Airport and some of our party will be taking a short tour of Paris. I plan to visit the Louvre Museum and Notre Dame Cathedral and any other points of interest I have time for. Going along as my guide to the Cathedral is a Monsignor, from Chatham, New Brunswick, who was in World War II saw a great deal of action. He was also familiar with the Cathedral and didn't care to spend as much time there as I would have liked to. I saw the famous Mona Lisa today, but I must admit I was a bit disappointed, it was so small. I had always thought it would be large. It was hard to really see it properly as it was encased in bullet-proof weather-proof glass, with a burglar alarm as well. No one would even consider trying to steal this painting. I was interested because my wife's name is Mona.

Libya ... I am here at the specific invitation of "strong-man" Colonel Mu'ammer Muhammad al Gaddafi. He issued invitations to parliamentarians from seventy countries to discuss various forms of parliamentary systems. I have had a young man working with me in Ottawa for a while now who is East Indian and has many friends among the Arab dimplomatic corps. And so it was through my researcher, Bupinder Liddar, I think, that I received the invitation.

I was surprised to learn that I am the only federal Member here from Canada. I had previously checked with the Hon. Flora MacDonald, our secretary of external affairs. I outlined the details of the trip and she said that she could certainly find no reason for me to pass it up. I also cleared things with our new prime minister, Joe Clark. He told me to file the details with the clerk of the House of Commons, and I have done that. We flew from Mirabel Airport in Montreal to Rome, and then on to Tripoli and then Benghazi.

The conference is taking place at the University of Benghazi and I have been very interested to meet Colonel Gaddafi who attended the official opening ceremonies. I said to myself, well, that will be the last we see of Gaddafi, but I was wrong. He is dressed in a very plain, Indian-style black tunic, with no decorations whatever. I think we all expected him to be in full military regalia.

The next surprise we received was that he has sat throughout the whole conference at a special desk provided for him in the audience. He has also sat through many of the question and answer periods. The conference is taking place in four or five different languages and translators are used throughout every session. I think we are all surprised to hear so many women here who are critical of Gaddafi and his regime, and are demanding more voice in the government.

Vanessa Redgrave, the movie star from England, is here with her very left-wing views. Sessions are taking place in a very modern theatre complex with elevated seats which give us a good view. We are staying at a lovely hotel not too far away, which has a beautiful bar. But as this is a "dry" country, we cannot buy a drop of liquor or beer. Soft drinks, orange and other fruit juices are very plentiful. I am a non-drinker of alcoholic beverages but it is interesting to see some of my colleagues longing for something "stronger."

I spoke today with some Libyan officials about the possibility of a Canadian trade mission to Libya in the near future and about 250 or so Libyans coming to Canada to do specific studies. Libya has a representative in Ottawa, not an official one, but we had met prior to this conference.

I also heard today that the turmoil in the Middle East, which we all feel strongly about, and which may be caused by the Arabs, has not received a fair hearing in Canada, or so some Canadian MPs seem to feel. But I was recalling today over breakfast that when I first came to Ottawa seven years ago, I figured there was only one side to the story and that was the Israeli side; that the Arabs were, to be perfectly blunt, a bunch of bandits and so on. Then I learned that there was another side to the story and that 3.5 million Palestinian people were refugees, so there are always two sides to any story. I think the public at large will agree with that opinion now. To learn more about this complex problem, I have attended a great many meetings in Ottawa, of both Israeli and Arab groups.

This is certainly a problem that will not just go away quickly as some people seem to think, and I am pleased to have been here and learned first hand how the Libyan people feel. We flew out of the Tripoli airport this morning, where a great many military aircraft are lined up and covered with canvas so we cannot identify them. There are, I would say, in excess of one hundred aircraft and we were told not to take pictures of them. However, I managed to snap one before we were given this order.

We stopped in Rome on the way back home, and have a day and a half to sightsee. I was able to visit St. Peter's Basilica, the Vatican, the Catacombs and the Coliseum, as well as viewing the magnificent statue of King Victor Emmanuel and the world-famous Trevi Fountain. We flew to Zurich and then back to Ottawa.

Ottawa, 1981 … I was asked today by the Conservative whip if I would like to join a group of Liberal MPs who required a Conservative Member to go along on a trip to Lahr and then on to Cyprus. As a member of the Defence Committee I was certainly interested in this trip and said I would go.

At the airport I realized that every member of the committee I was to accompany was French Canadian and would not be speaking any English. Not one of them was a member of the Defence Committee. The leader, John Claude Malapart, who later died of cancer, led us through visits to our troops in Lahr, and then inspections, troop performances and other manoeuvres, all in French. This certainly didn't please me very much.

A Canadian officer who sat beside me during most of the exercises translated everything as we went along, so I didn't feel too badly about missing anything.

When we arrived in Cyprus, one of the French Canadian MPs stood up on a question of privilege and said that she wanted the briefing to be in French; they had been given in English up to this point. I smiled to myself when the Canadian officer in charge who was wearing the UN blue beret said, "Madam, I am very sorry, but in the United Nations, the official language is English and all our briefings are in English."

This made me feel pretty good!

When we arrived back in Lahr, there was a special sale at the big PX Store at the base. Our "official visitors" loaded up with gifts, skis, ski boots, clothing, everything, to take back with them to Canada. They bought everything at half price. Going through Customs, when they were asked if they had anything to declare that had been purchased in Europe, they said no, and did not bat an eyelash or declare one single thing.

I felt that this was certainly rather bad form for government representatives to do.

I was glad to get back to Canada from what had certainly *not* been a fact-finding mission, but an after-Christmas bonus sale trip!

1992, Ottawa ... The Defence Committee has made arrangements to go to Europe and meet with high officials of the NATO countries, from February 1st to 12th. Mona is very ill, in the Ottawa hospital and in very good hands, so I can get away.

We met with heads of our armed forces in Lahr. Our position in Germany is changing and Canada is getting a great deal of pressure from other NATO countries who are requesting and imploring our government to let Canada have a significant presence in Europe. We were briefed today on the number of troops we have here and how many we will be continuing with in months to come. At the present time we have close to 7,000 troops with their civilian families, but it will be reduced to 400.

We flew from Lahr to Vienna, which is not a NATO country, and were met by members of the diplomatic corp and armed forces officers. Then on to Prague, Czechoslovakia, where we met with the armed forces. Czechoslovakia very much wants to become a member of NATO and is now, of course, a reasonably free democracy. [Since my visit in 1992 the country has been split, so things continue to change.] Arrangements were then made for our group to fly to Moscow on a commercial aircraft.

Moscow ... We were met today by members of the Red Army, and it was amazing to hear senior officers comment frankly on what a great failure the communist government was. I really had to hide my surprise when one bright young colonel, about thirty-five years old, said that if he had said these things a few years ago he would have been court-martialed and shot immediately.

He said that drastic changes would take place in Russia and in the Red Army as well, pointing out the problems that there would be when the Russian troops, presently stationed outside Russian borders, came back with their families. There would be no jobs, no places to live, and these would be very serious problems.

Our plans to visit Ukraine and Kiev fell through as arrangements could not be made.

Leaving Moscow, we flew to Bonn, Germany, and then on to Strasbourg where the former high command of the East German forces were located. This is now the headquarters for the Strategic Arms Reductions, where we were briefed on what is being done.

We met with senior officials of NATO in Brussels. The commanding general of the entire operation was there. He is, of course, an American, which is required by NATO regulations. Everyone we have met since leaving Canada has impressed upon us, in no uncertain terms, how vital it is for Canada to play an important, and visible, role in NATO operations.

We also learned that a great many NATO members are reducing their troops and expenditures in Europe, and upon returning to Canada we learned that Canada would remove all its NATO troops in the near future. This will not be well received by other NATO allies.

Burks Falls, Ontario 1992 ... Some of my constituents chide me about being away so much from Ottawa and Burks Falls but what they do not realize perhaps is that so much of what our government does is important to other parts of the world.

I never return from such conferences without having added greatly to my understanding of the problems facing the world, and how they can be solved, perhaps with the help of Canada. In many ways, the travels and conferences are exhausting and very difficult. The distances are so great, the climates are so different, time zones, strange food, long, very hard hours, always being at our best. It all takes its toll.

The sight-seeing that some of us manage to do is very much at our own expense both financially and physically, but I wouldn't change one day of it for anything.

Autumn 1996, London, England (Rotterdam and Williamsburg) ... We went to London, England for the occasion of the seventy-fifth anniversary of the CPA in 1986. The Britons put on a magnificent show. Her Majesty Queen Elizabeth did a most unusual thing – she invited all delegates attending the celebration to Buckingham Palace and very few people get into that magnificent establishment.

We were also entertained at the Guild Hall, the State Entertainment Centre for the Lord Mayor of London. I will always remember the announcer saying in a great solemn voice, "Great silence for the Lord Mayor of London."

I have used that phrase on several occasions since then.

I also attended a CPA conference in Douglas, the Isle of Man. Her Majesty the Queen was supposed to open the conference but an emergency arose and she could not attend. Her Majesty the Queen Mother took her place and did an outstanding job. Mona and I were presented to Her Majesty.

That was an island I will never forget – I never saw so many sheep in one place in all my life!

We also attended a conference in Rotterdam, at The Hague, where we were presented to Her Majesty, the Queen of the Netherlands.

Another conference of note was in 1976, when the United States was celebrating its bicentennial and was hosting a Canada/U.S. Parliamentary Conference.

We were located at the model Revolutionary village of Williamsburg, Virginia. There were special hotels there, on the grounds of the village, where delegates were given the royal treatment and entertained lavishly.

Our Canadian group was chaired by Tom Lefebvre, a Liberal Member of Parliament from Pontiac, Quebec. One evening Mr. Lefebvre had a special reception for all the Canadian delegates. There were a great many Canadian delegates attending because the Americans had said that they wanted "a good show of Canadians."

The Quebec election was being held in Canada at this time and Rene Levesque was running for premier. Of course, there were a few PCs in our group who were not jumping for joy over the thought of a Liberal victory.

As the results began to come in, it was seen to be a disaster for the Liberals. Rene Levesque won, and a great many of the federal Liberals there were just about in tears. In their ridings PQ members were being elected. One of my colleagues, Dan McKenzie, who is now deceased, was anti-French if anyone was. He was most happy with the results. It was quite an evening, seeing these Members of Parliament so dismayed.

One of the highlights of the conference was the reception hosted by

U.S. Vice President Nelson Rockefeller at the Carter Plantation. This huge plantation had been beautifully restored and had nothing to do with President Jimmy Carter. It was certainly an outstanding conference and some of us travelled on to Norfolk, Virginia, which is one of the main U.S. naval bases. There were some very interesting aircraft carriers there, which towered into the sky about twelve stories high, and there were many huge warships as well.

Key Largo, Florida, is one of the best places I know to have a winter conference. The Canada/U.S. Association met in February and we were quartered at a beautiful resort in Key Largo and entertained after the many conference sessions aboard a beautiful luxury yacht, owned by August Busch of the great brewing family.

Some of the most interesting political trips I have taken have been for the government groups such as the Commonwealth Parliamentary Association, the U.S./Canada Parliamentary Association, Inter-Parliamentary Union and others.

The Inter-Parliamentary Union is made up of all democratic countries in the world, and I was a delegate at only one of these conferences. Mona and I went to the conference in Lisbon, Portugal, and were able to steal away for a week's holiday to the island of Majorca, with a short stay in Spain.

But the most outstanding trip I have taken was around the world, in 1987. We attended a Commonwealth Parliamentary Association Conference in Kuala Lampur, Malaysia. The chairman of our group was Lloyd Crouse, a long-time MP from the South Shore in Nova Scotia. He became the lieutenant governor of Nova Scotia some time later. Mr. Crouse said that if we wanted to pay a bit extra above our travel expenses, we could leave a few days ahead of time and fly to Beijing for four days. We stayed at the luxurious Hilton Great Wall Hotel, and then flew on to Hong Kong for a day's stopover to catch our breath. We then flew to Singapore and on to the conference. After the conference was over, we stopped in Bangkok, where again our accommodations were luxurious and the sight-seeing was fascinating. Our secretary of state, Joe Clark, received many requests for our Canadian parliamentarians to visit Pakistan. We received a personal invitation from their president, General Zia.

We spent four days there, landing in Karachi, and then on to the capital city, Islamabad. Each delegate was provided with a chauffeur-driven Mercedes car, and we could not double up, because of protocol. We were also entertained at a state banquet in the presidential palace and had an hour's conversation with the President.

On this flying trip, we not only attended an important conference but saw the Great Wall of China, Hong Kong, Kowloon, Singapore, Kuala Lampur, Peshawar, not far from the Afghanistan border, where one of the largest refugee camps is situated, and the Khyber Pass, where we could hear shelling of the Russian troops. We saw special drills and army manoeuvres. There was a Scottish military band wearing their kilts. We also visited Karachi, Bangkok, Thailand and Moscow, where we refueled and then headed back to London and Ottawa.

In 1979, while attending another Canada/U.S. conference in Alaska and Yukon, we saw the oil pipeline which ran through such a large part of the country, and the chilly Arctic Ocean. A few hardy individuals, and I was certainly not one of them, paddled their bare feet in the ocean.

Environmental groups are, understandably, very hostile about the pipeline, saying that it will kill off the great caribou herds which migrate across these plains. However, despite this opposition, the pipelines were completed. As a compromise, a sort of stile has been built here and there, over the top of the pipelines, so that the caribou can go over the top of them. However, very few caribou use them. It would appear that they just crawl under the pipes. I was intrigued to learn that since the pipeline was installed, the caribou herd has increased tenfold!

There is a very famous restaurant in Anchorage called Molly McGee's. We feasted there on Alaskan crab legs which were out of this world. We also got to see the great salmon run in Whitehorse, on the Dawson River. The fish were huge, from ten to twenty pounds, and they swam up the fast water of the river to spawn.

Perhaps one of the most unusual conferences I have ever attended, apart from the many I attended for the acid rain committee, was the International Parliamentary Union in Lisbon, Portugal. It was made up of all democratic (?) countries from around the world and included delegates from Russia, Bulgaria, Romania, Poland, Czechoslovakia and other so-called democratic countries: there were about 180.

Nairobi, 1984 ... Our Canadian delegation arrived in Africa today to attend an environmental conference sponsored by IPU, the Inter-Parliamentary Union.

Nairobi is located a mile above sea-level, and because of the altitude, is lush and green, a stark contrast to the drought-ridden country bordering on the north. Like many developing countries, the division between the Kenyan rich and poor is very evident.

There are five of us here and the conference runs from November 26th, today, till December 1st.

November 27 ... It is interesting and revealing to hear the differences in attitude between the countries attending this environmental conference. There are fifty countries here and our agenda includes papers and discussions concerning drought, erosion, reforestation and the pollution of the land. Water and rain were also on our agenda and I was pleased to talk about Canada's acid rain situation, and acid rain control internationally. "Politicking" was alive and well in Nairobi and we all had our points to make.

November 28 ... The Muslim countries are well represented here and each time Israel representatives speak, the Muslim nations, with the exception of Egypt, get up and leave the hall. The Muslim contingent would also preface each of their speeches with the words, "In the name of Allah the Magnificent." We heard today from several sources, that some countries, such as Brazil, have no reforestation programs in place. Unfortunately, many countries merely harvest their trees with no thought of replacement. But I am aware that even Canada uses far more trees than are replaced by reforestation. We were entertained today by the Canadian High Commissioner to Kenya and then visited a game reserve where giraffe, rhinoceros, hyenas, wild boar and antelopes were roaming freely. We were entertained by native dancers and had the opportunity of buying some superb animal carvings which I will display in my Ottawa office.

November 29 ... The thrust behind the IPU conference is to show the interdependence between all countries in the world and the environment. When one country pollutes the sea, for example, it effects many innocent countries as well as the original culprit.

We learned this week that destruction of tropical forests could ultimately effect Europe and North American economies. Climate environmental hazards are rarely contained in the air, in the area which creates them. And so dialogue between nations is essential to survival of us all.

An acre of forest land is disappearing every second, in the south. Encroaching deserts are destroying 6 million acres of productive land, reducing to zero the economic productivity of 21 million or more acres every day.

The environment can also be a vehicle to international conflict, there is no doubt about that. There have been and will continue to be wars over oil, and conceivably in the future, over water. There are presently over 200 river systems that are shared by two or more states, worldwide and pollution and unsustainable withdrawal have already caused friction in some parts of the world and the pressure is escalating.

One startling fact I heard today bears noting ... Using current technology, industry will require four times the amount of water by the year 2000, just to keep employment constant with 1975 and as the population grows, we will need more water for consumption and irrigation yet we continue to pollute more of it each day.

Environmentally, mankind is moving 180 degrees in the *wrong* direction. I am coming to the conclusion that conferences such as this one could prove to be the silver lining in this ominous cloud. But so long as legislature world wide continues to maintain a consultation and dialogue with its fellow countries, the problems may, in time, be solved.

Ottawa, December 3, 1984 ... In looking over my materials and speeches from the IPU conference I am more convinced than ever of the necessity of our acid rain work between the U.S. and Canada. It is vital that parliamentarians approach their respective governments and insist on action. Too many environmental investigations are being ignored, just when they are needed most. Conferences such as the one in Nairobi can only be beneficial when the delegates take the messages home and shout them out loud and clear. One speaker in Nairobi put it in a nutshell: "If we can make peace with nature, we can make peace with our neighbors."

I agree wholeheartedly!

ATTRACTING INDUSTRY

Ottawa, 1992 ... I give a great many interviews every year and I recently did one with Mr. Tom Earle, who was with the CBC for some years. He asked me about the Georgian Bay Regional Development Council that I was active in the 1950s. It was the brainchild of the Ontario government, the Department of Economics, I think, and of a prominent civil servant there, Alec Crate, who went on to be a deputy minister. He worked with the great D'Arcy McKeough, and I had a few run-ins with him. But this particular regional council took in Grey, Bruce, Simcoe, Parry Sound and Muskoka. It's purpose was to point out to the Ontario Government that it was very important to have industry come up north to provide jobs.

I told Mr. Earle that our greatest export from my riding was its young people to Toronto and to other large centres with good jobs to offer them. I felt that something had to be done to attract industry so we could retain our young talent.

Well, in the fullness of time, many industries did decide to settle in this area but most of them went to Muskoka, and even more to Barrie. I have always taken a dim view that to some people, the "hinterlands" means Oakville or Oshawa or Barrie, which is 50 miles from Toronto. It was only the odd industry which filtered through to Parry Sound.

At that time, the government did provide incentive and capital grants, up to 25 per cent of the total cost. Many industries thought that maybe it was worth while taking advantage of it.

Mr. Earle asked me what I thought of Mr. Trudeau's government when they cut the size of the contribution to NATO by 50 per cent. Well, I told him I was not impressed any more than I was impressed with his lack of enthusiasm for the armed forces during the entire Trudeau regime.

Also, I did not like the idea of providing the three branches of the armed forces with one garbage-bag-green uniform. I have been screaming my bloody head off about it ever since the first day I got into the House. I went after it loud and clear. I remember Buzz Nixon of National Defence, who was the deputy minister for years, and a real tough nut, too. He would say, "Mr. Darling, it would cost $26 million dollars to reverse this decision and we do not have the money." I would say, "Are you telling me Mr. Deputy Minister that you are going to call in all the garbage-bag-green uniforms at once and burn them on Parliament Hill?" I would certainly have liked that! I said, "Surely you will be able to phase it in slowly and start with the Navy, our senior service."

I also pointed out that we had the only Navy in the world in garbage-green uniforms.

Needless to say, despite Minister Bob Coates having the guts to bring in the act to make the changes back to three uniforms, everybody seems enthusiastic about the way things are now, although there is still a great deal of controversy, depending on who you talk to. When I talk to members of the High Command at various defence meetings, they say, "Oh, there is no problem with the present uniforms at all, Mr. Darling."

Under my breath I say, BS! One of my research assistants asked me today if I had any phobias and it got me thinking. Yes, I do have two or three things that have become phobias with me during the years I was involved with defence. One was the unified service uniforms. One was when Paul Hellyer swore to me on a stack of Bibles that he had not intended the service uniforms to be unified. What was meant, he said, was that the High Command personnel would be unified – an entirely different story. Well, I don't know whether that was what he meant or not, but it really burned me up, the way things went.

I have always felt that the armed forces have been short-changed. They have not had the equipment they required; they have not had the numbers in their units that they required. I have kept on beating the drum about that. I have worked through six ministers of defence and have always pointed out that there is not one woman general, for example. I have tried to badger the defence people into doing something about it. The chief of the defence staff, and every minister of defence has said to me at one time or another, "Mr. Darling, you are right. We are going to appoint a woman as a general." I would then ask, "When?"

Some of the men I badgered included Lamontagne, J.J. Blais, Richardson and Coates. It should certainly have been done long before it was and I am happy to say that a fine woman general was finally approved and was written up in the Gazette on July 1, 1985. She is General Sheila Hellstrom and I am delighted.

MY FAMILY AND
EARLY TIMES

allander, July 16, 1911 ... No, I don't remember this far back, but it is the day I was born, in the home which has become the South Himsworth Museum. My family goes back for over one hundred years and my grandfather, Thomas Darling, arrived in the vast wilderness area to become superintendent of the J.R. Booth Lumber Company operations camp in Wasi, near Callander. He was given the task of establishing logging camps to harvest the fine pine timber in the area, and believe me, it required a great deal of skill and ingenuity. It was not long before a thriving community was built up, with houses, boats, and farms to provide food. My grandfather was born in Scotland, and he eventually married three times and had twelve children. His seven sons grew up to work in the lumber mill, on the boats in the area and on the railway. We have always had a great deal of pioneer spirit and have all worked hard all our lives.

My father, Jack, moved from Callander with his family when his children were young. When I was 17, I contracted tuberculosis, and I spent a year at the Mountain Sanitarium in Hamilton. Having had the bout with TB, I was not eligible to join the armed forces, so I decided to earn my living. After a variety of selling jobs, which started when I was quite young, I sold newspapers in Powassan, where we lived for a time, and also sold the Detroit weekend paper which was like the New York Times is today. I eventually turned to life insurance and, if I do say so myself, had a certain gift of gab to generate sales. I then branched into general insurance and real estate.

My family had, by this time, moved to Burks Falls, where my father worked for many years. My brother Peter studied to be an accountant and has worked all over Ontario, especially in the northern area. He also spent a time as a clerk with the Municipality of Burks Falls during the period that I was reeve.

Another brother, Don, moved to the West Coast after serving in the RCAF and then to California but is no longer living. My sister Doris took her R.N. degree in Hamilton, moved to New York and has stayed there for over fifty years. She also spent some time in the U.S. Army as nurse during the war.

I had some interesting jobs in Toronto and started my sales career selling coal, door-to-door, on commission. That was for Burton Fuels and I sold books of tickets and received one dollar for each ton of coal I sold.

I then answered an advertisement in the newspaper for Meyers Studio, which was looking for a salesman to sell photographs on commission. I sold a $1 coupon which entitled the individual to a free color picture and I was allowed to keep the $1 deposit. I did very well in this and eventually worked in the studio. I lived at 64 Shuter Street when I first arrived in Toronto and paid $6 a week for my room. I graduated to the Frontenac Arms at $40 a month and then the general manager of Meyers, Bert Cook, asked me to join him in the Park Plaza Hotel. I think we paid $80 a month for the apartment, and my share was $40. Bert Cook was a high flyer and quite a drinker. I bought my first car, a Ford Model 60, priced about $850 in 1937. I can still remember that it was a six-cylinder, two-door coach.

While I was working for Meyers Studio there was a beautiful young lady who worked as an artist there, coloring portraits. Her name was Mona Beatrice Collyer and I was immediately taken with her. We began going together and were married on October 5, 1940. Mona had been working for a short while in Hamilton and then Sudbury for a rival photographer. When we decided to marry, we were told to set a date before July 1, as I would then be classed a married man for the draft. But I said, "To hell with that," and we did not move the date forward.

I tried to enlist in the Royal Canadian Air Force. However, because of my previous history of tuberculosis, I was turned down. Later on, I received my call for the armed forces and was again turned down as 4F. During the war, I served on many voluntary organizations and did a fair job selling Victory Bonds.

I met a very unusual character around this time named Bill Daniels. He was a regional supervisor and used to stay in Burks Falls. He was also a great bridge player and played with Dr. Hallam, Harve Fowler, Mr. Fraser and myself. Fraser's wife was very jealous of him and used to phone several times during the evenings we played bridge to see if he was really there.

Bill Daniels used to drive her crazy by answering the phone, "Hello, Kelly's Pool Hall." She would apologize and hang up. The next time she phoned he would say, "Burks Falls Fire Department." And she would hang up again. We used to think this was only her due as she needn't have worried about her husband being faithful.

Mona and I had moved to Burks Falls a few years before this and I continued with my insurance and real estate business. I was working from the kitchen in our house in Burks Falls and it used to drive Mona crazy. She eventually persuaded me to get out and find an office to go to every day so she could have her kitchen back for getting meals for her family. In 1972 when I first became active in federal politics, there was no federal financing for a constituency office, so I used my own insurance and real estate offices and staff to take messages and type letters. When I went home on weekends, I did my political business from my old insurance office until, eventually, in 1979, we received funding for a riding office.

I was getting a lot of flak from my sons, Peter and John, who were then running the business in my absence. They said I was taking up too much space and staff time for my political career. So we opened a small riding office on Ontario Street. Eventually I was fortunate enough to find Ina Trolove as my constituency secretary and she was with me until I retired.

NATO

February 1993, Ottawa ... On my desk this morning were some briefing notes prepared for the House of Commons Standing Committee on National Defence and Veterans Affairs. I have been a member of the committee for some years now.

Entitled "Peacekeeping," the notes concern Maj.-Gen. Lewis MacKenzie, commander Land Forces Central Area. Major-General MacKenzie has announced his intention of retiring from the forces after thirty years in the military. During those years he participated in peacekeeping operations in such areas as the Gaza Strip, Cyprus, Vietnam and Central America.

I understand that Major-General MacKenzie has been involved in the implementation of the Central American peace plan and was deputy commander Land Force Central Area, before serving as director General Land Development and then chief of staff for the UN Protection Force in the former Yugoslavia. He was then appointed commander Land Forces Central Area.

An enviable record!

According to these papers, Major-General MacKenzie became a media celebrity when he was in Yugoslavia, especially when he served as commander of Sector Sarajevo. He stated at that time that the number one weapon he had to deal with in that situation was the news media. He could bring pressure on the combatants by making or threatening to make statements to the news media about their lack of co-operation.

But he also pointed out the dangers of letting the news media have too much influence on foreign policy because actions might be taken in response to slanted or incomplete stories produced, since the media does not have access to all the facts or to the combat areas.

These stories can also make life difficult for the UN forces if they feel that the UN is not neutral.

Among other things since the Major-General returned from Yugoslavia, he has argued against Western military intervention in Yugoslavia because of the complexity of the situation, and the heavy casualties that might result. And he has strongly criticized the way the UN administers peacekeeping operations and shortcomings in logistics and planning.

And enclosed with this brief are some very intriguing questions such as, "Are there problems with the training Canadian soldiers receive specifically for peacekeeping operations? Having observed the implementation of the Total Force Concept over the years, are you still convinced that this is the best way to proceed to ensure the effectiveness of the land forces? Do you believe that Canada should participate in the UN standing force? Are there situations where UN forces should take sides during peacekeeping operations?"

It would be interesting, in lieu of the situation in Europe today, to have seen the answers to those questions.

Another memorandum from the Standing Committee in February 1993 was headed, "Notes prepared for the appearance of the Hon. Kim Campbell, minister of national defence."

The paper was subtitled, "Increase in the number and size of peacekeeping operations."

It said that the 1987 Defence White Paper for the Department of National Defence policy was to keep a pool of 2,000 Canadian Forces personnel, out of the total of around 86,000 regular force people, ready for peacekeeping duties at any one time. In early 1993, 4,700 personnel were directly involved in peacekeeping, a sudden increase in numbers. It would appear that in one year UN forces in peacekeeping operations have shot up from 12,000 to over 45,000 owing, to some extent, to the end of the Cold War, the collapse of the Soviet Union and the easing of East-West tensions. World public opinion has been the key factor in the UN's decision to take some action in these situations. However, some peacekeeping operations to oversee implementation of a peace plan in Cambodia have come close to paralysis and may soon require more U.S. troops. Other UN duties have included operations in Somalia, where U.S.-led operations consisted of 18,000 U.S. troops and 14,000 soldiers from other countries, including Canada.

Size and number of peacekeeping commitments put a big strain on land forces. Budgets and regular force personnel are being cut, and Canada, among other countries, is having a hard time in meeting the NATO/UN obligations.

With the total number of regular force personnel, including land forces, air command and maritime command, being cut from 84,000 in 1991 to 75,000 by 1995, peacekeeping duties may have to be rethought. The use of reservists must also be given a considerable amount of thought. As one of my colleagues stated today, "Part of the problem, Stan, is that the Total Force Concept is still in the process of being implemented while budget and personnel cuts are being made, as the number and size of UN peacekeeping personnel is escalating."

It's not a problem with an easy solution.

Other documents in my NATO file include such headings as "Peacekeeping, a role for Canada," "Peacekeeping needs to be defined or redefined for the post-Soviet era," "The Bosnian conflict will not fade away or resolve itself in the short term," and "The situation in the former Yugoslavia puts the issue before the Committee in bold relief." The White Paper suggested, "Clarify the role of the Canadian military in the new Peacekeeping activity."

A news release dealing with this same issue crossed my desk today. It was headed "End the Arms Race" and came from Vancouver, B.C. Peter Coomoes, co-ordinator of the group said, "We believe an essential aspect of peacekeeping is prevention." Amen to that.

Another memo came from Roger Prefontaine of the Veterans against Nuclear Arms with yet more suggestions for peacekeeping and Canada's role in this escalating problem. "NATO and NORAD are becoming irrelevant," he said, "and only sovereignty and UN support retain their validity as roles of the Canadian Armed Forces."

And yet another memo about peacekeeping from Peter Speck of Vancouver, with some interesting suggestions.

Maj.-Gen. Lewis MacKenzie spoke to the conference of the Defence Associations Institute in Ottawa last night and brought down the house. He said he had returned to Canada the long way around by way of Yellowknife, New Delhi, Heathrow and Toronto. He had attended a thirty-four Pacific nation conference co-sponsored by the Indian army and the American army to address the basic UN principles of mounting peacekeeping operations. Major-General MacKenzie had stated then that "the UN knows about mounting peacekeeping operations. In fact they tended to get in the way of countries who do mount peacekeeping operations like Canada and Australia and New Zealand, India and some others."

His talk was very frank indeed and one statement he made bears repeating here: "Countries don't give their troops to the UN in trust to be killed trying to implement a really lousy ceasefire agreement arranged by a bunch of diplomats and politicians, which is what is happening in Yugoslavia. It was an impossible plan that was put in place, it never had a chance to work. Soldiers said, "Nobody listened to us, and now people are dying. The plans have to be better."

December 29, 1992, Ottawa ... Sean Murray of Victoria, B.C., made a statement today to the Standing Committee of National Defence and Veterans Affairs: "I feel that world peace should be the preeminent goal of Canadian Foreign Policy. Unfortunately muscle has to be used to ensure this goal. That means military expertise, professionalism, significant regular full-time military. Reserves should be downsized, returned to a voluntary non-paid force, with the surplus funds used to erect another regiment of regular infantry to sustain peacekeeping commitments."

And legal minds were also at work. Eric L. Teed, QC, BCL, said in a letter to our Standing Committee, "Canada should continue to give leadership to all nations and ensure our forces participate in peacekeeping roles throughout the world as a contribution to world peace." An international peacekeeping chart listed the peacekeeping operations Canada has participated in since 1947 up to and including the present. There are thirty-four different countries we have served, ranging from Korea and Cambodia to Egypt, Lebanon, Syria, Iran and Iraq, Central America, Haiti and the Dominican Republic, to name a few.

November 9, 1991, Huntsville ... General John de Chastelain, chief of defence, was asked to address the Huntsville/Lake of Bays Chamber of Commerce at Grandview Inn last night. He was talking on the role of the armed forces in a global economy. I attended with Mr. and Mrs. Frank Miller, Mr. and Mrs. Terry Clarke and Mr. and Mrs. Bruce Evans, and de Chastelain's speech targeted the future of the armed forces in a global economy. He mentioned that countries which used to comprise the Warsaw Pact now want into NATO. He said that the compelling argument is that since there is no longer a threat from the Soviet Union, for example, there is no need for an armed force in Canada. Can Canada continue to spend on defence when the threat is now global instability? He said that over the years, the armed forces have allowed military equipment to deteriorate and new equipment is a priority. Changes, he said, will also be made to the size of the regular force with increases going to the reserves and a decrease in the size of the regular forces.

November 14, Ottawa ... Over lunch today in the dining room I recalled with some of my colleagues a terrific evening I attended in October 1979.

On the twenty-fifth anniversary of the North Atlantic Assembly, a gala performance was held in the Opera Salon of the National Arts Centre with the Central Band of the Canadian Forces, the Canadian Brass, the Royal Canadian Mounted Police Band, and Maureen Forrester and others.

Presented under the auspices of the secretary of state, it was a full house and a very enjoyable evening. Another enjoyable evening sponsored by the North Atlantic Assembly was a reception given by Their Excellencies the Governor General and Mrs. Edward Schreyer, on October 23, 1979. And in 1985, I received an invitation to attend a special meeting on the occasion of a visit to Ottawa by the Rt. Hon. Lord Carrington, who is secretary general of the North Atlantic Treaty Organization. Lord Carrington gave a noteworthy address in January and said, "In my view the alliance is as important now as it ever was, and so is the job it has to do. Three main priorities are: maintain defences and deterrents necessary to avoid war; make a determined effort to negotiate with the Soviet Union to improve the quality of peace; maintain in good repair the essential bridge between North America and Western Europe."

October 9, 1984, Ottawa … As government leader in the House of Commons, the Hon. Ray Hnatyshyn, PC, MP, addressed their Atlantic Treaty Association Thirtieth Annual Assembly in Toronto, filling in for Lord Carrington. He said that as Canada was a founding member of NATO, Canada's commitment to peace defence is strong as ever.

He outlined three highlights of NATO's non-military character: effective collective action; discussion of all essential issues; national consensus. He concluded by saying, "The strength and credibility of this Alliance depend upon its political – every bit as much as its military – character." He is certainly a good speaker.

NATO has several important purposes, of course, but the most important to my way of thinking is to combine the defensive strength of its members to deter aggression against any one of them, and thereby to preserve peace and the security of all.

MOTORBOAT CALVACADE

June 1993 … My secretary, and hard taskmaster, Ina Trolove, asked me to check over some items she was about to throw out today, and one of them was a flier for the Tenth Motor Boat cavalcade in Burks Falls where my riding office is. The tour was by courtesy boats from our town docks to Lake Cecebe, through the Magnetawan locks to Ahmic Harbour and back again. Points of interest were marked on a special chart; there were times set aside for lunch, swimming, fishing and although this was not a race, it did test the drivers' skill. I notice that there were numerous prizes for the lowest total errors, including the Rockwynn Trophy, presented by the Cameron family of Lake Cecebe, and a treasure hunt along the way. Harve Fowler and I were the registrars and he is still going strong in Burks Falls.

Also listed on this interesting flier is an unveiling of an historical plaque by the Ontario Hydro Electric Power Commission and a Shore Fish Fry, sponsored by the Lions Club of Burks Falls. For the eighth annual motor boat cavalcade on Sunday, July 17th, sponsors, the Magnetawan River and Lakes Tourist Association and the Burks Falls Yacht Club advertised two new paved launching ramps for participants. In that same file-folder I found a bright red bumper sticker that said, "SHOW YOU CARE – GET RID OF PIERRE." Now I wonder how I came to acquire that?

MEETING WITH ROYALTY

Apri 17, 1982, Ottawa … I look forward to being in Burks Falls most weekends despite avoiding the occasional moose as I drive through Algonquin Park. But this weekend Mona and I are attending a very special occasion in town here.

Her Majesty, Queen Elizabeth, is in Ottawa today to sign the new Charter of Rights with Prime Minister Pierre Trudeau. Mona and I have seats just to the east of the signing table, in the section reserved for Members of Parliament and Senators. I am always struck by how tiny Her Majesty is and how gracious. Following the signing, Her Majesty performed her walk-about around the grounds at Parliament Hill, talking with various people in the crowd and then a lovely reception was held in the Hall of Honor and the Railway Committee Room.

My son John and his wife Joyce were there and were presented to the Duke of Edinburgh. The Duke, who must meet a lot of people in a day, was a bit mixed up and thought that John was a Member of Parliament and I was just "the father." We corrected him and I said, "John looks after the family business in Burks Falls and is not in Parliament." The Duke replied, "Oh, you are taking care of the family business at home and you sort of sponsor your father." We all got quite a kick out of that.

That evening we were recalling another important dignitary who attended Parliament Hill to speak to the combined Senate and House of Commons. Indian Prime Minister Indira Ghandi was a great person and I had the opportunity of meeting her. It was as great shock to hear later of her assassination. I also had the privilege of meeting Chancellor Helmut Kohl of Germany after his address to joint Houses of Parliament. And while I'm name dropping, President Mikhail Gorbachev of the U.S.S.R. was also in town and I think I have a photo taken with him.

DEBATES IN THE HOUSE

Ottawa, 1990 ... I read in one of the papers on my desk today that an "unnamed writer" had said about me, "Darling has garnered a reputation for dogged determination, vociferous opinion and tough-as-nails right-wing politics. Darling is a Tasmanian devil in a three piece custom-tailored suit."

Well, I wouldn't mind debating that bit about being a Tasmanian devil, but the other things seem correct.

At the Prayer Breakfast this morning the people at my table got talking about how useful House of Commons debates really are and that started me thinking about some of the ones I've taken part in through the years. Certainly, capital punishment was one of the hottest issues we have ever had to deal with. I recall saying, "When young offenders are convicted, their names should be published, the same as if they were adults. In my opinion, the public should know who these people are. If it's going to hurt their families, too bad. If it happened in my own family, too bad. But if they are criminals, they shouldn't be able to hide, except for first time offenders, and for a lesser crime."

I believe there is nothing wrong with the concept of punishment for crimes and a sentence passed should be served in full. The public's protection should take precedence over the rights of convicted criminals and if I had my way, parole would be much stricter. I've gone on record as stating in no uncertain terms: "It doesn't matter what the hell a guy has done – if he's raped twenty women, killed ten of them, and is convicted, they should just throw away the key. The public is getting angry."

There were many things I think should have been debated. Another thing I fought like a tiger about was changing the July 1st holiday name from Dominion Day, which it is, to Canada Day. I did not like it, period. I said that in a very loud and clear voice. Of course I spoke on it in the House. I am aware that we have a very different make-up in our population now, but to me Dominion Day had a special connotation and a magnificent sound. Of course, my example was that in the U.S., July 4th is not United States Day, it is Independence Day. This is how I have always thought of Dominion Day, which has a magnificent, almost scriptural connotation too: He shall have dominion from sea to sea.

We also had many official discussions and in the corridors and dining rooms about the CBC. Some people called it the Crazy Broadcasting Corporation. I was reminded today by a fellow backbencher that I had stated that the CBC should fire the whole staff of the television program The Journal. This was because the program was going off the air for nine weeks for vacation as "the staff needed time to recover from the day-to-day pressures of the job."

Well, I stated in no uncertain terms that people in other branches of the news media were able to carry on without taking off nine weeks.

After all, the CBC is subsidized by the taxpayer of Canada to the tune of about $900 million a year. In my estimation, the CBC has not been the greatest exponent of truthful broadcasting or newscasting as far as the government is concerned. In the view of a lot of us, it is a very NDP-oriented corporation. Perhaps this is why I take a jaundiced view.

When the budget is brought down, or there is a Throne Speech at the opening of Parliament, or anything else of great importance, the CBC is here at the House a week in advance, with several tractor trailers of equipment and personnel all around the place. Global and CTV come in with much less equipment and provide their viewers with pretty well the same high-calibre coverage for, I expect, a lot smaller budget.

A friend reported a statement that Harry Boyle made a while ago. He was a fine broadcaster, writer and head of the CRTC. He said that one way to cure the ills of the CBC would be to select a few hundred top-notch broadcasters, put them on a island in the middle of Lake Superior, and blow up the rest of the CBC.

Tourism in my riding is of prime importance and I kept getting all kinds of feedback from visitors to Parry Sound/Muskoka about insensitive Canadian customs officers conducting searches at border crossings. Some were so rude and insensitive that they were damaging Canada's already-battered tourism industry, and we were getting a lot of flak about this in American newspapers.

Here was a hot issue for debate if there ever was one. Tourism is the number one industry in my riding. Well, I had a lot to say about this problem. One particular case was when the fishing season opened one spring. The pickerel season opens a minute after midnight and a great many fishermen arrive so that they can drop in their lines at one minute after midnight. Well, one American family crossed the border at Windsor/Detroit and were stopped cold by over-zealous customs officials. The visitors had, I think, $40 of groceries. They were planning to drive at night and our stores would be closed. They wanted groceries for early breakfast in their fishing camp. The customs officials charged the visitors with whatever the percentage of duty was on these groceries, and to put it mildly, the visitors were furious.

After this had happened three times, I brought it to the attention of the minister of revenue, who agreed that this was not good public relations. Many tourists confronted by this over-zealous attitude by customs people vowed that they would never come to Canada again. It wasn't the idea of paying an extra $10 or $15; it was the principle of the thing. They knew they would be spending a lot of money here and many paid municipal taxes on cottages they owned in the area. After a bit of haranguing on my part, one of the top officials in Customs had a few quiet words with the border officials and they became a bit more sensible.

In the early 1970s pay raises for us MPs was also hotly debated. As so many other things I can mention, my participation in this issue did not ingratiate me with my fellow Members of Parliament.

At the time that all this started, MPs were paid about $18,000 a year, plus $6,000 a year for expenses.

A pay raise was being discussed by all parties and caucuses including the government, in the late fall. It reached its crescendo as Parliament was recessing for Christmas.

The suggestion made by the government was for a 50 per cent increase and you can imagine what a heyday the press had with that! I spoke forcefully against it, saying that it was highway robbery.

I wrote some letters to the media and then went home to Burks Falls for a very enjoyable Christmas. However, the majority of the House Members said that, what with the publicity about the raises raging in their riding, those two or three weeks were like hell on earth and they were glad to get back to Ottawa.

I had been recommending to the House that an increase of 25 per cent would be adequate, and rather than having it retroactive to nine months previous to it becoming law, it should not come into effect until the governor general's royal assent actually made it into law.

In April, without consulting my colleagues, I went to talk with my eminent expert on House of Commons matters, Stanley Knowles and was roundly criticized for doing so by my colleagues. I told Mr. Knowles that I was very much against this pay raise, even though, at this time, it had been argued down in the House to 33 1/3 per cent, but still with the retroactive clause intact.

I also pointed out to Mr. Knowles that many of the Cabinet Ministers on the other side of the House were not worth the money they were making at this time. However, I made on exception, Jim Jerome, the Speaker of the House.

At that time, the leader of the House was Mitchell Sharp. He said to me, "Mr. Darling, we are going to accept the amendment of yours to increase the salary of the Speaker of the House to Cabinet Minister status. His salary will now be on the same level as Members of the Cabinet."

This worked out to slightly more than the 33 1/3 per cent increase the members and Cabinet Minister would receive and as the original royal warrant was for up to 50 per cent increase, the Speaker's new salary would come within that limit.

The Speaker of the House would now be the only one to receive a salary of slightly more than 33 1/3 per cent raise.

Stanley Knowles was a smart old codger and he pointed out to me that I was the only Member of the Opposition who ever got a money amendment though to provide more money. When I asked him how that was, he said, "Well, the additional pay for the Speaker made the difference."

When my son Peter asked me about debating issues in the House, I had to admit that I find them fascinating, whether or not I take part. It is always fast-paced, and brings out both the pros and cons of the issue in very fast order.

FUNDING FOR
SMALL-CRAFT HARBORS

Burks Falls, 1985 ... When I went down the street for a haircut today
I was stopped by three people in a row who wanted to know how
they could obtain funding for various projects they were working on.
Well, as a lowly backbencher in the House of Commons I don't have a lot
of influence but I said that I would see what I could do, and asked them to
bring over a proposal to my riding office on Ontario Street and leave it with
my secretary, Ina Trolove.

In my riding, one of the greatest tourist areas in Canada, there are many
recreation wharves which have to be kept in good repair and upgraded from
time to time. I can always count on receiving quite a few requests for government funding every spring and I get in touch with the Small Craft
Harbors Branch of Fisheries and Oceans which is located in Burlington,
Ontario. Jack Hall is the regional director and his district runs from one side
of Ontario to the other, plus Manitoba and up into the Northwest
Territories. I was told, this year, that funds are very scarce and I should get
in touch with the minister of fisheries and oceans and just lay it on the line
that the money is urgently needed for these repairs.

Tourism in Parry Sound/Muskoka is our most important industry and
it generates a great many federal dollars. Therefore, in my estimation, the
government should provide money to keep it going. Sales of gas, boats,
motors, cottages and so on provide millions of dollars to the federal coffers.
There are more pleasure boats in Ontario than in all the rest of Canada put
together.

July 1986 … I learned today how much money is allocated to repair small craft harbors in the Maritime provinces compared to Ontario and I am damn mad. In Prince Edward Island, for example, which is no bigger than Parry Sound/Muskoka, the number of boats is a fraction of the number found here. In Ontario, the budget for small craft harbor grants was $3.9 million. Of that, $2 million is for salaries and maintenance, and only $800,000 is to be spent on the actual harbors. As well, there is very little administration and not too many salaries in P.E.I. and on the East Coast millions of dollars are allocated for the building, repair and upkeep of the many government wharves, which adds to their grants considerably.

I think all us MPs from rural and vacation areas should get together and plan our strategy.

I must say that Jack Hall has been very helpful. I was able to get some much-needed funding for wharves in the Callander area, which is of interest to me as that is where I was born and where my family were located for many years. As well, when the Hon. Tom Siddon was minister of fisheries and oceans, I was able to arrange financing for an important development of the Parry Sound waterfront, totalling $1.4 million. I was also pleased to arrange for the minister to come up to the official opening of the waterfront.

Stan Darling presents a gallon of Almaguin Highlands Maple Syrup to John Diefenbaker.

Stan and Mona Darling celebrate the 1975 Bracebridge Centennial with Paul Hammond, Bruce McPhail and Archie Rintoul.

Stan and one of the Fall Fair queens, Ontario Association of Agricultural Societies check-out out the Burks Falls display.

Stan and Jean Charest say goodbye to Parliament in 1993.

At the Global '90 Conference in Vancouver. Left to right: Stan, the Hon. David Macdonald MP, Robert Wenman MP, visiting the Carmanah Valley Forest on Vancouver Island.

The June 26th victory party for the Progressive Conservative Party at the Royal Ontario Museum, with new Ontario Premier Mike Harris and his wife, Janice.

Canadian Consul General Chris Pearson in Dallas when Stan spoke to the Southern Methodist University about acid rain.

Corretta Scott King, widow of Martin Luther King Jr., at the National Prayer Breakfast in Ottawa. Stan Darling and Bill Bussiere were hosts.

Stan exchanges gossip with Senator Keith Davey at the North Toronto
Collegiate Institute's 75th reunion for former students.

The Hon. John Fraser, Speaker of the House in the Mulroney Cabinet, and Stan at the launching of the Greening on the Hill environmental project.

Jean Charest announces that he will run for the PC leadership, in Sherbrooke, Quebec, March 17, 1993. Stan and Bob Layton, and Charest's wife Michelle, share the moment.

The Hon. Robert Stanfield, Rt. Hon. John Diefenbaker and Stan.

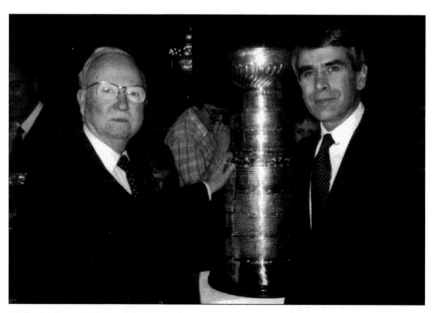

U.S. Ambassador to Canada Tom Niles and Stan approve inscriptions on the Stanley Cup in Ottawa.

Acid rain envoys in Muskoka for meetings are: Hon. Charles Caccia MP, Dr. Gary Gurbin MP, U.S. Envoy Lee Thomas, Bill Blaikie MP, Stan, and former Ontario Premier Bill Davis.

Acid Rain experts include Stan, Adele Hurley and Michael Perley of the Canadian Coalition on Acid Rain, and George Rejean, Federal Government.

At the May 5, 1995, reception for former parliamentarians at Rideau Hall in Ottawa, the Rt. Hon. Jean Chretien greets his friends.

As the crowd yelled "raise the shovel," Stan, Mayor Jim Lang and District of Muskoka Chairman Frank Miller take part in the Bracebridge Santa Claus Parade.

Stan's long-time friend, designer and clothing entrepreneur Lou Myles.

Stan does his best to help raise money at the McDonald's fund raising lunch for Ronald McDonald House in Huntsville.

The Dalai Lama of Tibet visits with Stan in the west block in Ottawa.

Although "not a great favorite of Stan's constituents," Minister of Finance Michael Wilson listens to Bill Kempling MP and Stan air their views on the GST.

Stan aims for a strike at the Bowling for Millions Fundraiser by the Muskoka Big Brothers.

Charlie Farquarson (Don Harron), and Stan find a lot to talk about at the Ontario PC picnic in the Bracebridge Fair Grounds.

The Hon. Flora Macdonald and Stan at the PC Leadership Convention in June, 1993.

In Dallas, Stan checks out the famous TV "Dallas" ranch and finds it very small.

On a visit to Belgium for the Defence Committee, Stan visits the Canadian cemetery.

Maharishi Mahesh Yogi and Stan at the group's Netherlands
headquarters in Voldrop.

The Acid Rain Committee in Washington, 1990. (From left to right.)
Rear: Marc Ferland MP, Bob Corbett MP, Bill Blaikie MP. Front: Pauline
Browse MP, Chairman Stan Darling MP, Janice Hilchie, clerk and the
Hon. Charles Caccia MP.

Friend and colleague John Crosbie with his wife Jane, at the PC Convention in Ottawa, 1983.

Father Shawn O'Sullivan was guest speaker at the Ottawa Prayer Breakfast.

Sharing the PC victory in Ontario on June 8, 1995. Ernie Eves and Vicki at the Jolly Roger Inn in Parry Sound.

Defence committee business took Stan to Gagetown, N.B. for military exercises. Included in the line of fire are Defence personnel and Maurice Harquail MP.

The Rt. Hon. Brian Mulroney and Stan Darling.

Mila Mulroney and Stan in Ottawa.

PC Party National Caucus welcomes an infrequent visitor, Rt. Hon.
John Diefenbaker to its weekly meeting in 1979.

MP Christine Stewart and Stan at the Earth Summit '92 Conference in Rio de Janeiro.

Stan's visit to the famous statue in Rio, Christ of the Andes.

Shanghai Grace Church, October 1991, where Stan presented a Dr.
Norman Bethune folder to the Rev. Joseph Lu.

From left to right: Brian Nixon, president of Burks Falls' Lions Club; Bill
Moody, international director of Lions International; Stan Darling; and Bill
Copeman. Brian Nixon, president, Burks Falls Lions Club, present Burks
Falls maple syrup to Bill Moody.

MR. DIEFENBAKER

onday, February 3, Ottawa … I am slowly finding my way around the House of Commons and parliamentary corridors. John Diefenbaker was sitting in his accustomed seat in the parliamentary restaurant today. It is especially reserved for him and no one else is allowed to sit there. From time to time I have seen him there, usually with other people but today he was sitting alone. Mr. Diefenbaker is someone I have always admired and so, with some trepidation, I went over to him and introduced myself. Despite my age, Mr. Diefenbaker said, "Well, my boy, sit down; I would love to talk with you."

So I sat down with this man I have admired so much, this fabulous individual. He seemed like such a lonely man.

John Diefenbaker when I first met him had an office that was very small, a quarter the size of my office. I was absolutely flabbergasted that a former prime minister was sitting in such a damned small office: it was an absolute insult. However, I didn't realize that Mr. Diefenbaker did have two other offices away from this one. But there he was, in this little cubbyhole, with his secretary Mrs. Eligh. I would go in from time to time to look at various mementos that he had, very famous things, that had been given to him, and I was always impressed. He said to me one day, "This is nothing, my boy, nothing." When I asked what he meant, he said, "You should see what I have in my home." I replied, "Mr. Diefenbaker, would I ever love to." By this time I had gotten to know him quite well.

The next day he phoned me and said, "Stan, you know what I told you: the archives are coming to move a great deal of this material from my home, and if you want to see it you are going to have to come right away." Well, I said, "Tell me when and where, midnight, anytime." He said, "What about tomorrow morning at eight o'clock. I'm in Rockcliffe and I will send my car for you."

At that time I had a young research assistant, Marlene Grace working for me. I was living at the Chateau Laurier Hotel and I said to her, "How about meeting me in the lobby of the Chateau Laurier Hotel at eight o'clock tomorrow morning." She sort of looked at me and was a bit cool. Then I asked her if she would like to go with me to see Mr. Diefenbaker's treasures at his home in Rockcliffe. She changed completely and said, "Oh my God. Do not tell me! My father is the greatest Diefenbaker fan. He has never met him." So I told her to be in the lobby of the hotel at eight o'clock sharp the next morning.

The next morning when his car came to the hotel to pick me up, Mr. Diefenbaker was in it, too, to take us to his home. We had a marvelous tour and saw Sir John A. MacDonald's famous whisky desk; thirty or forty university gowns which he had worn when presented with honorary degrees; Indian bonnets; a magnificent gift from the Emperor of Japan; beautiful china and sterling silver from the Nizam of Hydrobad. He was the richest man in the world – there was something from President de Gaulle – fabulous treasures and I saw them all, it was just amazing. A good many have gone out to the Diefenbaker Museum in Saskatoon. I even had my picture taken with Mrs. Diefenbaker's famous portrait in the background. Mrs. Diefenbaker had died some time before.

After Mr. Diefenbaker lost the leadership in 1967 to Robert Stanfield, he stayed on in Ottawa as an MP. I understand he gave Mr. Stanfield a hard time on occasion. I am well aware that Mr. Diefenbaker had a great many attributes. He also had some faults. He was a very unforgiving man, I am well aware of that. But in his final years, the Chief, as so many people called him, mellowed and he became a sort of folk figure on the Hill.

Thinking back about what might have been, it is tragic to see him alone so much of the time. He rarely if ever attends caucus unless he has something special to bring up, but I doubt if he has attended caucus more than two or three times.

Mr. Diefenbaker is very sensitive about bilingualism legislation. He has spoken passionately about this. I must concede that a great many of us from rural Canada, not in the province of Quebec, looked with some misgivings on some of the proposed bilingualism legislation. But it is amazing to see the affection that Mr. Diefenbaker is held in by so many, particularly in the rural parts of Canada. So many people purchased his memoirs and would say to me, "Do you think you could get Mr. Diefenbaker to autograph my book?" I would say, "Well, I will do my best."

Mr. Diefenbaker helped to set up the royal commission which led to medicare at the federal level, but the real battle for medical insurance was fought by the socialist government of Saskatchewan in 1962.

The John Diefenbaker I knew loved Parliament and knew how to bend it to achieve his ends. There was something in his character rather than in his record that makes him live on in the Canadian imagination. Peter Newman, in his book about Diefenbaker, called him a "renegade." I understand Mr. Diefenbaker claimed not to have read this book. But the Diefenbaker fascination was partly that he felt the right to kick over the traces from time to time. He was, I think, a nonconformist, an instinctive battler against establishments and he sometimes carried this to absurd lengths. Many people have told me they found him petty and petulant in his relations with other people. I never found this so with me.

A colleague pointed out to me that he found Diefenbaker messianic, that he so completely believed in his own mission in life and in Parliament that he did not have to adjust his opinion to fit in with others. They had to adjust to fit in with him.

I think there is a bit of the Diefenbaker ego in all of us, and perhaps a resentment of the pressure to conform. But I always found Mr. Diefenbaker a champion of individual rights by being, first of all, a champion of his own right to be as obstreperous and rambunctious as he pleased.

[The Chief would have been 90 years old today.]

Anchorage, August 16, 1979 ... I learned today that John Diefenbaker has died. His wife, Olive, died in 1976 and he has been, in many ways, a very lonely person since then. I can't help but recall how kind he was to me in the years I have known him, and how he had gone out of his way to help me when I first came to Ottawa.

Ottawa, August 25, 1979 ... At breakfast in the dining room this morning, a group at my table were talking about John Diefenbaker and what he had accomplished in the years he was prime minister and Member Of Parliament. I remember him telling me about his devotion to preparing a Bill of Rights for the Canadian people and at the age of 17 battling for such a bill in a debate of the Saskatchewan Boys' Parliament. As a young lawyer he also spent hours drafting a Canadian Bill of Rights and his time was not wasted. At 65, three years after he was elected prime minister of Canada, the 1960 government enacted his cherished bill.

He often said that it was his proudest legislative achievement. Mr. Diefenbaker said, in the second volume of his memoirs One Canada, "Critics condemned it as a pious and ineffectual declaration but court cases have proven the critics wrong. The Bill of Rights stands today as the protector of the liberties of every Canadian, however humble."

On a television station recently I saw an interview with Mr. Diefenbaker which had been done some time ago when he said, "I set out in life to bring about in this nation a recognition of the fact that regardless of race or origin, all are equal – one Canada, one nation."

Something not often discussed when Mr. Diefenbaker's name comes up is his "Vision of the North" into which he poured great efforts and funding in opening up Canada's last frontier. His government passed legislation aimed at producing Canadian investment in Arctic development and in his own words, "We enacted new northern oil and gas regulations that guaranteed independence, not continentalism, to the Canadian people. Inuvik was founded, the Dempster Highway from Whitehorse through the Northwest was recently opened."

Mr. Diefenbaker was proud of the South Saskatchewan Dam his administration sponsored, which opened up thousands of acres to cultivation. He said it was a project of national significance, of importance to all Canadians.

Ottawa, 1980 ... I attended a committee meeting today and during our coffee break, John Diefenbaker's name came up. It often does, as he is still remembered and discussed by former colleagues. I was asked what I thought his major failure was, why his government did not retain power. My own, and the considered opinion of many others, is that Mr. Diefenbaker was always a loner, he wasn't all that good at leading. He ultimately lost the support of key Cabinet members.

One major issue was the nuclear arming of the Bomarc missiles, to which Washington – contrary to Diefenbaker's position – claimed that Ottawa was committed.

At that time the minister of defence was Douglas Harkness and it was said that he led the revolt against Mr. Diefenbaker. Mr. Harkness said that the loss of Cabinet confidence started a year earlier during the 1962 Cuban missile crisis. Washington placed its armed forces on alert in October and asked Canada to do the same.

Mr. Diefenbaker balked, arguing that he had not been consulted and needed more time, but it was evident that the Cuban crisis shook the confidence of a number of the Cabinet had in the Prime Minister.

In answer to statements that he was anti-American, Mr. Diefenbaker stated, "I am a Canadian. I'm proud to be a Canadian. My message throughout the Cuban crisis was consistently pro-Canadian. Charges that I am anti-American are patently false."

Dalton Camp was, and is, an active political writer and supporter. He wrote in his Toronto Star column following Mr. Diefenbaker's death, "We are all diminished by the passing of famous men – who stand taller than most of us. But of course the death of John Diefenbaker is of unique personal significance to me since it was my lot to be his eternal nemesis and adversary. He was an adversary of estimable mettle and I shall miss him, and in a way no other of his fellow Canadians would know."

Headlines in a huge variety of national newspapers ranged from: "He's the greatest Canadian since Sir John A." to "Parliament's best storyteller," "Harsh partisan climate marked his years as PM," "Flashback: Downfall of Chief" and "He broke the rules with vengeful delight." The Toronto Star said, "The Day of the Long Knives, when opponents of John Diefenbaker manipulated the annual Conservative meeting to force a leadership convention, was one of the most dramatic episodes of Canadian political history. This was the day that the Toronto Tories determined that Dief should go, and ably generaled by an old Diefenbaker friend Dalton Camp, manipulated the annual Conservative meeting to force a leadership convention. Dief lost."

Mr. Diefenbaker said, just before he died, "My greatest mistake was to bring Bay Street financier Wallace McCutcheon into the Cabinet to appease Toronto businessmen. I became convinced he was a traitor."

There are probably several versions of what was called "The great conspiracy," but perhaps the real reason was that John Diefenbaker was raised too high to be allowed to exist. As Dalton Camp said one day as the knives were being sharpened, "By making a god of our leader, we have made cheap of ourselves."

August 1979 ... Christie Blatchford of the Toronto Star said, "Archie McQueen had been going to the Diefenbaker house every summer for a decade. He had nominated Mr. Diefenbaker for an honorary doctorate from his Waterloo University and Mr. Diefenbaker came to collect it. Mr. McQueen eventually became a volunteer special assistant with work to do, handling correspondence and research, living in the Diefenbaker house on his summer visits. When Mr. McQueen went into the Diefenbaker study on that August 16th morning to watch the television news, he found Mr. Diefenbaker dead. He said, "I'd never have done the work for anyone else. I really loved the guy."

August 1979, Ottawa ... John Diefenbaker, Canada's thirteenth prime minister, attended the First Baptist Church in Ottawa and as his body lies in state in the Hall of Honor in the Parliament Building, colleagues, friends, constituents, tourists to Ottawa, and the curious passed by his coffin to pay their final respects. I could not help but recall his words as I stood there, reliving the times we had spent together: "They did me in, in 1966. There are nothing in this party but ciphers and sons-of-bitches and I may be wounded but I am not slain. I will rest and rise and fight again."

John Diefenbaker had a difficult time speaking French. It was not from lack of trying but because of his inability to hear notes. Because he could not hear notes he could not sing, or could not pronounce unfamiliar words. It was said of him that when he tried to sing "God Save the King" at a family gathering many years ago, "When I heard him start, I couldn't bear it and thought that God indeed should save the King from his voice. He couldn't sing at all."

He was also noted as a great raconteur. His brother-in-law Harold Freeman said, "Once in a while if he was in town we'd go to his hotel or private railway car after a speech and he'd have poached eggs, toast, honey and maybe coffee or tea. Then he'd smile and tell all those stories."

August 1979 … John Diefenbaker made his farewell to the world today. Governor General Edward Schryerer, Prime Minister Joe Clark, MPs, Senators, the diplomatic corp and representatives from other countries packed into Christ Church Cathedral at 3 p.m. for the state funeral. His body will be lying in state from 10 till 3 today and from 10 till noon Sunday.

The inter-faith service will be conducted by Rev. Ralph Cummings, pastor of First Baptist Church where Mr. Diefenbaker worshipped. He will then leave for the Alta Vista railway station. There is a special train with two locomotives and seven cars which will leave at 5 p.m. making stops in Sudbury, Winnipeg and Prince Albert, Saskatchewan, before arriving in Saskatoon. These stops, lasting between two and four hours, will allow Canadians to pay their final respects.

There were over 10,000 people who paid their last respects at Parliament Hill to the Chief.

It was in every way the last of an era.

At the cathedral service in Ottawa were a great many friends who will miss their friendship with Mr. Diefenbaker. Seated together in the front row were Mrs. Carolyn Weir, his stepdaughter, her husband Donald, their five children, Cora Green, Mr. Diefenbaker's housekeeper, and Beatrice Eligh, his personal secretary, for whom I have had the greatest respect. Jon Vickers, the opera singer and a long-time friend of Diefenbaker, sang, his decorations were carried on a red cushion by a personal friend, Thomas Pickup, and there were sixty-one honorary pallbearers, including Alvin Hamilton, agriculture minister in the Diefenbaker cabinet, Bob Coates, PC president, former Liberal trade minister Jack Horner, and Paul Hellyer, former Liberal transport minister who became a Conservative. Arthur Maloney, former Ontario ombudsman, N.S. Premier John Buchanan, Senators Allister Grosart, David Walker and Robert Muir, Ray Hnatyshyn, Don Mazankowski and David Crombie.

Mr. Diefenbaker's coffin was placed on board the train by members of the RCMP.

As he was laid to rest in Saskatoon, tributes from around the world were received in Ottawa, and from Her Majesty the Queen, "Canada has lost a man of great stature. He never wavered. He was unfailing in his loyalty to his country and the crown."

As journalist Richard Gwyn said, "I know for certain I'll never forget him. Nor will anyone who met him. He'll be missed."

April 20, 1982, Ottawa … John Diefenbaker left his house in Rockliffe, Ottawa, to the government of Canada on the condition that it did two things: establish a museum and declare the house to be an historic site. If these two conditions were not met the house would be sold.

The government did not accept Mr. Diefenbaker's offer on his terms and the house will be sold in the near future. It is interesting to point out that the Diefenbaker Memorial Foundation offered $1 for Mr. Diefenbaker's house. The foundation, directed by an experienced fund director, has not been able to raise a sum sufficient to purchase the house and make it a museum in honor of the Chief's memory.

Mr. Diefenbaker's will stated that should the house become a museum, it would display documents, letters, pictures of pioneer days of the prairies, of the settlement of Canadians of all racial origins, which will emphasize his lifetime devotion that all Canadians, regardless of racial origin, shall be equal.

On August 21, 1979, my friend John Diefenbaker was laid to his final rest in the Prairie soil he loved so well, beside his beloved Olive.

MY SEVENTY-FIFTH

July 16, 1986, Burks Falls ... I'm not at all sure I like being called "spry," but that is how the Muskoka Advance described me on my seventy-fifth birthday today. They also said I am "spunky" and I would like to argue that word with them as well!

My family and friends threw together a big birthday party in the Burks Falls Armour and Ryerson Arena and there were over 500 guests by the time the day was over. I had my picture taken by Derek Billard of the Muskoka Advance, with good friend Liz Trolove, who with her mother, Ina, had a big hand in planning the party, and with Vicki and Ernie Eves. The Eves are really good friends and we meet often as they go about their duties for Ernie's Parry Sound riding.

There were seven MPs attending, that I counted, including Tom McMillan, minister of the environment, who I work with a lot, and Reg Stackhouse, MP for Scarborough West, Bill Scott, MP from Victoria/Haliburton, Ken James, MP for Sarnia/Lampton, Moe Mantha, MP from Nipissing and John McDougall, MP from Temiskaming, and others. I had no idea so many people would show up. I was almost speechless, if you can believe that.

Burks Falls, 1994 ... I was thinking about other momentous days as I drove to my dentist in Huntsville today and I recalled that I had had my pacemaker implanted inside my chest on May 13, 1987; I should have wondered about having an operation on Friday the 13th. The truth is, I never think about it or even know it is there. I needed it because I have low blood pressure, which is a good thing or I'd be dead by now. The odd time, though, if I'm going like hell, I get a little tired.

Another interesting thing in my life was in 1979, I think, when the

North Bay Nugget wrote an editorial headed, "Stan Darling has been an outspoken, energetic and capable MP and we definitely think he is cabinet material." That really pleased me. However, I was a backbencher for twenty-one years and enjoyed every minute of it.

In November, 1981, Speaker of the House, the Hon. Jeanne Sauve, honored fifty of us Members of Parliament at a private reception. We were all first elected to Parliament in October 30, 1972, in the federal election. Fifty-seven Progressive Conservative members were elected that year and of this number, thirty-two were still serving in 1981.

Another newspaper article I noticed while sorting through some files today was from the Gravenhurst News, one December. It stated, "Stan Rams Moose!"

I certainly remember that trip. I slammed into a moose on Highway 60, en route to Ottawa. It had been running across the highway and slipped on some ice and fallen right in front of my car. I had purchased a new 1990 Cadillac Fleetwood two days before and I did over $6,000 damage to it. Wayne Howe of Sundridge who happened to be on the highway at that time, helped me sort that one out. I estimated one time that I have driven over half a million miles during my Ottawa – Burks Falls – Ottawa weekly trips since first being elected to the House in 1972.

In a Muskoka Advance article, written by columnist John Challis, who visited me several times in Ottawa, he stated: "Stan Darling was one of the first to bring up the issue of acid rain in the House of Commons. The press snickered at his statements during Question Period, six or seven years ago, when the issue was unknown. Since then, he's become known as one of the experts on acid rain control."

I said to John Challis, "I never had a salary until I got into Parliament. I'd been selling insurance and real estate on commission for twenty years before getting involved in politics. I told him about coming to Burks Falls in 1931, when my first job was as a laborer in a local factory where my father worked and I was paid 15 cents an hour. A year later, it was increased to what was called a 'married man's wages' of 20 cents an hour."

Driving home from Huntsville in the rain, I remembered something Ernie Eves said at my seventy-fifth birthday party. "Stan Darling shares his birthday with actress Ginger Rogers. But, Stan, let me tell you, you have more moves than Ginger Rogers ever thought of having."

Ernie also mentioned my work in acid rain and said, "Stan is an individual who understands and cares for people and always puts his constituents before himself and anyone else. He goes to bat for these people every day."

That was a pretty nice thing for Ernie to say.

Tom McMillan, MP for Charlottetown in Prince Edward Island also said some nice things. "This is a special tribute to an incredible human being. I am amazed by Stan's stamina and by his work on acid rain."

Well, I was certainly surprised that so many of my friends and colleagues showed up at my seventy-fifth birthday party. It was a great day.

RCMP PROTECTION PLAN

June 25, 1986 … In my mail today was a letter marked "confidential." It was signed by Solicitor General Perrin Beatty and stated, in part: "In the event that you or your family receive a threat of physical harm, or you have reason to require personal security on an urgent basis, you should: contact the RCMP and identify yourself as a Member of Parliament, outline the nature of the threat and request personal security."

It goes on to outline how to handle other problems such as threatening letters (to be collected by hand by RCMP and handled as little as possible) to threatening telephone calls (try to establish identity of caller and origin of call, record relevant particulars and contact RCMP); attendance of unstable or bothersome persons at office (attempt to establish the subject's identity and address, whether they are staying in Ottawa, record reason for personal visit); suspicious package or mail (do not accept delivery of any suspicious packages unless delivery person is known personally, do not handle, suspect mail can be screened for explosive devices); all of which is good sound advice for anyone but it did nothing to make me feel more secure and relaxed for the day's work, let me tell you!

TRANSFER PAYMENTS

Burks Falls, 1995 ... Reading the news from Ottawa about the Chretien government's plans to slash provincial transfer payments. started me on a search for a report I wrote from Ottawa in April 1992. One of the items I reviewed for my constituents was headlined: "Federal Transfer Payments" and I wrote, "Recently, there have been numerous claims made by both the Opposition Parties (the Liberals), and some provincial governments that *our* government (the PCs) had been reducing its financial commitments to the long-standing tradition of transfer payments to the provinces.

These politically motivated claims are unfounded. Facts and figures on this issue are being provided for your information. You can decide for yourself who is coming clean!

We are not slashing nor massively reducing transfer payments to the provinces. If anything, overall transfer payments have been increased considerably since we first formed a government. In fact, total transfer payments to the provinces, including all cash and tax transfer points have increased by $12.5 billion since 1984/85, or almost 80 per cent.

I also outlined equalization program transfers and the established programs financing, which prove my point completely.

Every government, it seems, is accused of much the same things, no matter what party they represent.

SOME COMMENTS

I was asked recently what I thought of the idea of Canada having nuclear submarines, new equipment acquired recently by Defence Minister Perrin Beatty. Well, in my estimation, nuclear submarines are very controversial. I was at a defence meeting yesterday when the very eminent retired general Richard Rohmer was speaking against nuclear subs in the Arctic. I said, "Look, in my view we have a navy of about twenty-six ships in total, some held together with bailing wire, wax and so on. They have run their course. We now have three submarines that are at the end of their viability, most have been in service for twenty-five years, which is the usual life of a submarine. We are not in a position to buy one hundred ships."

I said that after the Second World War Canada had the third-largest navy in the world, now we have twenty-six ships. It is a lot better to have three new submarines. They don't have to be used in the Arctic only. With submarines, our enemy need not know where we are located. We should use nuclear subs for our protection. They are much faster, much more difficult to detect. We have the largest coastline in the world, 37,000 miles in length. I think my views about obtaining nuclear submarines is a proper decision.

I got into a philosophical discussion today with some former politicians in Parry Sound. One of them said he was glad he had chosen a political career and had spent the better part of his life at it. I said, "I think I have been one of the more fortunate Members of Parliament elected later in life, at 61, actually." When I look back over twenty-one years in Ottawa as a Member of the House of Commons, I wonder now at how many young MPs there are coming into the House, some have given up lucrative businesses: lawyers, teachers, professional men and women. Many have had to get rid of their businesses. And then comes defeat, or retirement, which is inevitable and many are not in a financial position to be able to go back and pick up the pieces. This is very unfortunate. All of a sudden, they are a nonentity, forgotten, and the phone stops ringing. Many people have been in a really tough financial position.

I have been fortunate. I had a reasonably successful business in a little town, with two sons both working for me. I am a real estate and an insurance broker.

My two sons didn't kill themselves working too hard, as long as I was there, the old man did it all! But when I had left for Ottawa, they eventually took over the business and surprised me all to pieces because they are operating a very successful business, bigger than it ever was when I was there. In my particular case, my business did not suffer at all.

July 1992, Burks Falls ... The Parry Sound newspaper had an article today by long-time friend Beth Slaney. She had interviewed me about my work in my riding and was, I think, surprised to find out how many hours I put in on the weekends. She started her column, Seniority, by saying, "How often have we heard that politicians are over paid, under worked and living in the lap of luxury?" She followed me around for the weekend and I filled her in on my schedule the week before.

I had been to Europe for two weeks in February with the Defence Committee, in Vienna, Prague, Moscow, Berlin, Bonn, Brussels and Lahr, a NATO Conference in Banff Springs, Alberta, a UNCED Summit in Rio de Janeiro, the International Trade Show in Sao Paulo, the commissioning of the frigate HMCS *Halifax* in Nova Scotia, in New York with Jean Charest for meetings on acid rain, and on the weekend in Port Loring to a sixtieth wedding anniversary, to Bracebridge to launch a new affordable housing development, a fiftieth anniversary dinner in Rosseau, another in South River, to the Rosseau Lake College for their twenty-fifth anniversary, to Camp Borden for the Standing Committee on Defence, to Huntsville to a Tourism meeting, to Parry Sound for the Learning Organization and then, of course, back through Algonquin Park to Ottawa and the start of another day. I met with people in my Burks Falls office, handled phone calls and correspondence and had my hair cut.

"People must love to see you coming, Stan," Beth said, but I had to admit that because of my party's low political standing in the polls right now, that I am often as popular as a skunk at a garden party.

Ottawa, Autumn 1986 ... I am always frustrated at getting legislation put through and passed into law. I had an unusual request last week from a solicitor in Parry Sound, Bruce Cunningham, who had a client, Lawrie Kingsland, whose company lost its charter through their forgetting to renew it. The only way it could be reinstated was through a private member's bill.

As Parliament was about to recess for the summer months, some fast action was needed. It had to be done immediately. I looked into it and was told that a special committee, headed by Marcel Prudhomme, and Senator Duff Roblin, would have to deal with it.

I approached Marcel, who is a good friend, and explained the circumstances to him. Lo and behold, they said they would get it throught both the House and the Senate in one day. Which they did!

I was pleased to be able to help one of my constituents.

BILINGUALISM – AN ONGOING PROBLEM

Ottawa, 1991 … Like so many contentious issues in Canada, bilingualism remains a hot topic in some parts of my Parry Sound/ Muskoka riding. I think that bilingual services should be available according to the Constitution, where there is a significant francophone or anglophone (minority) population. There is certainly a hotbed of anti-French sentiment in the North Bay/Powassan/Callander area.

APEC is a rabid group with a strong North Bay organization. Their name is Association for the Preservation of English in Canada, but they are just like the Ku Klux Klan in the U.S., fomenting dissension. This won't get us anywhere – in a country like Canada we must learn to get along with each other. I know that some Quebecers hate the English people's guts and they'd walk on red-hot coals in their bare feet and with the seat of their pants ripped out just to get separation, they want it so much.

But for all the bad things that I have said about Quebec at times, because I have often said that they want to separate from the rest of Canada, I say, if they want to go, let them go, and God bless them. But then I stop and think, well, my God, here we are now the greatest country in the world and with the breakup of the U.S.S.R., the biggest country in the world, with so much going for us. If there is any way to keep us all together, and strong, then we should be looking for a way to do it.

I'm not too fluent in French – *je parle français tres peu, tres pauvre, tres lentement*, and that is about the extent of my French – I took a very dim view of it, that anglophones and other than francophones were being discriminated against. In my early days in Parliament I would often say I spoke for the majority in Canada, in which a mere 20 million were, at that time, English-speaking, as opposed to 5 million francophones. A lot of us felt discriminated against because a document released recently indicated that no federal public servant could be appointed to a post abroad unless he or she was bilingual. Well, when I had revealed the contents of this document, the reaction was overwhelming in the English area of Canada, especially in my riding. I am one of those who concedes that Canada is a bilingual country. But, I take a dim view of it. A recent example was that members of the Royal Canadian Mounted Police must be bilingual, even though they are working in Alberta or British Columbia, where there is not a large amount of French spoken. If they have to be bilingual in B.C., I could see that it should be Chinese or Japanese they should be required to speak.

MR. FILZMAIER AND THE
MUSKOKA AIRPORT

Whon Beth Slaney asked me to explain the Roland Filzmaier Jr. Airport story to her today, as we were putting together notes for my diary, I thought back over ten confusing years. And, to the best of my knowledge, the story is not yet concluded.

On Mr. Filzmaier's letterhead, he states that he is an entrepreneur and that, "Co-operation is the Key That Serves Many Locks." Mr. Filzmaier lives in Toronto, Bracebridge and Carefree, Arizona.

I wrote to the Hon. Shirley Martin, PC, MP, on July 30, 1993, shortly after I announced my retirement from the House, asking her to help sort out this long saga of misunderstanding and confusion, but it is interesting enough to recount here.

1992: Transport Canada received from the District Municipality of Muskoka, copy of the approved draft plan of subdivision for Mr. Filzmaier's proposed industrial park, to be built, adjacent to the Muskoka Airport at Gravenhurst. Transport Canada requested clarification and by the number, type, size and frequency of aircraft to be processed by the off-airport developments.

1984: Transport Canada required that a feasibility study be carried out to show the potential for the aircraft related Industrial Park, to show its economic impact on the local economy. This was done and the report stated that the project was feasible and showed a great deal of merit.

1985: Filzmaier contacted aircraft related industries and obtained six commitments from companies who would relocate their businesses to the Muskoka Airport Park. Surveys and preliminary layouts were completed and submitted for approval.

1986: Planners reported their findings to Transport Canada and engineers confirmed that the project was viable, with economic benefits all around. Amendment No. 57 to the official plan was submitted and received approval by municipal and provincial governments.

1987: Planning and development continues on the industrial park. In June, Plan No. TP8502 showed Transport Canada that 614 jobs could be provided from the development, and $108.3 million would be brought into the area. Revenues generated in taxes would benefit the municipality. A scale model of the park in relation to the Muskoka Airport was built. Preliminary layouts and concept plans were completed and conveyed to Transport Canada and their consultants, 3M. Mr. Filzmaier's expenditures to date were around $500,000. Transport Canada and the Municipality of Gravenhurst began to negotiate the takeover of the operations of the airport, and all negotiations with Mr. Filzmaier were terminated.

1987 – 1990: The above negotiations lasted three years, and Mr. Filzmaier's plans were on hold during that period. Ultimately, the municipality and the Transport Canada officials said that, as they did not have the capacity to carry out airport management, Mr. Filzmaier should resume to negotiate with Transport Canada.

1990: After numerous meetings with Transport Canada, and the submission of various reports, he was encouraged to produce additional information for their review. The minister saw the industrial park development scale model, and was, we were told, impressed. He said he would like to encourage such projects and see that they materialize. Gravenhurst and Bracebridge mayors who were present, were fully supportive. The Hon. Doug Lewis praised Mr. Filzmaier's efforts, and thanked him for bringing this to his attention. The minister and Mr. Filzmaier also met in his constituency office in Orillia.

November 15: Transport Canada's Memo stated that the new parallel taxiway would be able to accommodate Dash – 8-300, Convair 580, DC-9, and Boeing 737. Things were beginning to hum along.

1991: A letter from the Hon. Doug Lewis outlined the criteria that should be followed and encouraged Mr. Filzmaier to obtain municipal and provincial approvals, thus eliminating obstacles outside Transport Canada's jurisdiction.

Further meetings with the minister were positive and Mr. Filzmaier was told that at that time the project should continue without hindrance.

April 1991: Mr. Filzmaier was told that all the approval he had obtained in 1987 were outdated and must be re-addressed to the various government departments for reapproval. This was done, plus contact with hydrogeological engineers, to satisfy the Ministry of the Environment. All departments reported favorably except the Ministry of the Environment. After three months they requested additional engineering work be completed and this was also done by Mr. Filzmaier.

The MOE then asked for still further studies and the installation of numerous wells to be installed. Then requests were received for yet more studies and the installation of still further wells.

After a further report that this had been done, the MOE asked for yet more studies, and more technical information which had already been reported in the initial 1991 report. This was done as well. These requests had cost Mr. Filzmaier $237,000 for the ten months work.

June 25, 1992: Mr. Filzmaier received approval from the MOE and clearance by Municipal Affairs with the results that were no different than they were in May, 1991.

Mr. Filzmaier commented recently, "After absorbing almost $2 million in costs for approvals alone, I find it ironic that Transport Canada has not made a positive commitment to upgrade the airport facilities to enhance the economic development of the Muskoka region. Muskoka Airport is absolutely necessary to a presently large population to which has been added the new prison, new tourist establishments and businesses."

April 1993: The Muskoka newspapers are carrying stories and letters from a man who gets my vote as the most patient man of the century. Roland Filzmaier! Headlines in the Muskoka Herald Gazette state: "Muskoka Airport venture explained." Mr. Filzmaier has written to the media asking them for co-operation in making his story known.

Until the Muskoka Airport is upgraded to an all-weather airport, Mr. Filzmaier's industrial park plans cannot go ahead.

Mr. Filzmaier is quoted as saying in one of the newspaper articles:" When I received the MOE's approval, I found out that the second airport for Orillia was now scheduled to be upgraded to a 5,000-foot runway, which would accommodate most jet aircraft traffic. It would be in direct competition with the Muskoka Airport and it has already received international status with full Customs services on-site. Further investigations show that an aviation related industrial park, very much the same kind of park I have been attempting to establish in Muskoka Airport, has been planned for next to the runway of Orillia's new airport, on farm land, within two years. This while I am still trying to obtain subdivision approvals from the Ministry of the Environment!"

Mr. Filzmaier brought this to my attention and to District Chairman Frank Miller, and to Gravenhurst Mayor Gord Adams.

I am asked so often by my constituents, why I cannot help them with one of their problems, and I always say that I do my very best. Perhaps Mr. Filzmaier's saga will give you some idea of what often transpires before something positive can be accomplished.

MY FRIEND LOU MYLES

I was at a PC meeting in Toronto today, I stopped by my friend and clothier, Lou Myles, who has designed and made all my clothes now for many years. An interesting thing happened last week. Beth Slaney who is helping me sort through my files and photographs, asked me if I knew Lou Myles. Well, I guess I do and told her so. When I asked her why she asked, she said, "Stan, I used to do public relations for some of the well-known designers and manufacturers of men's clothes and I recognize the cut and make of a super suit when I see it."

In the early 1950s I was selling insurance in Toronto and made a cold call at a men's clothing store in downtown Toronto. That is where I first met Lou Myles, he was working there. He needed insurance but couldn't afford to pay for it just then, and there was something about him that made me take a chance and trust him to pay me later. I have never regretted my decision.

Lou used to have one of the greatest men's wear stores in Canada on the east side of Yonge Street – above Dundas at number 363 – and I found that he carried everything I needed and better still, could design and make a suit for me that never went out of style. If there was one thing I needed in those days it was to look well dressed wherever I went. Come to think of it, I still do and so many of my clothes that look great today came from Lou some years ago.

Lou has moved to the outskirts of Toronto now and has a shop where he designs, makes, sells and accessorizes wardrobes for all kinds of people from politicians to first rate business people. He has certainly earned my respect and I have always felt that I could pack in an hour and be on my way to Prague or China or London, and be dressed for the occasion. It has been a nice relationship to have known Lou Myles all these years and I like to think of him as my friend.

DANGER PAY, TRAVELS AROUND THE WORLD

I have often joked that a Member of Parliament should receive danger pay. I've had quite a few narrow escapes in my business travels around the world. One night driving home through Algonquin Park, the roads were unusually slippery and although I was not driving too fast, my car slid right into and old parked car with the driver in it. My car was seriously damaged on the left front fender ánd the bill was around $900. The driver of the other car, a man from North Bay it turned out, looked at me and said, "Hello, Stan." I looked at his old Pontiac and there was not a scratch on it. He just laughed.

Another time I had just purchased a beautiful new car a week or so before Christmas and wanted to take it home on Thursday, but it would not be ready before Friday. My father had always said, "Never make an important deal or buy anything big on a Friday." Although I remembered that at the time, I said to myself, "Oh, what the hell," and picked up the car on Friday to drive home. Coming back on Sunday it was a cold night and I was not losing any time in Algonquin Park. Coming over the hill in front of me was a very big moose, crossing the highway about 100 yards away. I felt that I was perfectly safe but lo and behold, the moose started to run and he slipped on the icy road and fell down, right in front of my car. Well, there was no way I could avoid him, and I ran right over that moose. Had I hit him head on the chances are that it would have thrown the car into the ditch and I would have been seriously injured. The car had quite a bit of damage to it, steam was coming out of the engine, but I was able to continue on to Ottawa. But the smell nearly knocked me down. I had done a lot of damage to the moose, and most of it was stuck to the bottom of the car. Just after my accident with the moose, a man came along the highway and I explained my accident and the circumstances to him. He said that he would go back and take the carcass off the highway. When he returned to my car he said, "You're Stan Darling, aren't you?" When I said yes, he said, "Well, since I know you and your car can still run, I'll follow you out to the next service station at the east gate." I was thankful for his help.

When I had my first glider ride at the Parry Sound Airport, a while back, the glider pilots were all experienced, and one was a British pilot with the Royal Air Force. It was a wonderful experience to be with this man, gliding over trees and the water, without a sound of anything but the wind. As we turned to come back, the glider took a sharp turn and hit a current of air and made an 180 degree turn, and dug into the ground. People started running over to be sure that we were not injured, but again, luck was with me and I suffered no ill effects.

One time, after meetings in Germany for NATO, I was having a tough time to get a flight back home because of a variety of unusual circumstances. After a hair-raising drive across the country, I was told that the next plane which left Lahr in two days would have a space for me. There was a strike of traffic controllers in Prestwick, Scotland, with no international or overseas flights from Great Britain to North America. But eventually I got away. I was able to visit a long-time friend from Burks Falls, Captain Jim Thompson who was a fighter pilot and helicopter pilot. He is now a Colonel in Zagreb with the UN. I had dinner with the Thompsons and got on board my flight home. I could see sparks coming from the plane and we ground to a halt, and taxied back to the hanger. Lo and behold, Jim Thompson was right there and as an officer he was able to come out to the plane when the doors opened. Fire engines and ambulances were all around us, and Jim wondered what the sam hill was going on. He found out later that the plane had blown a window in the cockpit and the pilot had to abort the takeoff. As the plane was heavily loaded with fuel for our direct flight to Ottawa, they were quite right to be concerned. The tires were burned off the plane with the quick stop and arrangements had to be made to bring out a new set from Ottawa, before we could go on.

Once attending a Canada/U.S. Parliamentary Association meeting with Mona in Charlotte, N.C., at a resort on the Island of Kiau, we were coming in for a landing. Twenty-five members of our group were made up of Senators and staff and Members of Parliament.

The plane set down on the tarmac with a big bang and I said to Mona, "My God, the pilot must be new. He can't be very familiar with this plane."

At that moment the stewardess stood up and said, "Please keep your seats, please keep your seats, and in a few moments, proceed out as quickly as possible."

Well, instead of taking the usual stairs out of the plane, we were directed to slide down the emergency exits. Mona took one slide and I the other, which struck me as unusual. We were greeted by ambulances and fire engines but no one was hurt. Headlines in the Canadian papers the next day stated, "Canadian MPs were free-loaders on board a government plane which had a near crash."

THE PRIME MINISTERS

February 1972, Ottawa ... I was pleased to meet PC Leader Robert Stanfield again today. When I was campaigning in my riding of Parry Sound/Muskoka last year, he came through to visit three major towns. He was mainstreeting around the middle of July. We had decided to take Mr. Stanfield to Parry Sound on July 12th, but were criticized because we would be attending the "Orange" celebration. However, nothing much more came of that, but Mr. Stanfield received good exposure from his brief visit. However, during the October election the Liberals managed to get 109 seats, and the Progressive Conservatives 107, and so the PCs remained as the opposition by two seats.

I like Mr. Stanfield, he is a very honorable man and an excellent politician with many good ideas. I feel he would have made a top notch prime minister if he had been given enough time to develop a program for the future of Canada, and if the Canadian people had been given the opportunity of getting to know him as I had. Mr. Stanfield was a quiet gentleman, with a great sense of humor. It was said of him, "Mr. Stanfield was the best prime minister Canada never had."

During the 1974 election, the issues were wage and price controls – controls which Mr. Stanfield endorsed. The polls, however, showed that the people were opposed to this, and could not see past the fact that their wages might be frozen. Although Mr. Stanfield was warned that this would be used against him, he stated that he had given his word and would not back down on it. Well, he lost the election and shortly after, in 1976, and a new leader of the party was chosen.

January 1972 ... Prime Minister Pierre Trudeau has said a resounding "NO" to wage and price control and he and Mr. Stanfield don't agree on that.

I was never closely involved with Prime Minister Trudeau. In my maiden speech, where a Member can say what he pleases, I took exception to the constant heckling of the Prime Minister by my colleagues. I was hauled over the coals by my party about this but replied that it was the way I felt and that I didn't care about their opinion.

Prime Minister Trudeau was aloof, and was thought of as a keen philosopher who would have little or nothing to do with the Opposition Members of Parliament. He was always very polite to me when we met at a function, or in the stately halls of Parliament. I never felt any kinship or friendship with him, the way I had with Robert Stanfield.

I learned of a large and devastating oil spill in the waters of my riding, off Parry Sound, where a Shell tanker had spilled a great deal of oil during the winter. Parry Sound residents and cottagers, were, needless to say, concerned for their property and the 30,000 islands. They formed a delegation, came to Ottawa to see me. My colleague, J.J. Blais, who was a cabinet minister at the time, was able to persuade Prime Minister Trudeau to come to the meeting room briefly, to meet with the delegates. That was, I think, the only actual contact I had with Mr. Trudeau, who I always found to be a rather cold, remote man, and somewhat lonely.

In the 1972 election, the Trudeau government got 109 seats and the Stanfield group 107, but Trudeau was able to retain power through the support of the NDP, whose leader at that time was David Lewis. Ultimately, the roof caved in on Trudeau in 1974, when Lewis and the NDP withdrew their support.

When Robert Stanfield decided to resign in 1976, a convention was held to nominate a new Progressive Conservative leader. There were six or more contestants with the front runners being Claude Wagner of St. Hyacinthe, Quebec, and Brian Mulroney, also of Quebec. Others were Paul Hellyer, Sinclair Stevens, Flora MacDonald, Joe Clark, Heward Graftey, Jack Horner and Pat Nowlan. I supported Paul Hellyer on the first ballot; he had the support of more Members of the PC Caucus than any other candidate – thirty-five, I believe.

Paul Hellyer made a political statement and sent out a letter which, in my estimation, killed him. He withdrew before the second vote.

I then swung my vote to Joe Clark, who was the eventual winner, much to the surprise of a great many people.

Another contestant, Jack Horner, was a real sore loser who didn't like Clark and refused to support him. He eventually moved across the floor to the Liberal side.

April 1977 ... In the cafeteria this morning someone asked me why I had supported Paul Hellyer during the convention vote.

Originally, I was very angry at Paul for being the "father" of the unification of the Armed Forces – something I violently opposed. I fought it all the way down. However, in the long run I felt that with Paul's record as a very important Cabinet minister in the Trudeau government, he would have the support of a great many Canadians. I thought that he would do a great job as prime minister.

Joe Clark and Flora MacDonald had made a pact that whichever one of them was ahead in the first ballot would be assured that the other would withdraw and throw that support in with the leader. This is what gave Joe a shot in the arm and allowed him to come up through the middle and win the nomination.

May 22, 1979 ... Much to the surprise of a great many people, Joe Clark has won the election and has become prime minister of Canada with about 135 seats. Clark made a statement, though, which I will never forget and in front of the press, after his Cabinet was appointed. He said that he would govern as if he had a majority and I felt that this was a very foolish thing to say. There is no doubt that Joe would live to regret saying it.

December 13, 1979 ... The John Crosbie budget was voted on and the government has been defeated. As the former Prime Minister Pierre Trudeau has handed in his resignation, the Liberals are without a leader. Perhaps this was why the Conservative government felt they could risk the vote and push through a very controversial budget.

I had made a couple of bets with Ken Binks and Sinclair Stevens that we would be defeated. Stevens, who was the minister of trade and commerce, and Binks were both sure we would survive. We were doomed from the start as several of our Members were away: Alvin Hamilton was ill in hospital, Flora MacDonald was abroad, so was Lloyd Crouse. There had, unfortunately, been no concentrated effort to woo the Social Credit members although I believe there were only six of them, and in the long run it wouldn't have made a great deal of difference if we had.

Be that as it may, our government went down in defeat December 13, 1979. Mr. Trudeau was called back from the dead and became prime minister and the Liberals won a majority government in 1980. The next election did not take place for almost five years, in September 1984.

In the interim, of course, Joe Clark re-assessed his position. At a leadership conference in Winnipeg he issued a statement that unless he received the support of at least two-thirds of the delegates, he would call for a leadership convention. I thought that this was a very foolish thing to do and said so.

Well, the vote has taken place and Joe Clark received about 65 per cent instead of the 66 2/3 per cent required. As he had given his word, he was now faced with calling a leadership convention, which will take place in Ottawa in 1983.

This time around, leadership contenders were Joe Clark, Brian Mulroney and John Crosbie. I supported John Crosbie on every ballot except the last one, as he had been defeated. It was then a contest between Clark and Mulroney, and the Crosbie delegates swung to Mulroney. It appeared that Clark had received his total commitment on the first vote. I felt from the start that he either had to win or lose on the first vote.

I can say now that I pleaded with a great many Clark loyalists in the last vote to switch their vote to Crosbie. It was the only way they could defeat Mulroney. However, that did not happen. On the last ballot, I voted for Brian Mulroney, pointing out to him that the ones who voted for him on the last ballot only were the ones that ultimately elected him, and that he should not soon forget it!

In the 1984 election, Mulroney won a landslide victory. It was on September 6th. Two hundred and eight PC Members were elected. He reminded me at that time about our first meeting, in 1976. It was at his reception in the Railway Committee Room. At that time I was a supporter of Paul Hellyer as was my colleague, Dr. Bruce Halliday. We decided to stand at the back of the hall and hear what Mulroney had to say. He came into the hall, led by a Highland Piper and his retinue. It was quite impressive. He came right over to where Bruce and I were standing and introduced himself. I guess I shouldn't have said this, but I did say, "Brian, I didn't know I was going to have the pleasure of meeting you or I would have brought a pin with me." He asked, "What did you want a pin for?" I said, "I want to stick a pin in you and see if you really bleed. You appear to me to be the Bionic Man."

It struck me then and for many years, that he was so well programmed that everything that happened in his public appearances was planned well in advance.

In the following months, I was impressed with the way he handled affairs and in the way he was able to control the Caucus. It was fractious with a strong representation from Quebec. Mulroney was a great orator and was able to formulate and sell his ideas and legislation in the Caucus and retain top support. In many ways, I admired him in those early days very much.

However, there were many things which did not make me too happy and I made my position to him very clear – and also to the Caucus, but I was a member of the PC team and therefore supported my government's policies.

April 1988, Ottawa ... I attended a reception today at one of the beautiful embassies here and several guests got talking about elections. I was asked what was the most important election for me and I replied, "Well, 1972 when I was first elected to the House of Commons, of course." I have a pretty good memory and I told my friends that on my first day in the House I went down to Ottawa feeling very nervous. I saw the great John Diefenbaker sitting alone and introduced myself. I said, "Mr. Diefenbaker, I've been involved in politics for 31 years, but I am here to keep my ears and eyes open and my mouth shut.

"Mr. Diefenbaker said, 'My boy, this is a wonderful attitude. It's too bad a great many others here wouldn't do the same.'"

I told my friends at the reception that when I was elected in 1972, fifty-five new Conservatives, twenty-three Liberals, eleven New Democrats were elected and three members of the Social Credit Party were elected for the first time. Only eleven Conservatives and two Liberals with unbroken electoral records have remained. I also told them about running for the federal government in 1953, against former hockey player Bucko McDonald and losing. I thought my political career was at an end.

Speaking of Flora MacDonald, I recall one interesting conversation with this terrific woman. One of the early committees I was elected to was the Standing Committee on Indian Affairs and Northern Development. The minister was the Hon. Jean Chretien and the PC critic was the Hon. Flora MacDonald. I used to tell her that I was sitting on that committee just to make sure she did not turn the whole country over to the native people. One of the hot issues back then, as it still is, was the native claims for Northern Quebec.

The Quebec government was developing the James Bay Hydro Project. I made the suggestion that all native people be transported to Montreal to live at the Queen Elizabeth Hotel. They could live there with free room service thrown in. This outlandish suggestion would probably have saved us a great deal of money. I believe the eventual land settlement for the hydro property was in the neighborhood of $150 million. Most of the land, which had been expropriated, was of very poor quality, with trees no bigger than the size of your arm. I told Flora that I was under the impression that she thought the whole area in question was covered with giant trees and lush fertile ground. As I recall, there were approximately 700 native inhabitants involved.

I was attending a Canada/U.S. Conference in Anchorage, Alaska, in 1979 when i was told of the death of the Rt. Hon. John Diefenbaker. My colleague David MacDonald, secretary of state in the Clark government planned the state funeral for Mr. Diefenbaker. It was certainly a great one. Held in Christ Church Cathedral in Ottawa, I was one of those marching alongside Prime Minister Joe Clark and the Rt. Hon. Pierre Trudeau. We walked from the Parliament Buildings to the church, a matter of a few blocks.

A special state funeral train was arranged for Mr. Diefenbaker's casket, and the train made stops at various points along the way. The state train took Mr. Diefenbaker to his burial place, on the grounds of the Diefenbaker Centre in Saskatoon. Each year I have a special Christmas card designed by Gravenhurst artist, Frank Johnson. He designed one for this Christmas of the Diefenbaker home. I presented the original painting to the museum where it hangs today.

Ottawa, February 1987 … I asked Prime Minister Mulroney the other day for some facts and figures about what our government had been accomplishing in the past three years. He replied immediately and I was interested in some of his facts:

- Federal/provincial relations have improved greatly since this government was elected, and the economy is much better since September 1984, when we took over.
- International relations have improved greatly, especially with the U.S., despite recent friction over softwood lumber, acid rain and other issues.

Our government has slipped in the area of government ethics. Problems created because of Cabinet ministers' shortcomings hurt him. He has made 2,000 appointments, the majority non-political, some Liberal and NDP. The prime minister said, "When appointments for Conservative members have been made, they are no longer classed as 'friends' or 'associates' of mine. They become cronies and hacks. I no longer am allowed to have friends and associates."

In 1982, with a Liberal government, polls indicated that the Liberals were down to 23 per cent, unemployment was high at 16 per cent, and the Trudeau government was just two years into its mandate.

In the early 1980s, interest rates stood at 22.75 per cent, and the country was torn with the constitutional crisis. There were no Atlantic or Western Accords, and many ministerial resignations. Newfoundland and Quebec wanted out of the re-constitution.

Every government has its own problems.

August 12, 1987, Ottawa … I have just finished writing a letter to Prime Minister Mulroney. Prior to our summer recess he had sent me a personal letter requesting input and suggestions for our last lap prior to an election. I am sure letters to other members of our party were also sent. Throwing aside my shyness, I wrote back to him, in part: "One thing I would like to emphasize, and which would give you strong support across the country is a real forceful and strong approach on acid rain with respect to our neighbors to the south. I am well aware that you have accomplished more than any other prime minister with respect to the environment and are getting rave notices in the U.S. You are the only one who has been able to get the President to admit that there is an acid rain problem and to state that he will give serious consideration to recommend that controls on emissions be approved in the U.S. Congress."

I also brought the Prime Minister up-to-date on my thinking on the immigration problem. "The refugee question has been a hot issue in my riding but nothing compared to city ridings. It seems a damned shame that with all that has been accomplished, you are still being vilified by the bloody media, and of course the opposition parties." I also pointed out to the Prime Minister that he had created 800,000 new jobs, had negotiated lower interest rates, lower unemployment, more housing and construction, a new white paper on defence and one on tax reform. I also stated that, "much against your own personal wishes, you fulfilled the promise to have a free vote on capital punishment." Needless to say, I was not ecstatic over the outcome of that. I told him, "Keep up the good work re: acid rain and let the President know, without mincing any words, that he has to deliver on that promise. Here's hoping that we will be able to rescind Murphy's Law, and have things break for us in the next year and a half. My heart really bleeds for you when I know the great job you are doing and the tireless work you and Mila put in as prime minister and first lady."

I was changing my mind about Brian Mulroney.

Ottawa, 1992 … I came across something in my files today that I can't recall reading before and it astonished me. Headed "A selection of comments: Pierre E. Trudeau" on various areas of government involvement. Some of them bear out my personal feelings of Mr. Trudeau:

"Get off your ass, get out there and work." (Vancouver, B.C., 1979)

"We have brought down the worst plague we have had – inflation. It's not on its knees yet but its coming down slowly, so you may as well relax and enjoy it." (St. John, N.B., September 1976)

"Canadian have to be told they're soft. If Canadians don't discipline themselves, we will discipline them." (Ottawa, 1977).

"A Liberal approach begins with the proposition that the roots of inflation must be eradicated. We cannot wish it away. We have to take action." (Toronto, 1981)

"We can't make an obsession of the deficit. We say, what is the deficit for, let's keep it under control, as we did in the past three years, but let's not make a fetish of it and say we have to balance the budget if it means causing slower growth." (Ottawa, 1980).

"Maybe Canada is too big for us. Maybe we can't hold it all together … but at least we should ask ourselves the question, and should seek the answers. I don't believe that we are really doing that, but Canadians are not really concerned about their country, now really, are they?" (Vancouver, 1981)

"It is more important to maintain law and order than to worry about those whose knees tremble at the sight of the army." (October 1970).

"There are a lot of bleeding hearts around who just don't like to see people with helmets and guns. All I can say is, go on and bleed, but it is more important to keep law and order in the society." (October 1970)

"Historically, French Canadians have not really believed in democracy for themselves; and English Canadians have not really wanted it for others." (Quebec, 1958)

"If the people don't think that unity is an important question now, I can only wring my hands." (March 1979)

"Since I was a little boy, I have heard about threats of Quebec separatism. It never frightened me, and I never thought it would happen. When I said separatism was dead and you all laughed at me, it was true exactly in the sense in which I said it, that no party would win an election on the separatist mandate in Quebec. They had to use all kinds of gimmicks to try and get the party which supported it elected, the referendum gimmick – and that they didn't even use the word separatism or independence in the referendum itself. (Ottawa, 1980)

"I'm glad I won a majority. Now I can go back to being arrogant and telling everyone to fuddle-duddle off." (Ottawa, 1971)

"The political philosophy of the Liberal Party is simplicity itself: "Say anything, think anything: Better still, think nothing, but put us in power for we are the best fitted to govern." (April 1983)

"I'm sorry if I insult you. I really was giving you more credit for your intelligence than I know you deserve." (Vancouver, 1981)

And people complain about Prime Minister Mulroney!

In looking back over the prime ministers I've worked under, I still feel sorry for Joe Clark. I think he got a bum rap. Let us not kid ourselves, there are a lot of hatchet men in the media. Joe was downgraded in every way possible and belittled as well, but in the fullness of time, he has come along to prove that the media were a bunch of rats – period! I will go no further than that. But Joe Clark has conducted himself in a most gallant and gentlemanly manner. He has a wife who is not a shy and retiring violet. I like Maureen very, very much, but I know that she has caused Joe some problems, and again, he has been a perfect gentleman in every respect.

During the leadership convention, Joe said that his decision to remain as leader was based on his getting 66 2/3 per cent of the vote. Well, he didn't get that, and as a man of his word, he called a leadership convention in 1983.

I think Joe was very unwise to call the leadership convention because he knew that everyone who was against him would just all get together to do a hatchet job on him and see that he was defeated. There were elements in the party that never liked him in the first place, people who couldn't stomach the idea that he was chosen leader over them. They felt that their view and superior abilities should have been recognized and for this they did not give him a fair chance. I felt that Joe Clark was growing in stature and would be a much more seasoned leader the second time around. What I felt then has proved to be correct and as secretary of state for External Affairs in the Mulroney government, Joe Clark did a great job.

The Crosbie budget was the back-breaker, and the 18 cent tax on gasoline was a big controversial item. The government's phrase, "short term pain for long term gain," just backfired on them. I had pleaded with Crosbie and said, "For God's sake, John, phase the tax increase in 6 cents at a time. Don't give the voters a chance to be upset." But the Prime Minister and John Crosbie didn't listen. I bet Sinc Stevens $5 that we would lose the vote, and we did. To me, John Crosbie was a charismatic individual, and a great speaker. I felt he would have made a good prime minister of Canada. I supported him when he ran for the leadership of our party, right up until he was defeated.

I had a great deal of admiration for John Turner, who held many senior Cabinet positions including minister of justice and minister of finance. Mr. Turner ran against Pierre Trudeau for the Liberal leadership in 1968 and finished second. He had the opportunity of serving as prime minister only for the spring and summer of 1984. When he took over as prime minister, he was leading in the polls by eleven points and yet in September Brian Mulroney won. It is interesting to point out that in every election the

Progressive Conservatives ran behind the Liberals in the polls. In 1984, Turner called the election in early July for September the 6th. He was eleven points ahead in the polls. It wasn't until a couple of weeks before the election that the Conservatives surged ahead. In earlier elections, where I was involved, the same thing happened. The Liberals were always in the lead. I remember particularly in 1974 when Prime Minister Trudeau won the election it was pointed out that the only reason I held my seat was because of my high profile and a long involvement in municipal politics. I believe I won that election by about 2,500 votes. In the first election in 1972 I won by about 5,000 votes. In the 1979 election when Joe Clark became prime minister, I won by 8,000 votes. In 1984, my plurality in the Mulroney era was over 13,000 votes. This was the highest ever recorded of any winning candidate.

Ottawa 1989 … I was asked today what I think of our Question Periods in the House. With items for debate such as Free trade, for example, both sides have good arguments but I am not sure just how much is grasped by the electorate at large during the televised sessions.

The Opposition in Question Period and in every opportunity during television shows, are saying that Free Trade is no good. Listening to Mel Hurtig of Edmonton and other great nationalists, you would feel that everyone is against it, no matter how good it is for the country, because that group caters to a particular segment of the economy – the unions. They represent only 30 per cent of the employed sector in Canada. Well, I am aware that televising the Question Period is not such a good idea, apart from the incredible costs involved. However, there is no way it can be changed now. But I am aware, as a Member of Parliament, that it is not possible for every Member of the House of Commons to sit in the House for seven or eight hours a day from 11 a.m. till 6 p.m. But the Canadian public love to see the proceedings on television. They can turn it off if they don't want to see it, but it is amazing how many people do watch every session. I concede that a television cameraman in the House might embarrass Members from time to time. If a Member is speaking to a group who has heard the same speech five times over, MPs will probably take the opportunity to sign letters, read a newspaper or their correspondence from constituents, or, from time to time, doze off. At the beginning of the televised sessions, the lights used were much hotter than they are now and we would almost cook with the heat. This made us sleepy and we would often close our eyes against the glare and heat. However, now that the public can see what we are doing, some of the catcalls and worse than that, have been toned down. Prior to television, there was only the Hansards to keep the public caught up. Now there is the "electronic Hansard." Mr. Trudeau found out to his dismay when he started the great "fuddle-duddle" controversy that people do watch the sessions.

But there is no doubt about it, a charismatic speaker makes a lot of friends when he delivers his addresses or answers questions in a televised debate or session in the House. But we sure have to mind our manners!

My relationship with Brian Mulroney was always cordial and friendly. Although his schedule was long and hectic, he always had time to listen to his ministers and backbenchers. In July 1983, I wrote these words in my diary: "Parliament has just now recessed for the summer, and still the longest session in our history staggers on.

"The government has desperately been trying to shed the effects of some of its more disastrous policies, in an effort to regain some of the popularity they for so long assumed was theirs automatically. It has tried to lay the blame for its failures at the feet of the Official Opposition, but it simply will not wash."

The Trudeau government had its own problems in 1983, just as the Mulroney government (and every other government if it comes to that), would in following years. Brian Mulroney polled his Members each year asking for their frank views on the past year's activities and although I am not known for my shyness, I think my letter of 1992 to the Prime Minister really laid it on the line. It had somehow been "leaked" to the headquarters of the National Rifle Association in Alberta, and received a lot of press coverage. No one seems to know how leaks occur, but this one certainly received a lot of publicity, not all of it bad!

Among many areas I discussed with the Prime Minister were:

- "There is no denying that we are still stuck in neutral at the bottom-end of the polls. Some days the light at the end of the tunnel seems further and further away.
- "If our political fortunes have not begun to take an upward move by the early spring of next year, we are toast. I believe we have taken a significant step toward a major comeback with the appointment of Hugh Segal as your Chief of Staff. Don't get me wrong. I have no gripes about Norman Spector. It is just that the times dictate calling up a trench warrior to marshal the troops and Hugh Segal fits the bill.
- "Postal service remains a contentious and emotional issue and regardless of justifications given and the number of fancy public relations programs undertaken by Canada Post, franchising is not being accepted in my riding.

- "Gun control is a total fiasco in Parry Sound/Muskoka. On this issue alone our government may be in for the payment of a heavy electoral price in the next election.
- "Bilingualism continues to be a sensitive, contentious and highly emotional issue in the riding.
- "My constituents in Parry Sound/Muskoka are tired of the debate and rhetoric on the Constitution. They are more preoccupied with kick-starting the economy. Frankly prime minister, there is just no way that the 'distinct society' provision of the Constitutional proposals in any shape or form can be sold in my riding, regardless of how it is presented or the pill is coated.
- "The mood, to say the least, is ugly in terms of any special concessions to Quebec and any move in that direction is unacceptable. Immigration is another touchy issue, with general frustration for the whole question of refugee status.
- "As for GST, Free Trade, Unemployment Insurance reform and Free Trade with Mexico, none of these policies are selling well in my riding. As a government, we have done a very poor job in communicating these policies.
- "The general perception on taxes is that they are too high. And the electoral support base of the PC Party in my riding is being challenged.

"As to the environment policy, my constituents are strongly supportive of all measures to maintain a healthy environment. My constituents recently raised these issues at the Snow Fest in Parry Sound:

- "Many English-speaking Canadians feel that they must be French to get a job in the federal government.
- "While we are a multicultural nation, maybe it would be better to become a melting-pot like the United States. The federal government should learn to say no to many projects and handouts, various cultural and special interest groups who should be required to obtain funding on their own initiates. Turbans being permitted for the RCMP and other police forces have been soundly criticized.
- "Senators should serve without salary."

I concluded my letter to Mr. Mulroney by saying, "Beyond a doubt, prime minister, it would be easier for us to bury our heads in the sand like successive Liberal administrations and say that there are no problems with our current economic structure. However, that would be totally irresponsible and reprehensible.

"I hope these thoughts will prove useful as you grapple with the many hard decisions I know you will have to make over the next few months."

Brian Mulroney was prime minister of Canada for nine years. I was ultimately deeply involved with him time and time again. I recall him saying to the Caucus, "I can be a popular prime minister if I just keep spending money and spending money and never say no. Or I can be a prime minister who, by bringing in things in Canada's best interest, will not be so popular. We will wait and see if the future bears me out."

Brian Mulroney was viewed as a front-run statesmen, but sadly, mostly outside of Canada. It will be interesting to see what future historians have to say about the Mulroney years, but I am pleased that I am a part of them.

The leadership of Prime Minister Kim Campbell was altogether different from the Mulroney years. Even though we were down in the polls in the early part of 1993, I felt that Brian Mulroney would hang in, that he could turn things around. Jean Chretien was not too popular a leader, and on the world scene, there was no comparison between the two men. Mulroney had tremendous prestige internationally, and was highly respected by other world leaders and, in fact, was one of the senior leaders himself. A great many others had fallen by the wayside, during Mulroney's nine years as prime minister. I am thinking of Margaret Thatcher, Ronald Reagan, two or three Japanese prime ministers, Gorbachev and others. There was a good deal to say in favor of Mulroney staying in power and fighting the coming election. I was holidaying in Florida with my son Peter and his family, on a three-day cruise, when I heard the news that the PM had resigned. A leadership convention was called for June 12th and 13th and the obvious front runner was Kim Campbell, the minister of defence.

April 1993, Ottawa … The Hon. Jean Charest, minister of the environment, with whom I have had the pleasure of working for some years now, made his announcement in March that he would run for the leadership of the PC Party. I looked at him very seriously and felt that he would be an outstanding candidate. First and foremost, I have a special affection for him. I weighed many things in the balance; even though I don't like it, I realize we must recruit strong support from the province of Quebec. Charest can deliver that. He is a bright young man with a charming wife and family. I feel he will be an asset, over Kim Campbell who has been twice divorced.

Well, I've gone out on a limb and said I will support Jean Charest, much to the disappointment of quite a few of my colleagues. They can't understand the oldest Member of the House throwing his support behind the youngest contestant for the leadership.

1995 ... As things turned out, I made the wrong choice, but I was quite happy with the choice I made. I still feel that Jean Charest will one day lead our country and of course, our party.

Jean Charest lost the election by about 187 votes. Jim Edwards of Calgary and the third contestant, garnered a good number of votes and we had every hope that his delegates would throw their votes behind Charest if he did not finish higher. As it turned out, the scenario left Kim Campbell the winner and, in the fullness of time, a short-term prime minister.

In retrospect, the whole roof caved in before the election. Hindsight is always better than foresight but I guess if Kim Campbell had grabbed the bull by the horns, and immediately called an election, she would have done much better. Initially, she was getting a lot of good publicity and was the highest in the polls, among all the leaders. However, during the last ten days before the October vote, the whole roof fell in. The voters just decided that they didn't like Mulroney and they were going to make sure that no member of his party was going to win the election. A great many members of the NDP knew that they didn't have a hope of winning. They switched to the Liberal Party and it was a resounding Liberal majority with about 185 seats.

In the June 14th Globe and Mail, Geoffrey York of the parliamentary bureau said, "It was a heartbreakingly narrow defeat for Jean Charest yesterday, but the curly-haired young man from Sherbrooke has emerged as a powerful force in the Progressive Conservative Party. Although he ultimately lost the leadership, in many crucial ways Mr. Charest was the campaign winner, in the debates, in the convention speeches, and in almost every poll, he consistently outperformed Kim Campbell. He performed superbly and was seen as the candidate with the substance and the ideas, so he should be playing a very important role."

Garth Turner, another defeated candidate, received seventy-six votes on the first ballot and was pleased with the results. Patrick Boyer, who received fifty-three votes on the first ballot, was the only candidate to throw his support on the second ballot to Jean Charest, whose views he said were the closest to his own.

But veteran journalist Peter Worthington wrote in the Ottawa Sun on June 15th, "Some thoughts on the Tory leadership contest – hardly the finest hour for the media which, mostly, seemed seduced by their own hype and lost their perspective, not to mention objectivity. Despite media headlines and hype such as: 'Campbell's speech on Saturday was terrible, a disaster' (Craig Oliver CTV), and 'Kim fizzles – Jean sizzles' (Toronto Sun), after the vote, the polls showed Campbell with 48 per cent, and it was thought by the media that 'only a lightning bolt can stop her.'"

According to Worthington: "The look of dismay after her final win of 1,664 votes, on the faces of Barbara McDougall, and Joe Clark, and other such cheerleaders, spoke volumes. They didn't want Kim, why? After the vote, Brian and Mila Mulroney seemed glum, the Tory establishment wanted Charest, not the Western upstart. Only Dalton Camp, commenting on CBC-TV after a heart transplant, was one of the few who saw this reality clearly. Camp may have needed a new heart, but his brain functions on all cells.

"On Campbell's side, Mike Wilson was concise, humorous and persuasive when he pledged 'absolute' support for her. And finding Flora MacDonald to stand at her side was a stroke of genius. MacDonald didn't lose the leadership in 1976 because she was a woman but because she was the wrong woman.

"Anyway, it's now history. With some exceptions, the media blew it again – by becoming too partisan."

An interesting, frank and perceptive column by a good writer.

A Globe and Mail article following the election stated: "In electing Kim Campbell on the second ballot, the Conservative Party made the politically riskier choice. As Conservative leader she will be weaker than Jean Charest against the Bloc Quebecois, and she may even be weaker than Jean Charest would have been in alliance with Alberta MP Jim Edwards against the Reform Party in the West. Ontario will be as tough for the Tories in either case. Her relationship with ordinary Canadians may be mercurial. It's going to be a volatile election.

"Most polls have shown that, the more Canadians know of Kim Campbell, the less certain they are of her leadership capacity, while the contrary is true of Mr. Charest. Although it is satisfying that Canada will have its first female prime minister, she will not be prime minister on the basis of a mandate from the Canadian people."

Ottawa, June 18, 1993 … The Conservative government's mandate expires this fall. Before then, we are all agreed, Prime Minister Campbell will strive to put her own stamp on the party and the government, and, perhaps, to distance herself from the unpopular Brian Mulroney. But giving the government a new look will take time, and it may not be possible to do so before an October election.

Putting a fresh face on the party begins with the kind of people Kim Campbell will surround herself with and will continue as she begins to construct a cabinet, fresh with new faces.

As Rick Gibbons in the Ottawa Sun stated, "These first crucial steps by

Campbell will be crucial in projecting an image of change and party renewal. If the public perception is simply that Campbell is Mulroney in a purple skirt, then start preparing the political obituaries."

1995 … Well, we all know what happened in October 1993. I had announced my retirement on June 13th, the last day that Parliament sat. I was the last to speak that evening, about 9 p.m. After twenty-one years in the House and as a very full-time politician for my riding of Parry Sound/Muskoka, it was a good time to retire.

The Progressive Conservative Party went down to a humiliating defeat and the brief Kim Campbell leadership of our country, was over.

I found a 1992 clipping today which was interesting, to say the least. It was in the Ottawa Citizen, I think. Headlined, "Thirty-two per cent of voters would back PCs if Clark was leader: Almost one-third of the Canadian electorate would support the Conservative Party if Joe Clark was its leader, a Gallup poll indicates. A survey of 1,024 adults conducted from June 3rd to 6th found that 32 per cent would vote for the Tories with Clark, the present Constitutional Affairs minister, at the helm, compared with 37 per cent for the Liberals and 18 per cent for the New Democratic Party. Seven per cent would vote for the Reform Party, 2 per cent for the Bloc Quebecois and 2 per cent for other parties."

Now that gives us all something to think about!

ABORTION – A HOT ISSUE

Ottawa, 1993 … I think that at least 70 per cent of the citizens of Canada would agree that abortion should be available under certain circumstances, such as after incest or rape, or where the life of the mother is endangered.

The opinion of government and our citizens seem to be pretty well split down the middle between those who feel abortion should be available without any restrictions, and those who are violently opposed under any circumstances.

In the years I have been in Ottawa, Parliament has spent many long, angry hours debating this sensitive issue and have still not come to an agreement. The last bill proposed to establish legislation in Canada, was defeated. As a result, there is no legislation in force at the present time. This means that an abortion can be performed at the ninth month, or on the last day before the baby is delivered into life.

In preparing legislation, the government must keep in mind that a number of issues relating to the Charter of Rights must be considered. Should legislation be too restrictive, the Supreme Court could strike it down. Should it be too lenient, it could be challenged under the special clause, Number 37, in the Charter of Rights.

It is my opinion that Canadians will *never* be unanimous about abortion law, or concerning the kind of legislation that should be passed.

Certainly not in my lifetime!

THE METRIC MESS

Friday, May 13, 1983, Ottawa ... In today's Toronto Sun, an editorial stated, "Metric Mess," and continued: "One of the most costly and confusing boondoggles of the Trudeau regime is the Liberals' mulish insistence on compulsory conversion to metric.

"It has cost Canadians an estimated $3 billion so far and it could easily cost another $6 billion to complete. It has caused needless confusion and presents golden opportunities to rook the public. What's worse, it's no longer needed or wanted."

The Sun suggested that "the feds" should swallow its monumental pride and scrap the compulsory metric conversion program. It should let the sale of groceries, goods, gasoline, etc., be in metric or imperial as the sellers and buyers wish. I could not agree more, unless the whole thing was just banished and we went back to the tried and true methods of the past.

Ottawa, 1982 ... In my Ottawa Report this month I wrote: "The federal government continues to charge ahead in its efforts to convert everything in Canada to the metric system. As in most things that the Trudeau government has undertaken in the last nine years, the metric conversion program is marked by an excess of zeal, and total contempt for the wishes of the majority of Canadians.

The government's plan to convert all roads and highway signs in Canada from miles to kilometres is a very serious mistake for two reasons: municipalities across Canada will have to bear responsibility and costs of this conversion with the lion's share of costs falling on the towns and cities.

The United Sates Highway Administration has announced that it has scrapped plans to convert its highway signs to kilometres, following a survey of public acceptance showed that 98 per cent voted against conversion.

To my way of thinking, the Canadian government should make the same democratic exercise rather than have the metric system shoved down our throats.

Small businesses in Canada are having a tough enough time to survive without having the financial burden of metric conversion imposed on them arbitrarily. Andre Ouellet, Pierre's Minister of Metric Mess, still insists that most Canadians want, need and must have metric. Nonsense. Let's make it voluntary, says the Sun.

Twelve years after the metric mess started, it is still being pushed down our throats. We were told then that the Americans and the British were converting and that we must go along or face a trading disadvantage, so we mumbled a bit and went along with it.

Andre Ouellet stated that Canada would change to metric at exactly the same speed as the U.S., but he obviously forgot the promises he made to Parliament and certainly did not keep his word. Because of the difficulties and cost of trying to change equipment, printed matter, and training staff to deal with metric, many carpet and fabric businesses went bankrupt. Others were fined heavily by the government for not converting swiftly enough, and because of this many businesses were lost.

The U.S. and Britain have both backed off and made conversion voluntary. President Reagan and Prime Minister Thatcher scrapped their metric commissioners long ago, but Trudeau has twenty of them on the payroll, each paid $250 a day, and all but one are Liberal hacks feeding at the bottomless Ottawa trough. The lone exception is an NDPer. The commission's budget has swelled to $32 million a year from an original $44,000.

These facts come from the Toronto Sun, but many of us faced with this needless expense, to say nothing of confusion, agree completely. I know I get a lot of angry comments from my constituents in Parry Sound/Muskoka who have troubles enough just surviving without all this additional expense.

FREE TRADE

April 1993, Ottawa … In my twenty-one years in Parliament, I can't recall anything more controversial than Free Trade. Whether Canadians realize it or not, we are a country of 27 million people and we are highly productive, producing a great deal more than we can consume. And so, we have to trade. There is no way, in my estimation that we can trade with anybody if it's not a two-way street. Internationally, Canada and the U.S. have the greatest two-way trading market between any two countries in the world. This may come as a big surprise to the people of Canada. In 1993, we traded over $200 billion worth between us, with sales very much in favor of Canada. In other words, little Canada is selling more to the United States than we are buying from them; that isn't a bad deal.

At a reception after work today I heard a statement which bowled me over. A few years ago, President Reagan was asked, "Who is your greatest trading partner?" And of course, the very knowledgeable president of the United States said, "Well, I guess it is Japan." He didn't even know that Japan isn't even close. Now people are furious because when the Free Trade Agreement came in three years ago, jobs were lost but jobs were also created. The same thing will apply with NAFTA. There is no question in my mind about that. Everybody seems worried about Mexico and the low wages there among their workers. And about the fact that Mexico will be terrible competition for Canadian products, with hundreds or thousands of Canadians losing their jobs.

I think people are not considering that Mexico, with a population of 83 million plus, is a potentially great market. Canada and Mexico and the U.S. can become one of the greatest trading entities in the world. We see how serious the European economic situation is, where they have torn down trade barriers, and immigration barriers to try and better their situation.

They are moving to one currency now. Whether or not they will achieve that, I don't know. But Britain is not too enthusiastic about giving up the British Pound.

We all have to compete on a worldwide basis these days, no question about it.

If there is one thing I'm convinced of it is that Canadians are terrific workers who can outproduce Mexican workers anytime. Another thing to consider is that the cost of labor in a unit, whatever is being made, a car or small product is about 7 per cent. Many people think it is 50 per cent. So you can see, it is a small part of the cost of the product. Canadians are not aware that, at the present time, Canada/Mexico trade is a $2.5 billion two-way trade, a year. But the most important thing is that there are very few duties or tariffs to contend with. The bad part is that Canada sells Mexico $600 million worth of goods a year and buys $2 billion worth in return. Now is that a good deal? We can't help but improve on that.

But along come the unions. Bob White and his gang, screaming their heads off. They were against the automobile pact years ago when it first came in. They said, "It's going to be a disaster for Canada." But it has proved the very opposite. In fact, the Americans are very unhappy that Canada has got the best of the deal.

Over lunch in the Dining Room today, a constituent from my riding asked my views on Free Trade, saying that many companies will move their businesses to Mexico with Free Trade because labor there is cheaper.

Well, I pointed out in no uncertain terms that it has been that way for years and why in hell haven't they moved to Mexico before now? I pointed out that if the North American Free Trade Agreement is passed in Canada but ultimately didn't go into law, the Free Trade Agreement between Canada and the U.S. can be abrogated and cancelled on six months notice by either country. I don't think most Canadians are aware of that.

Burks Falls, November 1994 ... I read in a Toronto paper today that when Prime Minister Chretien visits President Clinton in Washington he will try to make a "fairer deal" about free trade. Well, International Trade Minister Roy McClaren, who is no fool, is an acknowledged "free trader." Let's not kid ourselves, the Prime Minister appointed him to that important post because of his experience in the area. I saw Mr. Chretien on TV recently and he said that "there are certain differences that we will try to work out." But if they break the Free Trade Agreement and ask for too much, then it will work the other way. A great many Americans are also unhappy with the Free Trade Agreement. They aren't unhappy with the Mexican Trade Agreement or for the potential for Mexicans to take American jobs. I think that should discussions be reopened, we might not come out as well as we did in the original agreement. But in my estimation, the future will prove that the only way to go is with free trade. The future will prove, long after I am dead and gone, that our three North American countries will have an agreement of some sort to protect themselves against European trade and against the Pacific Rim countries. They are very, very tough customers.

January 1991 ... My secretary brought me in a big stack of mail today with one huge folder about free trade. Many letters are from senior citizens in my Parry Sound/Muskoka riding, who, in all fairness, are not aware of the ramifications or do not understand what it is all about. I plan to talk with as many, person-to-person, as I can over the next few months. But the main fear is that Canada will lose its identity and become the 51st state. Baloney! I keep telling them and telling them that, if we were ever going to lose our sovereignty and identity, it would have been one hundred years ago. Canada is a big boy now in the world political scene and to not worry about us become the fifty-first American state.

I write to these people that free trade will mean more prosperity in Canada, and lower prices, but there is still a long way to go on our side in explaining the free trade issue so that the voters can grasp what it will mean to our future. But there are people who argue against it no matter how good it is for the country because they are catering to a particular segment of the economy, the unions, who represent only 30 per cent of the employed sector in Canada.

December 20, 1992 ... In the Muskoka Advance today there was a reprint of a letter from Margaret L. Boyce of Gravenhurst with her version of the free trade debate. She said, "Any one who takes the trouble to look over the way Canada has gone since the first so-called Free Trade Agreement can only wonder at the audacity it takes to promise anything good without doing the same thing over again. Of course not all our troubles can be blamed on the Free Trade Agreement, but to ignore universal opposition and rush into another agreement when the promised benefits of the first have not materialized and the drawbacks are plain to see, is either blindness or callous indifference to the people's needs."

Well, that is what a democracy is all about – free discussion. But to have the last word on free trade, and this is *my* book, I'll just quote from my Ottawa Report of May 6, 1992: "There were other compelling reasons for Canada joining in the trade talks with the United States and Mexico.

Mexico has modified its import regulations and has reduced its tariffs and other barriers to trade since 1986, when Mexico joined (GATT). Mexico is now Canada's largest trading partner in Latin America and our two-way trade is growing steadily, leaping to $2.6 billion in 1989. Our negotiators are continuing to produce a North American Free Trade Agreement to secure barrier-free access to Mexico for Canadian goods and services and to make sure Canada remains an attractive centre for foreign and domestic investment.

However, contrary to what the Liberals, NDP and other detractors of free trade would have us believe, we have no other options to make the transition to a more efficient and world-scale economy. If we fail in that task, the tide of world events will surely leave us behind as an economic backwater.

And then would I ever get piles of mail!

Without the Free Trade Agreement, Oshawa, instead of making a million cars a year, would make 200,000 because 80 per cent of the cars made in Oshawa are exported. Four years ago, the United States had a trade deficit of $170 billion a year. At one time, Congress was debating 400 pieces of legislation that would bar products from certain parts of the world, put quotas on others, and set high tariffs for others, in order to protect their own industries.

Canada had an opportunity to sign a free trade agreement which protects us from some of this. Every job that is lost in Canada is blamed on free trade; yet, 3 million Canadians, every year, change jobs. Factories close – they've been doing it for a hundred years. They used to have a flourishing business making buggy whips and wagons. But we can't blame *that* on free trade.

A FEW WORDS ABOUT THE SENATE

July 14, 1993 … Burks Falls. I buy and read six or seven newspapers every day including the Bracebridge Examiner. On the editorial page on Wednesday, one of the headlines stated: "Senate is most despised group of political hacks." A letter to the editor was signed by Keith G. Farraway of Bracebridge who said, in part: "Happy Birthday Canada. So you're all excited about the Senate grabbing you for another $6,000 each. That is small potatoes compared to their wages and perks.

"Did you know they get up to sixty-four free flights per year anywhere in Canada and their servants can accompany them, and their children, grandchildren, and the Mrs., all at the expense of the taxpayer? They are the most despised group of people in Canada."

Well, this is tough stuff and it triggered some thoughts of my own about the Senate.

It costs the Canadian government about $70,000 plus perks to appoint a senator, for, in some cases, forty years. But I am unhappy with the Senate the way it is now, appointed by the government, actually the Prime Minister, and overloaded with Liberals. What is it, seventy-five or so to twenty-five or twenty-six? It will take twenty years to rebalance the Senate, so I figure that anything would be an improvement over that. I think some good appointments could be made if the provinces had their input into the selection of Senators and Justices of the Supreme Court.

My understanding is that a list with new proposals for the Senate is sent to the Prime Minister. He does not necessarily have to accept it. If he doesn't care for the suggestions he can request another one until an agreement has been made between the province and the federal government. I was asked recently what I thought of Senate reform and I know the West is agitating for an elected Senate. And it is also suggested that each province could elect the same number of Senators. But I cannot see Ontario and Quebec, who have twenty-four Senators each at this time, agreeing to reduce their number to two as in the United States, for example, and Prince Edward Island which has four, and so on. I don't think this is ever going to happen.

I think the Senate is a pretty nice set-up, or that is what I thought until last year. There are some brilliant men and women in the Senate, as well as a great many political hacks, but they have contributed greatly to various bills.

In the last couple of years, there have been three particular incidents which I have found interesting. One was when Senator Allan MacEachen held up a borrowing bill, a year or so ago. In my opinion just to be ugly and stubborn because they had been defeated – in fact just to embarrass the government. It cost the taxpayers a few million dollars in extra interest because of that stupid ploy.

The other time was the drug bill, which they delayed, delayed and delayed. Finally, I think at the behest of MP John Turner, they grudgingly gave it up and the bill is going through. And, of course, there is the latest charade, where the Senate is holding up two refugee bills – C-55 and C-84 – despite the fact that Canadians as a whole agree these loopholes should be closed. I think they are just flexing their muscles to once again embarrass the government.

If I had my way, the Senate would be abolished and this is not sour grapes. In 1986, columnist Claire Hoy suggested my name, and I think, Hal Jackman's (he is now Lt. Gov. of Ontario), for the Senate. He had no idea of my age but I would have been 75 years old in July and this was early summer, May or June. As the oldest a Senator can be to retain his seat in the Senate is 75, I would have been in the Senate for about six weeks only, if I had accepted this honor. When I told Claire later that year how old I was he said he was very surprised. I continued on in my capacity as backbencher for another six years.

THE GRAVENHURST PRISON

July 1992, Ottawa ... On the 29th of July, the Gravenhurst News headlines stated, "Gravenhurst wins prison bid. $60 million project will create about 200 permanent jobs: beginning of renaissance, says [Sylvia] Purdon." It continued: "Federal Solicitor General Doug Lewis was to hold a press conference this morning at Beaver Creek Minimum Security Prison, to officially announce the news. The $60 million project will create roughly 200 permanent jobs for this heavily depressed area. The prison is expected to be located adjacent to the existing Beaver Creek Correctional Services of Canada facility."

Several people have tried to get in touch with Frank Miller who is the District Chairman, but he knew nothing beyond the news story. However, Frank did compliment the municipalities for working together to bring the prison to Gravenhurst. Sylvia Purdon who is the acting Mayor of Gravenhurst, called it a victory for all Muskoka and the beginning of a renaissance for Gravenhurst.

Well, there is always more to a news story than the headlines. The federal government has owned 300 acres of land here for some years. It was used during the Second World War to train Norwegian pilots. The prison will accommodate 440 mostly non-violent first-time offenders between the ages of 18 and 35; those who will be serving a two to five year sentence for anything from fraud, break and enter, criminal negligence, to impaired driving.

Two hundred and sixty correctional officers, security guards, psychologists and administrative staff will be employed with about $16 million returned to the local economy each year. Construction will start in the spring of 1993 and a "normal environment" for inmates to live in will be created, according to the news story.

This is a big surprise to me. I have been shivering in my boots for months now, wondering if my riding would be chosen. When I heard the good news I let out a whoop of joy. However, when the officials saw our brief, they would have been damn fools to pick any other place. I'm glad that the prison will be built here – Gravenhurst has had a real tough go.

Frank Miller said a few kind words about me to the newspaper: "If you don't think your Member of Parliament makes a difference, you will never understand the political process. Stan Darling continued the pressure on his party for months on end, and simply would not give up." I certainly put in a lot of hours and effort into getting the prison situation completed.

However, it was not all roses. The Huntsville Forrester said in August 1992: "Practically everyone who lost out (on the new federal penitentiary) started screaming about trying to buy votes and all the rest of it.

"Well," they continued, "whether Doug Lewis, supposedly in trouble in his Simcoe North riding was trying to buy votes or not is immaterial in this case. The location is a good one."

However, not everyone agreed with the decision. The North Bay Nugget on August 4, 1992, said, "Ontarians across the province can be forgiven if they greet the federal government's plan to construct a $60-million medium security prison in Gravenhurst with more than a hint of cynicism. After all the news came from Federal Solicitor General Doug Lewis, who just happens to represent the riding of Simcoe North, near Gravenhurst. Mere coincidence? Not likely."

I pointed out, of course, that the new facility had to be located somewhere, and the same kinds of catcalling about patronage would probably take place no matter where it was located.

The Nugget said, "While it's undoubtedly good news for a region that has grown dependent on a sagging tourism industry for economic survival, it's perhaps the first of many similar patronage announcements packaged with the express purpose of boosting Tory support in time for the next federal election, which could be called next year."

Baloney!

IMMIGRATION

Burks Falls, April 1993 ... I am blessed with the fact that as a Member of a rural riding I have not had to deal with too many problems in immigration. Toronto, and other huge cities have hundreds, if not thousands of such problems. All in all, I have had to sort out only five or six in past years. They are getting much more complicated every year. They are also very time-consuming, mostly because of the autocratic behavior of immigration officials.

In Huntsville recently, an East Indian man who had a hotel, was trying to get visas for his wife and children to come from India to join him. It took almost three years before final approval came through. He was reunited with his family just a short while ago.

Another case I recall was that of a young woman from India who came to Canada to study at an Ontario university for two years.

She was then able to obtain employment in a Toronto-Dominion Bank and I was told she did very well. She became a mortgage officer and when she was well established she was informed by Immigration Canada that her time in Canada was up and she would have to return to India. Needless to say she was very upset.

She came to my office in Burks Falls to see if I could do anything for her. She said that if she had to go back to India she would be forced into an arranged marriage and would not be able do anything about it. She was transferred to Bracebridge which is why I became involved. I spoke personally to the officials at Immigration and to the minister, the Hon. Bernard Valcourt. I had another case before the minister at this time.

While attending a PC convention in Toronto, the minister came over with the wonderful news that he had obtained clearance on the young bank employee's case, but the other case in question was still in discussion. So I was batting .500 on immigration. This case had a strange twist to it.

After the woman received Immigration approval, I received a telephone call from a woman who had sponsored the bank employee. She was furious about the whole situation and at me for obtaining her visa. It seems that the young lady had stolen the heart of this woman's husband. She wanted the girl returned to India, but I have no idea how it all turned out.

Another interesting case involved a man from Nobel, just north of Parry Sound. Mr. Kang had invested $300,000 in a shopping mall, which also included a convenience store and gasoline station. An immigration lawyer had told him that with this type of investment Mr. Kang would have no problems being admitted to Canada permanently. This situation had started over three years before this time and he was still no farther along with getting his permanent papers. As far as he could tell, no action had been taken and so he approached me.

I learned of information that was most distressing. Immigration stated that Mr. Kang had not disclosed his criminal record from the time he lived in England. He had been a British subject, had raised his family there and had been an official with an insurance company. The incident which was holding up his papers and which was classed by Immigration as a "criminal record," was this: As he was crossing a parking lot in the city where he lived in England, a gang of teenagers started to harass him because of his race. He was a Sikh, and wore a turban. When he tried to fend them off, and defend himself, the teenagers accused him and then charged him with assault, which of course was a lie. Before the case went to court, his lawyer told him he would have a very hard time proving his case, because he had six witnesses against him and no one to speak on his behalf. The lawyer advised him to plead guilty and to accept a fine and he did. But, when applying for permanent status in Canada some years later, this "record" showed up and had held up his papers. Eventually Immigration officials proved very helpful, especially David Johnson, of their Orillia office who believed Mr. Kang's story. Because official sanctions had to take place at a consular office outside Canada, we were dealing with the Buffalo, New York, office, one of the busiest offices at any border point. But finally, Mr. Kang's papers were received, a statement from the British police had arrived and we understood that it was "just a matter of time" until the final documents would arrive.

Well, I am no longer an MP and a new government is in power. At this time, I understand that Mr. Kang has still not received his papers. I got in touch with Mr. Kang in January and he was still waiting to hear from Immigration. Well, as I had started all this I wrote to the Liberal minister of immigration, the Hon. Sergio Marchi and sent a copy of my letter to Mr. Kang. He phoned me yesterday with the good news that he had finally received approval. To say the least, I am quite pleased that I have been successful in this case.

April 1993, Burks Falls ... Ina Trolove, my secretary, received a call yesterday from a Toronto woman who wanted an appointment with me when I got back to my riding office. She said it was personal and would not divulge the reason, so Ina arranged an appointment.

She was a refugee from Lebanon, had been kidnapped and raped by a group of Shiite fundamentalists in Hezbollah and had, somehow, escaped to Canada, and had been living here for two years. She spoke both English and French and managed to get a job teaching refugees and immigrants English. She also had another part-time job, and she used part of her salary to put her brother through McMaster University in Hamilton. Needless to say, she was trying to get landed immigrant status but last winter was told that she would be deported.

I wanted to know why she had come to see me, when she was living in the centre of the riding of the Secretary of State for External Affairs Barbara McDougall. The woman said that she could never get an appointment to see her and that Ms. McDougall's office just gave her the brush-off. A friend who lived in Muskoka told her that I would probably give her every help I could. Well, I explained that I probably could not help her, but I got in touch with the Minister of Immigration Doug Lewis who eventually came back to me with a little different story on the case.

The woman had been told to leave Canada by March 26th, but she had married a Canadian citizen on the 26th of May. A wedding like that is bound to be viewed with suspicion. I wrote a letter to the Hon. Barbara McDougall, outlining the case and the woman also had a lawyer working on her behalf, but she just slipped out of sight as far as I was concerned, although several months after my involvement she was still in Canada. I have often wondered what eventually happened to her case.

June 1992, Ottawa ... The United Nations has proclaimed something that we all have known for some time: Canada is the best place in the world in which to live. It has placed Canada first on its human development index, up from second place last year. The survey measures education, life span, literacy and purchasing power to rate the quality of life in a country. We are well ahead of the United States, which was rated sixth and we are now recognized around the world as we celebrate Canada's 125th birthday.

In my summer report from Ottawa, I talk about the Immigration policy changes and the many reasons why people decide to make Canada their new home. Some seek to start a new life, while others come to join their families. Others look to escape persecution, and today 80 million people around the world are on the move with the number growing. This is a strain on immigration systems around the world.

June 17 ... I have just heard the sweeping changes that Employment and Immigration Minister Bernard Valcourt announced yesterday to the Policy which include: establishing three application streams for various categories of immigrants with a higher priority for some classes over others. To be fast-tracked would be wealthy investors, immediate family members of immigrants already here, and Geneva Convention refugees.

Also outlined was a policy to revamp the immigrant investor program to attract more immigrants with capital and business expertise. And high on the list in my estimation are: Creating a one-hearing Immigration and Refugee board to replace the existing two-hearing system.

And to speed up the process of granting landed status to genuine refugees and, after they become landed immigrants, allow them to begin the process of sponsoring their relatives as soon as their claims are approved.

Although I have not been too involved in the immigration problems in my riding, some have been quite intriguing, and all have been very, very lengthy and time-consuming.

RUNNING MY RIDING OFFICE

Burks Falls, October 1993 ... Ina Trolove and I locked the door on our riding office today. The election yesterday was a disaster for the Progressive Conservative Party and I certainly don't regret my decision to retire from the House of Commons after twenty-one years.

When I first obtained a budget from the federal government to open my riding office in 1979, I was fortunate indeed to be able to hire Ina Trolove as my riding secretary. She tells me she came for a few months, but she has been here ever since and it is impossible to think of functioning all these years without her.

Ina was active in the Progressive Conservative Party from 1949 on. She said that her father was a very staunch supporter of the party and she just grew up with it. She worked with J.N. McDonnell when he was a candidate for this riding. Mc Donnell had been defeated by Bukco McDonald in 1949. McDonald had been a high profile hockey player for the Toronto Maple Leafs. (She was also the secretary-treasurer of the riding association for twenty-three years).

What a lot of people don't know is that Ina ran against me for the PC nomination in 1953. Dr. R.H. Dellane of Powassan, who had been my doctor when I lived in Powassan, was also a candidate.

I won the nomination but lost the election to Bukco McDonald by 1,200 votes.

Well, Ina didn't run for public office again and I didn't either, until I ran for nomination in 1957, provincially, and lost to Gordon Aiken by ten votes. I ran federally in 1972 and won by 5,500 votes, at the age of 61, and headed up to Ottawa.

Ina was a member of the Canadian Women's Army Corp with the rank of captain during the war and was, she told me, the second-last woman to leave the army at the end of the war.

Prime Minister Mackenzie King declared that he wanted all women out of the army by September 30, 1946, and that command was carried out.

Her training in the army certainly came in handy, during the years she worked for me.

After Ina married, she retired to Burks Falls with her husband, Ron, who had been with the RCMP. They had a tree farm and huge conservation program, north of Burks Falls, and they planted 85,000 red pine trees by hand on their 230 acres.

Ina has always been a very energetic person and she needed it at our office as I was in Ottawa and travelling around the world for my government most of the time. I tried to get back to Burks Falls every Friday night and would leave again to drive through Algonquin Park after church on Sunday. In the meantime, Ina ran things and kept everything in good order. She was also a Justice of the Peace and worked very hard at that. One thing that was difficult to deal with was the fact that people came to our office constantly; from early morning until we locked the door, and then they tried to reach us by phone.

Ina dealt with every kind of problem anyone could dream up, from people who had lost their birth or marriage certificates and needed them immediately, to people who couldn't get their passports when they needed them; people who wanted funding for projects they were starting; people who wanted legislation passed immediately for one reason or another, from boat safety to making their estranged husband pay child support.

"It is a day-to-day operation," Ina often told me. And, of course, she was always on hand on Saturdays and many Sundays when I was in the office. As well, when I couldn't make an event, the presentation of a certificate, or greetings from the prime minister, Ina would always be there on my behalf. She is certainly a good public speaker.

I read somewhere that Ina said that working at my office is like working in the eye of the hurricane. But she also said that we work well together, which we do. But for much of the time we worked independently of each other. She was far, far more than just someone who typed up my letters – there wasn't a problem that she couldn't and didn't solve in all the years she was at the riding office.

Someone told me the other day that Ina hadn't had a holiday since she came to work for me. I used to plead with her to take some time off, if ever anyone deserved it, it was Ina Trolove, but she said there was so much to do that she didn't want to get behind, even for a few days. We've been known to shout at each other from time to time, but, on the whole, we have gotten along very well.

I often run into people who can't say enough about the work Ina has done for me and how kind and helpful she was to them when they needed it. One woman said that Ina frequently loaned money to people in need and that if she ever got paid back, she could travel around the world on what she received.

In our constituency office, we handled everything from requests for funding for Fednor projects to providing help for people who wanted jobs, letters of recommendation, information about buying property or starting a business, immigration problems, but by far the biggest headache came from people who wanted help dealing with Revenue Canada. There weren't many days that went by without a cry for help from one of my constituents. Ina dealt with it all in her calm and efficient way and most of the time I was not even aware of many of the jobs and problems she dealt with everyday for sixteen years.

I know how it is for me and the same for Ina; we can't walk down the street to the post office for the mail without people stopping us, asking for advice and help. A big issue in my riding has always been acid rain, and the maple syrup producers are hot on my trail. The producers around here say they are being hit hard, every year, by quantity and quality going down because of acid rain. And many of the tourist operations are also on our tails. They say reservations are cut in half because fishing is at an all-time low with acid rain problems getting worse. I know Ina deals with everyone in the same professional and patient way and she certainly keeps me up-to-date on who is saying what in the riding.

We also get a lot of requests from hunters in the area and people who run hunting camps because of gun control legislation. Hunting is a provincial decision, but all the same, gun control is a federal issue and very contentious, in my riding.

We've also had to deal with the changing of election boundaries and I lost three full townships recently; that's 10,000 wolves, thirty-five deer and maybe ten votes, the way I calculate it.

I read in an article by Roy MacGregor, of the Ottawa Citizen, that Ina told him some years ago, "I came to Stan's riding office in 1979 for a few months. And now it has been over ten years. I guess it's going to be a race to see which of us goes first."

Ina pointed out an article by Michael Armstrong of the North Bay Nugget of a few years ago which said, "Stan Darling, MP for Parry

Sound/Muskoka is holding up the next election." It was a statement that had been made by Flora MacDonald, MP for Kingston and the Islands. When financial critic Sinclair Stevens told the House of Commons the new Liberal slogan was "Show You Care. Get rid of Pierre." It evidently threw the whole Liberal election out of kilter.

July 1991 ... I was 80 years old on the 16th and friends and family threw a big party for me. Muskoka Publications also produced a fine magazine called, "Stan." Some of my long-time friends contributed columns about our work together. Frank Miller, who was a recent Premier of Ontario had a few nice things to say. "Stan simply defies description. The party thought he would be a one-term Member as he ran first at age 61. Stan tackled his new job at once, and never slowed down. His riding is immense. And Ottawa is a grueling five hours drive from his home. But like the old postal adage, 'Neither rain nor snow can keep him from his duties.' He drove all over the twin districts to visit those who were lucky enough to have him as their Member."

Frank also pointed out that some Members look after their ridings at the expense of their parliamentary duties. I don't believe I did that. I have always taken my duties to my constituents very seriously indeed.

A major issue in my riding has been the level of the Muskoka Lakes. The cottagers association annual meeting was held a short while ago, and I usually try to attend such meetings. On the agenda was an item about the level of the water in the lakes. Docks on the different sides of the lakes were either out of water or were underwater, depending on when they were built.

The local newspaper said, "Heated controversy ensued." There were many speakers during the afternoon meeting, each with his or her own thoughts and the level of the water on the lakes was the issue. I found all of this exasperating, to put it mildly. When it was time for me to speak, I thought the situation needed a bit of humor, so I said, "Well, there is only one solution, I guess. we'll have to tilt the damn lake!" Things eased up a bit after this and the meeting was soon over.

July 1991 ... I read an article today by my long-time political friend, Hugh Mackenzie of Huntsville that really pleased me. He said, "It is fair to say that during his [then] nineteen years as a Member of Parliament, no one has represented his constituents more effectively than Stan Darling. He is the textbook example of a good constituency man and this is the prime reason that, in all the elections Stan has faced as an MP, his fate was never in doubt. His greatest political strength is his innate ability to recognize that as long as he speaks up for the people, the people will never let him down."

When I first went down to Ottawa, I replaced Gordon Aiken, who had retired. He had done some good work in the Parry Sound/Muskoka riding and I had some big shoes to fill. I met Mr. Diefenbaker about this time and told him that I had replaced Gordon Aiken, my predecessor of fifteen years. Mr. Diefenbaker looked at me and said, "My boy, I am delighted to welcome you. You bring a new fresh air from that area."

I did not know the significance of this remark at that time but learned later that Gordon Aiken was one of the group out to replace Mr. Diefenbaker with Robert Stanfield. Needless to say, he did not have too much affection for Gordon Aiken.

July 1993 ... I am trying to clean up some things in my riding office today. My upcoming so-called retirement has made me as busy as ever in Burks Falls but our office has never had so many visitors and people wanting help. At the Lions meeting last night someone asked me how I got into politics. It seems to me that the first person who suggested it was Mr. A.A. Agar, a feed merchant and the owner of some steamboats in Burks Falls at one time. He nominated me for council in 1942 and I've held one political office or another ever since.

I have admired many political people including one of the first women in politics, Agnes McPhail. Another woman I admire is Flora MacDonald, who has made a great contribution federally. And John P. Robarts, Ontario premier for two terms was also a fine man and politician. Leslie Frost was also a hard-working premier. But political people certainly don't get the respect that they used to. Investigative reporting by the media often means that they just dig out the dirt about politicians, things that happened 40 years ago and don't amount to a hill of beans in their later careers. I remember once when I was running for office, in 1972, Gordon Aiken came to me and said, "Stan, I don't know how to say this to you, but there is a story going around that your younger son, Peter, is involved in drugs and is a drug dealer and that he has been picking up drugs in Halifax." Peter had never been to Halifax in his life and I said I would check out these allegations which I did, with the Ontario Provincial Police.

Well, they traced the story back to some old busy-body of a woman outside the village and I think the police scared the hell out of her for circulating such a false story. She was a known trouble-maker and had the habit of calling my office often to try and get help in solving her problems, during the years I was reeve of Burks Falls. The whole thing just died because of lack of interest.

Another time, Liberal candidate, Ed Fisher, and Paul Gray, his campaign manager, had something going around about me which they felt would harm my chances of winning the next election. When Mr. Gray was asked about this smear, he replied that he and Ed knew it was not right but that was politics. They just hoped it would work!

In 1988, a young driver, Chris Edwards, was taking me around the riding and he had heard the story that I was going to run in the election and right after I had won, I would resign and take a seat in the Senate – so why vote for Stan when he wouldn't fulfill his term? I was doing a radio show that night and told the listeners what nonsense this was. I was then two years too old, at 77, to even be considered for the Senate. Their age limit for a seat in the Senate is 75.

Another time, in 1986, Claire Hoy of the Toronto Sun wrote that as there was one vacancy in the Senate, and he suggested two candidates to fill it: Mr. Hal Jackman, who was a millionaire and insurance executive; and the long-time Member for Parry Sound/Muskoka, Stan Darling. I collared him outside the chamber about this "offer." Well, I told him how ridiculous it was to even consider it as I would be 75 in six weeks and would have had to resign and would, of course, already have given up my seat in the House. As it was, I still had two years to run before the next election.

For some reason, he was surprised to hear that I was almost 75 years old. It was certainly no secret – half my opponents had used it for years when trying to think of reasons why I should not run again!

Ina and I spent a good many hours getting funding for businesses in my riding. It was a grueling business as some of the funds were provincial and some federal. Time and time again, after receiving these funds, the companies would simply fold up inside of a few months. We both found this very discouraging.

We hoped that by getting additional funding for some businesses, it would help to get people off the unemployment insurance rolls and save our riding a lot of money. We both worked very hard over the years on this issue.

Fednor grants, of course, were for Parry Sound district only, as they did not apply to Muskoka. And that provoked people in Muskoka, let me tell you.

Ina has often voiced the opinion that it might be better if we all had to stand on our own two feet, and there were no government grants at all.

A prime example of businesses which did not continue after receiving a grant was right here on our own doorstep. Thompson-Heyland received a major grant but were not able to continue business after re-financing. They employed about seventy or so people and this was a great blow to the Burks

Falls economy.

Ina built up wonderful contacts in the years she was at my office. People would come in with unemployment insurance problems. We were deluged with them. At one time there were two UI offices in the area, one on our main street and one in South River. To "streamline" their operations, UI closed both offices and people came to our riding office for help instead.

Ina told me many times that she worked seven days a week and twelve or fourteen hours a day so that she wouldn't get behind in the work. In my Ottawa office I had two secretaries and an executive secretary/research assistant. We were busy all the time. Many times a day our two offices were in touch, but in Burks Falls, there was just Ina. Occasionally she would have to be out of town and her daughter, Liz, who is very capable and talented in her own right, would fill in for a day or two. But the amount of work the Burks Falls office accomplished was incredible.

Ina said to me one time that she never had a problem she couldn't solve and that she tried to send people away with a smile. She said, "There but for the grace of God go I."

When I hit the 80-year mark, I found out that Ina was the same age as me. Her birthday is in November and mine is in July. But I can't recall either of us ever discussing or considering age as a factor in our work.

When I get back to my riding on Friday night, and, as Ina says, "sweep into the office," there has never been much time to talk about what happened during the week. We just got busy on the work I had brought with me and with the dozens of people and issues that came up on Saturday and Sunday. And Ina would, of course, have my schedule for the weekend in good order.

"I hardly had time to go to my husband's funeral, we were so busy," Ina told friends recently. "The hospital phoned me in the afternoon to say my husband had passed away and I said thank you and went on with my work until the office was clear. It was extremely hard and very, very sad," Ina said.

I helped Ina with the notice of Ron's death, and getting it placed in the Globe and Mail. The funeral was arranged over the weekend for Monday noon at the Anglican Church in Burks Falls. We had wanted members of the RCMP where Ron had maximum years of service, to be there too, but this did not work out. I knew Ina was disappointed because she knew that her husband would have wanted them to be present.

October 26, 1993 ... Ina was a bit surprised that the moving company from Parry Sound arrived this morning to clear out the riding office. The phone and fax were disconnected, the furniture and file cabinets were loaded onto a truck and away they went. That's the way riding offices work, following defeat at the polls for their party. But it left our office in a bit of a mess, let me tell you. There was Ina, standing in the pile of files which she had unloaded onto the floor, her desk and chairs were gone, no phone or fax to keep in touch with anyone. And still people coming into the office for help, despite the fact that I was now retired. It took some weeks of kneeling on the floor and hunting through the files on the floor to sort through boxes and boxes of constituency records, including the many which had arrived from my Ottawa office. We were trying to carry on for our former constituents and also trying to carry out a smooth transition of help to Andy Mitchell, who had won the riding for the Liberal Party, and make sure he had all the help he needed.

I don't think I was much help to Ina, but we eventually managed to close down our office and move everything over to my insurance and real estate offices as there was a big store room on the second floor that my sons said I could use.

It is a strange feeling to see twenty-one years of my political life in Ottawa and Parry Sound/Muskoka packed up in boxes. Our next job is to get things unpacked and sorted out.

Ina has assured me in no uncertain terms that she is now retired!

And I am considering writing a book of political memoirs.

THE *HAIDA* COMMEMORATION

ugust 28, 1990, Ottawa … On my fax machine today I received a twenty-page briefing about the commemoration program to take place at Ontario Place in Toronto the day after tomorrow. I am one of the platform guests and Diane Morin of Environment Canada in Cornwall has arranged an interesting program.

The HMCS *Haida* is the last surviving example of a Canadian tribal-class destroyer, and is to be declared of national historic significance. I will represent Environment Minister Robert R. de Cotret at the unveiling of an Historic Sites and Monuments Board plaque to commemorate the forty-eight-year-old vessel. The *Haida* saw heavy action with Australian, British and Canadian navies during World War II. She also served two tours of duty in the Korean War and took part in numerous NATO exercises and training cruises. She was moved to Toronto and in 1965 became part of the Toronto Historical Board's Marine Museum. I am looking forward to my visit.

Toronto, August 30, 1990 … We are gathered together onboard the *Haida* for our 2:30 p.m. ceremony. For a Thursday, it is a busy place, with the Canadian National Exhibition in full swing and a great many visitors coming to Ontario Place as well. The Stadacona Band of Maritime Command is playing and in a few minutes there will be the Vice-Regal salute and greetings from Her Majesty the Queen, by the Hon. Lincoln Alexander, the Lieutenant Governor of Ontario. Also part of the official party are, Professor Thomas H.B. Symons, who is the chairman of the Historic Sites and

Monuments Board of Canada; His Worship Art Eggleton, mayor of Toronto; Clare Copeland, chairman of the board of Ontario Place; Robert A. Willson, commander RCN (retired), captain of HMCS *Haida*; the Hon. Ken Black, minister of tourism and recreation; Sonja Bata, commander, Naval Reserve; and myself.

After the *Haida* was decommissioned in 1965 by the Canadian Armed Forces, an association of former shipmates and friends was created to preserve it and ensure its continuation as a living museum. The Ontario government took her over in 1971 and through the efforts of Tourism and Recreation, she was moved to Ontario Place.

Lincoln Alexander has been interested in the ship, and serves as personal patron and honorary patron of the Friends of the Haida as well as honorary noon-time gunner.

This is a very well-organized program. We were met at special parking adjacent to the *Haida* by Walter Haldorson, Superintendent of Niagara National Parks. We were met by the Sea Cadets and brought to the marquee tent in the *Haida* compound and escorted to reserved seating where we awaited the Lieutenant Governor's arrival. He was escorted to the tent by his Aide de Camp, Commander Tony Pitts, HMCS *York*. Jane Roszell who is Director general, Canadian Parks Services, Ontario Region was also with our platform party and Dan Heap, MP, Trinity-Spadina; Joel Shapiro, Acting Manager, Ontario Place; Dr. Alec Douglas, Director of History, Department of National Defence; Rear Admiral P.C. Martin, Maritime Command, Halifax; Vice Admiral H.G. De Wolf, who was the first commander of the *Haida* and others.

I made my few remarks on behalf of the minister, and unveiled the plaque and was certainly pleased to be a part of this historic occasion. Ontario Place is certainly a great credit to its creator, Premier John P. Robarts of Ontario. He had said many times that it was very tough going indeed to get the approval and funding for Ontario Place but he had the vision, patience and guts to see it through.

MUSKOKA LAKES AND THE COTTAGER'S ASSOCIATION

Burks Falls, August 1, 1993 ... John Challis. a journalist with the Muskoka Advance covered a meeting I attended recently and wrote an accurate report. John and everyone who reads the paper know that I have been trying to organize a water safety bill, called C-46, for eight years or more. The federal bill, that was supposed to allow for ticketing speeding boaters, has been passed into law but it's still not being used.

The bill received Royal Assent last fall and to me, that means the bill is law. But Justice Minister Pierre Blais says the law has to be processed by the provincial solicitors general offices, in every province and the territories. They must each work out an implementation separately. I have offered to write to the ten solicitors general and the ones in the territories to get them going but the powers that be feel this may not be "expedient."

When we started out with this bill, it was to control water safety and boating infractions. Period! Today, however, the bill includes around 4,000 federal regulations to be policed through the provincial courts using tickets, the same way as minor infractions such as parking and speeding are currently handled.

Since boating is conducted on federal waterways, even recreational boating, and there's a lot of that in my former riding, it is controlled by the Canada Shipping Act. Constituents in my riding have watched the peace, quiet and safety of their recreational waterways be disrupted by bigger, faster and noisier pleasure boats, driven by inconsiderate showoffs, and we have wanted to help do something about it.

The crunch has been that speeding boaters could not just pay tickets for infractions of the law; they have had to appear in court to answer charges, under the Criminal Code of Canada. And Bill C-46 will change all that.

When it finally is implemented, it could reduce the number of court cases by as many as 400,000 a year. But I attended a meeting of the Muskoka Lakes Association in Milford Bay last Friday with a heavy heart. President John Patterson who conducted the annual meeting told the association that he was disappointed Bill C-46 has not been implemented. I told them, "I come here pretty downcast tonight because that damned bill isn't in effect yet." It was the one objective that I wasn't able to accomplish during my twenty-one years in office.

Muskoka Lakes Association is probably the biggest cottagers association in Canada, with many influential members headquartered in Toronto. They approached me eight or nine years ago to see if I could obtain legislation to deal with dangerous boating practices on the Muskoka Lakes. I met with the Hon. Doug Lewis, among many others, initially when he was minister of justice, with very little success. I kept at it for years, until I finally was able to arrange legislation with Justice Minister Kim Campbell in 1992. It was to be presented to the House in the fall.

October 1992 ... Bill C-46 has been passed into law and I am delighted to tell the Muskoka Lakes Association that the bill has received third reading, has been passed by the Senate and received Royal Assent. I expect that it will be in effect soon.

It has taken such a long time to come to this – I couldn't believe my ears when I heard that what started out as a bill on water and boating safety now included over 4,000 items including such misdemeanors as picking flowers in our national parks! I had suggested that the area dealing with water and boat safety be separated from all the other items and put into practice immediately, but this has still not been done by the provinces and territories. Until each solicitor general has settled the legislation to his province's liking, it cannot be printed in the Canada Gazette, the official organ of Parliament.

I recall Justice Minister Kim Campbell saying, "Bill C-46 should be called the Stan Darling Bill, because you have been the one person to persue it from the beginning to the end."

I hope it won't take some really bad accidents on the Muskoka Lakes before this bill finally is put into practice. And I hope that I am around when it is finally law.

CHINA
an Unforgettable Experience

O ctober 10, 1991 ... A group of Canadian parliamentarians have been invited to visit the People's Republic of China. We are to be called the Canadian-China Inter-Parliamentary Friendship Group, and will pay $1,000 toward our own expenses for the trip. Once in China, however, their government will be our host. Ten of us are set to fly to San Francisco and then on to Beijing. Our group includes Dr. and Mrs. Stan Wilbee of Vancouver, Beryl Gaffney, and our leader, Robert Wenman, MP of Fraser Valley, among others.

October 12 ... When I arrived at the Capitol Hotel in Beijing today, a letter was waiting for me in a well-prepared press folder, from the Hon. Fred Bild, who is the Canadian ambassador. He said, "The National People's Congress is pleased to arrange a schedule of events for your stay in Beijing. My wife and I also look forward to hosting a buffet luncheon at our residence on Monday. Mr. Wan Li will host a banquet in your honor."

Everything seems very well prepared for our visit and our itinerary in Shanghai is both detailed and lengthy. It includes a visit to the Number Seven Stock-Raising Farm, a visit to Nanpu Bridge, the Pudong Development Office, the Friendship Store, Yu Garden and a Bazaar. A series of banquets including one hosted by the Standing Committee of Shanghai Municipal People's Congress will be held when we get to that city. But we are in Beijing for two days only.

Wherever we go in busy Beijing, we are focusing on environmental and economic cooperation and on human rights. The emphasis is on co-operation with each other through parliamentary exchanges. Our sessions started today and our ten-member delegation heard a fine address in the Great Hall of the People, which led to a long discussion by Gu Min, former secretary general of the state council and current member of NPC Standing Committee. Mr. Robert Wenman, our Canadian chairman, addressed a wide variety of current international environmental issues, including destruction of global habitat, sustainable development, waste management, climate change, and biodiversity. This took up over half the allotted three-hour meeting. Both Mr. Li and Mr. Ming speak English but most of the sessions are translated for us as we go along.

Gu Ming, whose environmental qualifications are excellent, (he was the deputy-delegate leader to the U.N. 1972 Stockholm Conference and has held a variety of environmentally-related economic portfolios in the PRC government), responded at length to Mr. Wenman's initial comments, stating that the PRC recognized the necessity of pursuing environmentally sustainable development policies and had achieved preliminary success in cleaning up their domestic environment.

However, despite this record, they still required substantial external development assistance to control domestic pollution, he said. He suggested that this assistance would be best provided by unconditional transfer of clean coal-burning technologies.

Well, I must admit that Gu Ming received considerable sympathy from our contingent, especially from me. (I was introduced as a long-time House of Commons acid rain activist). I had the opportunity later this afternoon to speak, at length, (several members of our group pointed out the "length" part to me later), on the environmental impact of acid rain in Canada.

Before our meeting ended we arranged for me to handle correspondence from Canada, and Gu Ming to handle it from the PRC.

Both sides of our meeting expressed satisfaction with the state of the current economic relationship and the desire to enhance trade with each other. Our delegates called for greater Chinese purchases of Canadian goods, with China responding that Canada must take action to reduce its long-standing trade surplus with China, if it is expected to sell more goods to their country.

We were getting along fine until Liberal critic Beryl Gaffney, a member our Canadian contingent, stood up to express her disappointment with the lack of progress achieved by the PRC in democracy, and the lack of response to letters from herself to the PRC leadership, She expressed her concern for the plight of Tiananmen detainees. And then gave them a list of names of the political prisoners! She asked that Gu Ming seek clarification on their current health and status.

Those of us not in on this part of the agenda were embarrassed to say the very least. An experienced, mature politician in his early seventies, Mr. Gu Ming accepted the list graciously, I thought, and responded by reading, at length, from a position paper which had obviously been prepared well in advance of our visit.

He quietly emphasized the legality and necessity of their government's decision to act resolutely and to protect the right of the majority from subversive challenge. He said that some of those held had been found guilty of subversion by independent criminal courts. I thought I detected a note of irony when he said that their system in China was not perfect but that it was improving.

Wan Li – who is the third-highest ranking official in the PRC – then said, "We are considering sending a Chinese delegation to Canada in the near future to investigate your country's treatment of Canada's native people."

No one in our party made any comment about that!

We decided to meet annually in alternate capitals; Canada will host the meeting next year in Ottawa.

In following discussions, we were given to understand from several senior officials of the PRC, that leadership in China has further refined its position and their hard line on legality and legitimacy of their government will be even further refined in the future.

I think the bottom line is that China has entered a new phase in its relations with the developed world countries and a belief that Western memories of Tiananmen Square are fading however, there is, apparently, a harder line being taken domestically in the wake of communist countries collapsing all around them. This, I feel, has been a deciding factor in their internal "adjustments."

One brief mention of the re-uniting of Chinese families was touched on by our group. They replied that problems with family reunification rested mainly with the inability of People's Republic of China citizens to obtain Canadian visas! Over to the Canadian Government once again!

In a summary made by the PRC, the phrase they used with which I agree, was, "Visit by the Canadian-China Inter-Parliamentary Friendship Group: the first visit to the PRC by the group went well."

October 14 ... As we are in Beijing for only a couple of days, we want to see as much of the country as we can and today we took a train from the old city of Canton to the new city of Ganzhong, which has grown from a minor settlement of 30,000 ten years ago to a new, very modern, throbbing city of a million and a half. It is in every way a super city; the skyscrapers and modern factories everywhere we look are impressive. There is a tremendous amount of trade between the two cities of Ganzhong and Hong Kong, with a rather unusual feature; they will not accept Chinese money, the yuan. All trade is done with Hong Kong dollars only.

We were not thrilled with our train accommodation today as no private or reserved seats were available and the train was jammed.

This afternoon we were taken on a visit to a very modern aluminum sash and door factory which had the latest machinery for every phase of the operation. It is an interesting tri-ownership arrangement, with the Chinese government owning one-third, (for which they put up no money), Canadian financing for one-third, and the final third owned by the Japanese. It is all very impressive.

October 16 … We were met and entertained by the Governor of the province, tonight, following a visit to the Stock Market Exchange which is in its infancy. Shares were being traded much like those on the Toronto Stock Exchange. It is unusual for a communist country to conduct business in this way, very much as the Western countries do. We are also amazed at the great number of private entrepreneurs, shops and stores everywhere in Ganzhong.

October 17 … We are heading back to the old city of Canton by train, with a beautiful private compartment this time around. We plan to make arrangements to fly to the giant city of Shanghai tomorrow.

October 18 … We are quartered in the new, sumptuous Hotel Jinjiang in Shanghai where I have a suite of rooms suitable for a family of four! My suite is just below the suite used by President Reagan on a earlier visit here. Its appointments are comparable in every way to Mr. Reagan's former suite, I have been told. Seniority must have some compensations.

We have a lengthy and well-detailed schedule of events planned for us in Shanghai, including a visit to historical gardens, and several banquets and luncheons. We are being entertained royally and breakfast is served each morning in a skyscraper around the corner from the hotel, in a room forty or fifty stories above the city.

Today, we were taken on a tour of a huge bridge under construction which will cross the famous Yangtze River. New building developments on either end of the bridge are mostly commercial. One unusual fact about this building project was explained by the project officers. They said the bridge building is ahead of schedule and under budget!

October 20 ... This is our last day in China. As it is Sunday, we were asked by our guide, a very pleasant woman, if we would like to attend church. I, and another colleague said we had great interest in doing so. Dr. Stan Wilbee, and his wife, of Vancouver, said they would very much like to go with me. Arrangements were made to have a car take us there and the driver drove very fast indeed through the narrow streets. There wasn't a lot of traffic at that time, thank heavens, and I still shudder when I recall the car swerving off the street right into a solid wall which lo and behold, opened up in front of our eyes. Behind the wall, gates opened into a huge old church courtyard. We went in and were introduced to the Pastor, who was, of course, Chinese. A former Baptist Church, it is now non-denominational.

As soon as I arrived, the officials pinned a beautiful red rose to my lapel. I wondered what this was for and found out later that it was a service dedicated to senior citizens. I certainly qualify for that!

There was a long line of worshipers going into the church but we were given preferred space in the gallery. I was amazed to see such a large crowd. The church was packed to overflowing with benches placed outside in the courtyard and loud speakers placed to hear out there as well.

There must have been two or three thousand people inside and outside the church and I was certainly impressed. There was a beautiful choir and the sermon was given in a Chinese dialect by a senior citizen. He informed the congregation that senior citizens, despite their advanced years, have much to contribute to the country and to the community. Following the church services, I had photographs taken with the ministers and some were taken outside the church, which, incidentally, has over 3,000 members, with regular meetings held without any interference. The size of the enthusiastic congregation that day was very impressive.

In the afternoon we visited the very large, government-owned department store, the Friendship Store, where I purchased a soft pouch-like suitcase, to carry the quantities of papers I had collected at meetings, a lovely pottery Chinese horse, several beautifully crafted collectible boxes and other unique items. There is certainly no lack of nice things to buy.

We've done quite a bit of sight-seeing in the city of Xian. We had an unusual opportunity to see the historic site of life-size terracotta warriors and horses of Emperor Qin Shi Huang. This rare site is hailed as the Eighth Wonder of the World, and was uncovered in 1974, quite by accident, by a man digging for a well. It is at the foot of Mount Lishan. Each of these astonishingly life-like warriors has his own unique facial expression, and it is estimated that over 6,000 warriors had been buried originally. The ones we saw included cavalry, infantry, chariot guards, generals and horses, in full battle array and position. We were told that this was an artistic recreation of the Chinese army at that time. In 1980, evidently, a pair of bronze chariots and horses were also unearthed near the General's tomb, not far away. This was certainly one of the most eerie and startling experiences we had had in China and one we won't forget for a long time.

October 20 ... We were told at the outset of our visit to China that tipping for any service whatever is illegal in China but we've received so much kindness and good help during our stay that we all wish we had some way to express our thanks. Mr. and Mrs. Fred Bild have entertained us all in their home several times and have been of great assistance to our delegation. We are delighted that arrangements were made for us to visit Canton, the new city of Ganzhong, and, of course, to tour Beijing, before we start back on our twelve-hour air journey from Shanghai to San Francisco.

November 9, Ottawa ... An interesting footnote to our China visit has just recently come to light. Three members of the House of Commons, one of whom had been a delegate on our trip to Beijing several weeks ago, Mrs. Beryl Gaffney of Ottawa, had an interesting experience. She and Geoff Scott, MP Wentworth, and Svend Robinson of Vancouver, were invited to China by a group violenty opposed to the communist regime. The Canadians were able to obtain visas to get into China and talk with several Chinese government officials. The Canadians demanded to be taken to a prison where some of the political prisoners were being held, but were refused permission. However, they did manage to get there on their own and made quite a scene at the doors of the prison, demanding to be allowed in and waving their diplomatic passports. They shouted that they were members of the Canadian Parliament. They certainly got a bit out-of-line and were roughed-up a bit, and grabbed by the guards and thrown onto a bus.

This has made headlines around the world, especially in Canada and especially in their home ridings. For a few days there has been a great deal of sympathy for the Canadians because of the way they were treated and threatened. But the last day or so has brought out the whole and the true story; we found out that our Members of Parliament seemed to forget that they were in a foreign country and subject to the laws of that country. That they were trying to dictate to the Chinese people how to take care of their own internal problems evidently did not occur to them. Naturally, the authorities in China did not encourage this sort of thing, nor would Canada if the roles were reversed. In any event, they received a lot of very bad publicity and came back to Canada with their tails between their legs.

I feel that they have been very autocratic in demanding to see Chinese political prisoners and in trying to interview them, which, of course, was refused.

November 10, Ottawa ... In a meeting with Prime Minister Brian Mulroney today, I said to him that our visit to China was an extraordinary one, to an incredible country with its vastness and its complexities. I am delighted to have had the opportunity to visit there and to contribute whatever help I could, to their environmental rehabilitation. It was certainly a learning experience for me.

MAHARISHI MAHESH YOGI

D ecember 1992 … I've done many things in my professional career, I met people, travelled to far-off countries, but nothing has been more interesting than my meetings with Maharishi Mahesh Yogi, on several special occasions.

My introduction to Maharishi was through a friend, Rick Alexander, whose family I have known for fifty years. A couple of years ago Rick had been working at the Lake of Bays establishment, called Maharishi Ayur-ved Health Centre and he approached me to see if I could introduce him to Solicitor General Doug Lewis. And we have just gotten along very well since then.

The organization was very interested in contacting senior politicians in Canada and endeavoring to place before them a program and plan which would be of great assistance in reducing the prison population by having teachers instruct the prisoners in Transcendental Meditation.

I approached Mr. Lewis and wrote him a letter outlining the program and asking for his attention to it, and to not just brush it aside as another crazy scheme. Doug said he would look into it. I also spoke briefly with the Prime Minister and, of course, he was hesitant, as the head of our government could not afford to be criticized as being involved with some far-out organization.

June 1991 … In May and early June I was a delegate to the meeting of the North Atlantic Assembly in Rotterdam. During my work there I received a telephone call from Rick Alexander. I was very surprised to hear from him. He asked if I could possibly find time to spend an evening with His Holiness, Maharishi. This invitation was certainly a big surprise to me. I explained my very tight schedule both day and night but mentioned I did have one free evening, Sunday. So I agreed to meet with Maharishi. Rick said they would send a car for me and that I would be "returned" early the next morning. The group's headquarters is in Vlodrop, in the Netherlands.

At five o'clock Sunday evening, a delightful Swiss gentleman, named Lucas, poured me into a very long silver stretch-Cadillac limousine, which was to say the very least, luxuriously appointed. I told Lucas I preferred to sit in the front with him so we could get acquainted and he could point out the sights. We drove from one end of Holland to the other for an hour and thirty minutes and believe me, we were driving at top speed.

Lucas took me to a beautiful hotel on the outskirts of their headquarters, and I enjoyed dinner in their dining room. Lucas said he would return for me at 7:45. We set off for headquarters and in a few moments arrived. I expected to meet with His Holiness for a few minutes at the most. I was taken into a special section of their building which was an old monastery, dating back to the Middle Ages. His rooms were superbly furnished and appointed with beautiful red carpets. I was asked to remove my shoes before entering the apartment. I can only describe it as a throne room, beautifully furnished in white with hundreds of flowers, with beautiful perfume coming from them.

Shortly after, Maharishi entered and everyone stood and bowed. I informed him how delighted I was to have the chance to meet with him for a few minutes. We sat together with at least a dozen or so of his associates with the conversation between us being very warm. He asked me about the government, and Parliament and said that he was interested in endeavoring to improve the situation in most countries. After talking together for a while I glanced at my watch and found it was almost 1 a.m. I felt I had taken up too much of his time but he assured me this was not so. It was a fascinating exchange of ideas. His Holiness stated that he was hoping to meet with heads of state to outline his ideas and he hoped to persuade them to adopt the ideas. I pointed out that of course, as a lowly backbencher in Parliament, I had little or no influence. He then told me about his vast organization and connections. It seemed to me unusual that he had not been able to sell his ideas to other governments. He agreed and said that he had not been successful but would still continue to try.

My wife is very ill, with cancer and in the hospital. It is a great worry and I wish there was more I could do to help her. So it is with a heavy heart that I join a delegation of the National Defence for a visit to Europe, to discuss the Canadian situation and participation in NATO. We are going to several cities for a fact finding and discussion trip, including Lahr, Vienna, Prague, Moscow, Bonn, Berlin and then Brussels.

In Brussels, just before we were to leave for home, I had a telephone call from Rick Alexander, who had, somehow, tracked me down. He asked me if I could spend a short time in Vlodrop with His Holiness. I pointed out how tight our schedule was, but I found one free evening. The Maharishi told me about the party which he had formed, known as the Natural Law Party. It would be contesting elections in various countries, the most recent one being England. However no one had been elected at that time. They planned to provide a candidate in the next federal election in various centres the following year and he asked for ideas as to what programs the candidates should pursue. I pointed out my special interest in the environment and the damage caused by acid rain. I suggested that they would certainly be on the right track if they would use that program to emphasize to the Canadian public their involvement in this area. I then returned to Canada.

March 1993 ... I told my riding executive that I would be retiring in July and would be making the announcement soon. However, they asked me to wait a bit before doing so as the Prime Minister would be retiring and there would be a new leader. And so, of course, I waited.

May 3 ... An invitation today to visit Maharishi in Vlodrop, which informed me that complete arrangements would be made for me to fly to Amsterdam and be driven to their headquarters. I said that I really could not provide much information that would warrant a trip such as this. The Maharishi was most insistent, saying they would be pleased to put me up at their headquarters. I was there for a few days and we had many conversations about the election; about what the principle issues would be in the campaign. I said I felt it would be unemployment and the recession. I also hoped that the environment would be discussed. However, this proved to be a non-issue not often referred to as people are worried about unemployment and the recession, jobs and lack of industry.

I pointed out to His Holiness that a great many Canadians thought that it was a "Prime Minister Mulroney-made" recession and that other parts of the world were, apparently, not feeling the same recession. Dr. Neil Paterson, the new Leader of the Natural Law Party was there – just returned from Moscow – and he said he had returned early to talk with me.

Knowing the length of the drive back to the airport, I was getting a bit concerned. However, Maharishi produced a helicopter to fly me directly to the airport. Despite the cloudy, wet day, it was a thrilling experience to fly over almost the entire width of the Netherlands, at a very low altitude and see their beautiful country.

April 1993 ... I was struck by the fact that Maharishi is a very small man, probably not weighing more than one hundred pounds. He has a high-pitched voice and I had some problems, at our first meeting, in hearing him. I have a hearing problem to begin with and His Holiness speaks very quietly indeed. But we get along very well. The last time we met, we were in a beautiful summer garden, outside the main building. There were flowers everywhere. Maharishi told me that he had been able to convince one of the African heads of state, Kenneth Kuanda, to adopt his program. Unfortunately, Kuanda was defeated in their last federal election, shortly after their meeting. However Mozambique President Joaquim Chissanno is applying Maharishi's Transcendental Meditation program, to bring about political peace to Mozambique. President Chissanno credited the TM program for the major, positive events in his country, and to Maharishi Mahesh Yogi. The president had told His Holiness that TM brings peace of mind, relaxation of body, and coherence in society. People who practice TM always benefit.

May 1993 ... I have been a member of the National Council for a Crime Free Canada for some time now and it occurs to me that possibly the practice of TM could help prevent crime and possibly rehabilitate offenders. Ultimately, if it is a successful program, it could save the government upwards of $7 billion annually.

Maharishi told me about their plan to reduce the prison population and to rehabilitate young offenders. That really made me sit up and take notice. If meditation will save taxpayers money and is going to save younger criminals, then no matter how far out it seems, it's worth a gamble. I'm not afraid of being ridiculed and I am certainly going to look into it further.

Burks Falls, July 1995 ... Since my retirement in 1993, I have continued my involvement with the National Council for a Crime Free Canada and with my friend Rick Alexander. I have made several trips to Ottawa to help the group meet and talk with members of the present government. And I have attended an international meeting in the Netherlands where plans for the further dissemination of the council's programs have been discussed and expanded.

In Canada, I have had the pleasure of meeting with senior council people who are continuing their research into ways and means of introducing TM programs into the Army, and in to our correctional institutions.

We met recently with such well-known people as Lt.-Gen. Lew MacKenzie, with one of the senior people at Camp Borden, with the chief of police in Barrie, Ontario, and many others. There are currently some very senior and experienced people who have become actively involved with the council. Former police commissioner of New Brunswick Carmen Kilburn and former crime prevention program coordinator for the New Brunswick Department of Justice, Chris Collrin, who has implemented the TM program in correctional institutions, are both actively contributing to the council's work.

According to the group, a recent survey shows that 45 per cent of Canadians polled, favor offering TM in prison. In addition, research at maximum security prisons in thirteen countries including America's infamous San Quentin and Folsom prisons, found decreased violence and drug abuse and a 40 per cent reduction in recidivism among offenders practicing TM.

It has been quite successful and I hope our government gives some consideration to the introduction of the TM program, if only on a limited basis initially because nothing else works.

I am certainly in favor in doing something positive about our prison population because it's costing an arm and a leg as things are now.

The Council for Crime Free Canada and the Natural Law Party have met with a good many people concerning the use of TM in the military. One suggestion was to create a prevention wing in the Canadian military to practice TM, and to help prevent the rise of negative and destructive trends in their group.

Various presentations have also been made to the military and defence people showing how stress can be reduced in peacekeeping operation, not only among troops but also among the populations suffering from civil strife. Studies show that service people practicing TM techniques have benefited enormously from reduced stress, improved morale, and performance, and have radiated a peaceful influence of coherence and positivity.

Among those the council has met with are: Hon. Warren Allman, PC, MP, a former solicitor general in the Trudeau government and chairman of the Standing Committee on Justice and Legal Affairs; Hon. Bill Rompkey, PC, MP, chairman, Standing Committee on National Defence and Veterans Affairs; Fred Mifflin, parliamentary secretary to the minister National Defence, and member of the Standing Committee on National Defence and retired admiral; George Proud, MP, vice chairman of the Standing Committee on National Defence and Veterans Affairs; Lt.-Col. R.G. McLellan, chief social worker, Surgeon General Branch, National Defence; Kenneth J. Calder, assistant deputy minister, policy and communications, National Defence; Christopher Axworthy, MP, Saskatoon-Clark's Crossing; Jim Hart, MP, Okanagan/Similkameen/Merrit; and many others.

I must admit the interest has been great.

In a recent article by Robert M. Kahn, entitled, "Can good vibes reduce crime," he outlined the results of a test program conducted in Washington, D.C. Evidently, over 3,800 experienced meditators from sixty-four countries gathered in and around Washington, D.C. for most of June and July one summer, in an effort to slash the overall degree of violent crime experienced in Washington. The event was sponsored by an Iowa-based Institute of Science, Technology and Public Policy, a volunteer crime prevention group.

"Nothing else has been found to have an effective impact on crime," said one researcher, "so everybody tells us. We are told, 'if you can do something, we're for it.'" A spokesman for the Washington police force said, when told of the experiment to take place in his city, "Nothing short of two feet of snow in July would cut down on crime in this city this summer." The Washington Metropolitan Department agreed to provide the institute with data on violent crimes that occurred throughout the course of the study, which ran from June 7th to July 30th. Violent crimes, according to the police, includes homicides, rapes, robberies and aggravated assaults. Such crimes, on the rise in the District of Columbia since 1987 fell 14 per cent compared to the same period in 1992, following a TM mediation sit-in.

An official at the police department's Research and Planning Division did confirm, overall, that there were about 363 fewer violent crimes in the eight-week period. "We are going to take some of the credit for these reductions," said Dr. John Hagelin, a Fairfield native, now heading up the Iowa-based institute.

Other, similar, tests are being conducted in other parts of the United States.

John Smelcer, an assistant professor of management at the Kogod College of Business at American University who has been practicing TM for twenty years, was asked to sit on the review board because of his experimental research background.

He responded with a resounding "Yes" when asked whether TM was responsible for lowering the overall rate of violent crime in Washington, D.C. during the test summer.

"If you take the difference between the prediction for what crime should have been, compared to what it actually was, then this is great," he said. While saying that TM is a "novel approach to crime reduction," one scientist stated, "in the twenty-first century it will become quite commonplace for city and national governments to maintain large groups of meditators to create coherence in society. When people meditate together it is magnificent."

I was asked recently if I practice the art of TM. Well, yes, I have tried to occasionally but I don't meditate often enough, I find it very relaxing, no question about it but I keep forgetting to do it and frankly, I have so little free time.

THE LIONS CLUB – WE SERVE

In 1913, Melvin Jones, an insurance executive living in Chicago, came up with the idea of founding a club for businessmen, linked with similar clubs around the world. It would be, he said, dedicated to creating and fostering a spirit of generous consideration among the people of the world through study of problems of international relationships.

Out of this idea, came the International Association of Lions Clubs, formed in 1917.

Burks Falls, 1938 ... The Burks Falls Lions Club was formed this year. In our village and nearby Powassan, Lionism will be "tried as an experiment." Bruce Malcolm, district secretary of the Niagara Falls District A Club, is responsible for helping this club become a reality. District A takes in all of Ontario and most of the province of Quebec and there are twenty-seven members in Burks Falls. This includes most of the businessmen and merchants on our main street.

"This club is not going to work for very long," said merchant Charles W. Sharpe, "but I think I might as well join anyway."

Ernie Bolton, of Bolton's Restaurant, is president and dinner meetings are held there every Friday evening at 6:30. There is a very good meal served for $1.50.

Burks Falls, 1994 ... I have been asked to speak at the Fifty-fifth Charter Night of the Burks Falls Lions Club and I've been sorting through some files for a bit of club history. I am pleased to see that Harvey Fowler, the only

Charter Member living, will be at the meeting. He is almost 80, a bit younger than I am.

I joined the club in 1940, although my father was a member before that. The second president was Ernie Warner, who published the Burks Falls Arrow each week, and, if I recall, both Ernie Warner and Ernie Bolton went on to become Deputy District Governors. The third president was my father, John M. Darling, who was very reserved and quiet, not unlike me!

Father told me one day that he was planning to withdraw from the club because of the expense, but I knew what the real reason was. He didn't want to take over as president and when I tackled him about it, he said that was true. Well, he stayed with the club and was a very good president and was still president in 1942, when our club sponsored a new Huntsville club.

I was president in 1945/6 and went on to become Deputy District Governor in 1946/7 and District Governor of A5 in 1947/8.

Burks Falls 1952 … For years the Lions in Burks Falls produced a sports day to raise funds but I wanted to do something different. After talking with Dr. J.J. Wilson, a magistrate and a dentist in town, and with Bob McLaughlan, a blacksmith, they suggested that the trotting races, which used to be held in town should be brought back. I got quite excited about this suggestion, and got on the telephone to the horse owners to line up some race events.

We had nine horses, nine races, three heats each and a purse of $600. When the first event was over there was no money left. I asked Dr. Wilson and Mr. McLaughlan how they had made any money for the Lions in the past. They said, "Oh, we forgot to tell you. We used to go up and down the street to get donations for prizes from all the merchants."

Despite this set-back, we ran the races annually for over 25 years and it was one of the great summer events in the area and a real money-maker for Lions.

Burks Falls Lions are unique. We have provided four District Governors which is more than any other club our size. They were, myself, Dr. Bev Hallam, Dick Hyndman, and Earl Box.

Our club was often praised by people like secretary Bruce Malcolm, as one of the most unusual, as far as getting things done in our community. Our reeve and councillors were Lions, members of the utilities commission were Lions, Lions members comprised the school board – we were always assured of a sympathetic ear!

In the early 1940s, District A5 ran from Gravenhurst to Noranda, and from Duparquet, Quebec to Wawa and Hawke Junction. At that time I told a Lions Club I was visiting, that there were 330,000 Lions from 39 countries. Today there are 1.4 million Lions in 177 countries, with over 30,000 clubs. It is the largest service organization in the world.

I have had the pleasure of presenting charters to two clubs, Espanola and Mattawa, which are still active after almost half a century.

I have been a Lion for almost fifty-six years and it has had a very positive effect on my life. Despite my work in Ottawa for the twenty-one years, I have endeavored to keep active as a Lion and have attended clubs in far-off places around the world. I've been welcomed in every one, from London, England, to Nairobi, Kenya.

Some years ago, I was speaking to the newly-elected Secretary General of the Commonwealth Parliamentary Association, David Tonkin, from Australia. There are over 10,000 members. Dr. Tonkin was a medical doctor and he noticed my Lions pin and said, "Oh, you are the Past District Governor," and I said I was. "I was the District Governor in my area of Australia and have been an active Lions for many years," he said.

On the elevator of the Waldorf Astoria Hotel in New York City one day, two men were wearing Lions pins. I immediately introduced myself and shook hands and received a hearty welcome. When I looked at their business cards I was most impressed. They were both international past presidents, Robert Uplinger and J.L. Wroblewski. Several times in my life such situations have occurred and when some international Lions presidents have visited me in Ottawa, I always tried to arrange for them to meet the prime minister as well. One such man was Bert Mason from Ireland, and also the international president from New Zealand. Another time I was asked to bring greetings from our government to the international convention meeting in Montreal in 1979.

All members of the House of Commons are given a special House of Commons Pin to wear; it's very distinctive, with the mace of Canada on it. Believe it or not, I seldom wear mine, but I always wear the Lions pin. Wives of Members also have a pin, and Mona was very proud of hers. She wore it to bed on occasion, I think. She used to give me the devil for not wearing this pin and I told her in no uncertain terms, "Look, very few people know what the pin is but my Lions pin is recognized worldwide. That is the reason I am very proud to wear it."

One day a woman, spotting my House of Commons pin, asked me what it was. I said it denoted membership in one of the most unpopular clubs in Canada, and it was restricted to only 295 active members. She said, "Is it the Ku Klux Klan?" I replied that it was not quite as bad as that and that I was a Member of the House of Commons.

As District Governor one year, I was to visit the Thessalon Lions. Their president owned a hotel and I was travelling with the secretary, Bruce Malcolm. As we entered the hotel lobby, the president came over to introduce himself to us. He had the Rotary emblem on his lapel and I nearly fell over. He could see that we were embarrassed and he reached up, removed the Rotary pin, took his Lion pin from the bottom of his vest where it was pinned, and pinned it to his lapel. He thought that the Rotary pin had more prestige and that more travellers would be impressed by it than by the Lions pin.

On one official visit to Hawke Junction from Sault Ste. Marie, I walked from the station across the street to the hotel where the meeting would take place. I was to go by train from there to Wawa the next morning for a special ladies night. I was told the train would leave at 11 a.m.

The next morning I sat with my packed bags in the lobby. The hotel was only feet from the station and I kept watching for the train to show up. Finally, at 11 a.m. I took my bags across to the station and asked the agent where the train was. He said, "The train doesn't come in here. It's down the siding and you'd better hurry because I think it is starting to move."

I lit out of there like a bat out of hell, running and running after that train but I didn't seem to be getting any closer. Finally, the train pulled away and I was stranded in Hawke Junction. I tell you I was pretty despondent.

When I asked how far it was to walk to Wawa, I was told it was nineteen miles and even at my young age, I thought it was a little too far on a bitterly cold January day. The agent got in touch with the Road Master, by telephone. His name was Jack Thompson. He was a Lion. He explained the circumstances for the call and Mr. Thompson said, "leave it to me." He called back with the message that all the arrangements had been made to have a special train made up which would leave later that afternoon and would get me to Wawa in time for the banquet. He told me that because of regulations I would have to buy my ticket and I paid over my seventy-five cents, pretty cheap for a special train.

There was a large crowd in attendance when I arrived in Wawa and at the banquet I was told that the Lions had decide to run a pool on the time of my arrival, with tickets and a prize for the person who came closest.

That was a Lions gathering I won't forget for a while!

Burks Falls, 1995 ... I recalled today when talking with club President Bryan Nixon, that there is only one Lion in our club with a perfect attendance record for his fifty-seven years of membership. That is Harvey Fowler who still attends faithfully. Lions are able to make up any meetings they miss by visiting other clubs. We are not always able to make the dinner meetings because of illness or other commitments.

Harvey was a school teacher for some years and then a merchant on the west side of Ontario Street.

I asked Bryan to have lunch with me today at Costas Restaurant. He has been a Lion since 1982, and works with the Darling Real Estate and Insurance Company. He will be starting his fifth term as president soon.

"I thought it was mostly social, that we would help to sell tickets for various functions, get to know people in town, that sort of thing," Bryan said about joining the Lions Club. "But it didn't take me long to realize that it was much, much more than that. I think that members get a quiet pride of doing things for people who are down and out, helping to make a difference in their lives. I can wear my Lions pin with pride and say, "I did everything I could yesterday and today I will try to do the same thing."

Bryan and I talked over what has kept the Lions Club in Burks Falls, and around the world, going strong for so many years. "Every member of the club is equal," we agreed. Both Bryan and I have received many awards of recognition for work we have done with our club and we accept those awards on behalf of our club. We know we have made a difference in our community through our work together.

"Some of us do more than others," Bryan said and I agreed. "I often wonder what that person has joined the club for, when others are busy all the time. There is always a core of movers and shakers, the people who are not afraid to work and who make things work and happen, like you, Stan," Bryan said.

Bryan and I often work together on things, and, in all honesty, neither of us want any recognition for what we do. What one Lion does, all Lions do.

Bryan told me that his wife commented: "'Bryan, you must be out of your head to work so hard for the Lions, you never stop.' But she works right along side me on most projects. Lions wives and relatives are a big and important part of Lionism."

Bryan and I got talking about Dr. Bev Hallam, who had been District Governor and a Lion for many years, until his death in March 1992. He said, "Stan, you and Dr. Hallam have always talked right from the heart. If there was something that had to be said, we could always count on you two to say it. We respect you as we did Doc Hallam, for what you have done."

I appreciated that, especially as he also said that I always wanted everything to be done yesterday!

I pointed out that other long-time Lions had the same philosophy, including Earl Box, and Scott and Art Thompson. "Dr. Hallam told me when I first started with Lions that, if I wanted recognition, I was in the wrong business. "We are in the people business," he said. "Sometimes we fall flat on our faces, but at least we tried to do what we think is necessary. Should someone say, thank you very much, Bryan, that will be a bonus."

Perhaps a shortcoming of the Lions is that we do not publish the good deeds we do every day.

New members are needed so much today in Lions Clubs. There is a great deal of competition for free hours: skating, hockey, baseball, bowling, theatre, television. But the world is changing and there are so many needs that must be met. We are in it to make a difference.

Dr. Hallam told Bryan, when he first joined the Lions in 1982: "Keep your priorities straight. First comes your family, then your job, and then the Lions. If you keep them in that order, you won't have any difficulties."

It is so easy to get involved in the projects that are vital to our community. But I still tell myself, as Bryan does and other Lions, keep those priorities in order.

Bryan has some wonderful insight into what makes Lionism work. "The secret of being a good Lion is to be able to spark a little fire in the club, in the community. To be able to grab a moment to get the job done and take pride in the sense of accomplishment. I've wanted to quit a million times, but when I quit, it will be for my reasons, not because I am angry at something someone said or did. If you know in your heart that you have done the best you could do, that's your thanks."

We talked for a few minutes about the Burks Falls Club's involvement in the drug awareness program.

Bryan said, "We participate in training teachers to deal with young people who are, quite often, experimenting with drugs. Teachers are often the first to know this and in east Parry Sound, many of the teachers have already taken courses in this area. We also try to keep a few thousand dollars as a contingency in case something comes along such as a family which has been burned out. This money will help them stay at a motel for a few days, until the insurance companies get organized, and to buy some clothes for the family."

A year ago, the Burks Falls Lions took part in a program called, Sight First. It prevents or cures preventable blindness in countries around the world. Money is used to remove cataracts, give kids vitamin supplements, and to help youngsters with other sight problems in Third World Countries.

In such countries, clean water is precious and so children often use the polluted streams and rivers to wash and pick up all kinds of infections which can cause blindness.

"For ten cents a pill, we can keep these kids from going blind, for a year. Is this something we can ignore?" Bryan said.

Two years ago, Bryan was chairman of that project with fifteen co-chairmen in A5. They raised 102,000 American dollars for this project out of a worldwide total of $147 million. Bryan said, "Stan, there are 40 million blind people in the world today. If we don't do our part now, there will be 80 million in ten years time." Such fund-raising is administered by the Lions Charitable International Foundation in Chicago. The funds are banked, and work is done by spending the interest only on these projects. Lions International is told, "We need a certain kind of hospital, or treatment equipment, or medication supply," in India perhaps, where the disease is so rampant. And the Lions take it from there.

Recently, a resource centre dedicated to helping the hearing impaired, was spearheaded by past-Governor Bill Ross. It was eventually opened in Sudbury, with clubs around Ontario contributing what they could. Another centre, the Daffodil Terrace, was arranged for by North Bay Lion James Leek for relatives, patients and friends to use, also in Sudbury, with contributions from many Lions Clubs.

Bryan told me about one Lion who he feels is outstanding and I agree. His name is Ed Kincaid and he is blind. Ed used to be an RCMP officer and he played football for the CFL. "He is a big, strapping guy, over 60 now, who had a terrible accident and lost his sight. He is now a spokesman for the Lions Foundation of Canada and he and his dog go everywhere together. He tells people how lucky he is, because he can hear, and talk, and relate to people. He can communicate with his friends and that he is fortunate to have a dog to help him, supplied by the Lions Canine Vision group. People like Ed Kincaid point up to us all what a difference we can make for people, some ray of hope and assistance to get through a tough time, and to make our efforts worth while. Listening to Ed Kincaid recharges my batteries," Bryan told me.

"Most people ask us how we decided on the projects we do each year. We go over last year's projects and budgets, we make a Wish List of things we would like to do and try to ask for volunteer chairmen to do them. We are asked often by our communities for help and we weigh every request and try to do something. In Burks Falls we support youth activities such as Scouts, Guides, hockey, baseball, Christmas and Halloween parties, the food bank and many others. Last year our club raised and spent $47,000 in the Village. Our mandate in Lions is, if we raise $30,000 then we spend $30,000. We don't have a big bankroll in the bank, because we don't want to get lazy. The need is too great. We installed an elevator in the Burks Falls

Arena last year, and we supported patients with Cystic Fibrosis in this area. We also support the Lions Sight Conservation Program in other areas. Just because we don't have any blind people in Burks Falls, doesn't mean we don't recognize the need for this support. Hopefully, we never will have the need locally, but if we only have a hundred dollars to send, it will eventually help someone in another community, that's what it is all about," Bryan said.

"Lions around the world are particularly interested in helping the visually impaired or blind people and those with hearing problems or deaf people. In doing this we are associated with clubs in Toronto, England, Chicago, Japan, everywhere."

Each Lion pays his dues of $50 per year. He pays all his own meals and entertainment, unless he is a guest speaker at another club. A portion of the dues go to their district and a portion to MBA which means that of $100 raised for community projects, $100 is spent on community projects.

"There are 1.4 million Lions in the world today, and 285,000 Lionesses and numerous Leos. With husbands, wives and other partners working toward a better community, that makes over 3 million partners in service," said Bryan.

In District A5 there are fifty-three Lions Clubs, eighteen Lionesses Clubs and one Leo Club. Until recently Lions Clubs were made up of men only but the world is changing. In the Lions constitution, there is no place for sex, color or race discrimination. But, we must admit, the changes were hard fought by some of the older members.

Lions have a program called Lions Quest which teaches skills for adolescents, skills for growing, for working towards peace, working towards action. It goes from Kindergarten to Grade 12. It teaches kids about drug awareness and how to say NO, how to get along with others, how to prevent violence, how to do service towards others. It is an incredible program and we help pay the lodging and food for the teachers while they are taking these courses. Teachers touch on all the children's lives, and we are, in essence, the expediters. If we train thirty-six teachers at a cost of $10,500, for example, we reach over 1,000 youngsters who are in need of these skills. We must find innovative ways to raise this money, to give the donors something back for their financial involvement. It keeps us on our toes.

Both Bryan and I realized as we were talking, how tough it is these days to bring up youngsters in a small village. Kids want something to do, and they don't know what. If some of them are not trained properly to avoid problems, where is their future? Lions of course work with the local police, such as the Ontario Provincial Police in Burks Falls. We plan bike rodeos, drug awareness programs, and many others. Lions are focused on their community and have an investment in its future.

I asked Bryan what Lionism had done for him. "It's changed my perspective, made me more understanding and aware of other people's needs, more enthusiastic. Every day is a new day to do something for someone in need," he said. I had to agree.

Lions have always been interested in public speaking projects and in 1947, when I was district governor, there was talk of abandoning our annual contest. I fought pretty hard to keep it going and the following year assumed chairmanship for the district to make sure it was kept alive. We joined forces with the Canadian National Exhibition, a few years later so that the contest could be held there and this went on for some years.

Effective speaking projects have gone through many changes in the following years. I have donated a trophy for winning girls in District A5, and then one for winning boys a few years later. There is now one for French-speaking contestants as well. It is open for all young people from Grades 9 to 13 in Ontario and is a very high profile involvement.

Well, my lunch with Bryan Nixon was one of the highlights of the week. We certainly both enjoy talking about Lionism and that night, as I climbed into bed, I thought of a speech I had given to the Espanola Lions a short time before. The next morning I found a copy of it in my file at my Ontario Street Office.

I said, "Lions often pride themselves on reaching the top as a leading club in their District, without, perhaps, giving thought to how difficult it is to remain at the top. Some of the things it takes to stay there are: hard work, brains, the exercise of intelligence and the ongoing training of new Lions members. Those who entrust the work of organization to assistants after they reach the top are on their way out.

"I've seen some clubs which, because they became self-satisfied, lose the spark of initiative and determination.

"Lions should constantly be working to bring in new members, and to thoroughly assimilate them into Lionism. I cannot state too strongly that a club's continued position at the top depends on new members and the kind of future Lions, leaders help those new members to become.

"Lions should always work with a goal in mind and take every opportunity to serve their community and fellow human beings. That is the only way to keep a Lions Club at the top of their efficiency.

"Remember, it's harder to stay at the top, than it is to get there.

"If it is to be, it is up to me."

MONA DARLING

Thursday, March 26, 1992 ... A day I will never forget. Mona died today at North Bay Civic Hospital. We were married in Toronto in 1940 and although she has been very ill with cancer for some time now, I think we both thought that somehow, she would recover and outlive me.

Mona was always a fine artist and it was her artistic work for Meyers Studio in Toronto that first brought us together. She was beautiful with large, expressive eyes and we got along right from the start. Mona was always a very private person, and didn't follow me to Ottawa when I was first elected. She had so many friends – and of course our boys – in Burks Falls and had been president of the Burks Falls Art Club and a member for years. Mona was a great volunteer in Burks Falls and worked with the Canadian Cancer Society, the Red Cross and the Armour Ryerson and Burks Falls Agricultural Society. She had a keen interest in the flower section and won many prizes there and in the domestic science section. I have talked with many people who said her help was invaluable including members of the Good Companions Senior Citizens Club in Ottawa and later on she was a member of the Parliamentary Wives Association.

Mona loved to travel and was a great companion. She could pack her suitcase in two hours. She was a great shopper and I used to enjoy listening to her haggle with merchants in the bazaars overseas. She always came home with something different.

Mona was just 76.

March 28, Burks Falls ... Our church, Burks Falls United, was packed to the walls today. I was surprised to welcome Prime Minister Brian Mulroney and Mila, who came all the way from Ottawa for the funeral service. They had both known Mona through the years and she and Mila were very good friends. Jean Pauley who is our minister and former minister and friend, Bruce Thomson conducted the service. And Peter gave a fine eulogy for his mother. He said, "We have a church filled with loving family and friends, and the thoughts and prayers of the many who could not be with us today. She inherited her mother's Scottish eye for a bargain and to shop with mother was a lesson that the greatest economists and accountants would have praised. I am sure many a finance minister asked her for advice on forming the Canadian budgets.

"Accomplishments? Love, beyond the call of duty, always there, never expecting anything in return. Understanding. I hope in future to come close to her gift. Wealth, based on the above, limitless."

Mona was diagnosed with cancer of the lung about a year ago but kept it from me for a week or more.

Mona was a wonderful woman and enjoyed meeting Her Majesty the Queen, Prince Philip, prime ministers and presidents, Premiers – she always had something to say that brought a smile to their faces.

Mona was always interested and involved in the family business, taking messages, day or night, when I was away, she chose the color and design for our new offices in Burks Falls and our home on Ryerson Crescent and as I am color blind, she certainly had a lot to say in what I wore. On our fiftieth wedding anniversary, one of the members of Parliament asked the Speaker of the House, the Hon. John Fraser, if it would be possible to have Mona declared a Saint for having put up with me for fifty years.

Mona was a wonderful grandmother and I have taken some beautiful pictures of her with the grandchildren on her knee.

Mona faced every problem in a calm, humorous way. Her unique turn of phrase and comments were always unexpected and to the point. Our home was never dull and I always looked forward to getting home from Ottawa on weekends. Mona would have everything in good shape.

March 30, Ottawa ... I have received so many wonderful letters from friends and colleagues who knew Mona. This morning Ramon John Hnatyshyn wrote saying that he hoped I would find some measure of solace not only in the expressions of support from other family members and friends, but also from thoughts and prayers of the many people we know. It is appreciated from the busy governor general of Canada and means a lot to me. Bryan and Mila Mulroney also sent a letter saying that "as a mother, a wife and friend, Mona obviously had a good deal of love to share."

Sunday, December 20 … A beautiful memorial window designed by artist David Morgan was installed today on the east wall of the United Church in Burks Falls. It shows the nativity scene and is dedicated in loving memory of John M. and Kathleen Darling, and Mona B. Darling. My father and mother were very close to me, and dedicated members of the Burks Falls United Church when they lived here.

I think David Morgan has done a wonderful job of designing and making the window. He used to live in South River and now in Barrie and is noted far and wide for his talent as an artist.

It was a beautiful service with so many members of our family here including my brother Peter, who now lives in Owen Sound who read the scripture during the service. We all went back to our home for a visit and something to eat after the service. I think Mona would have enjoyed the gathering she was certainly there with us in spirit.

John and Peter will certainly miss their mother, they were all very close as Mona had so much of their upbringing to do when I was away. And the grandchildren particularly will miss her – Jason, Stephen and Patrick, Joyce and John's children and of course, Peter and Martina's daughter, Victoria. They all had a very special relationship with their grandmother.

Life will certainly take some adjusting without Mona. I spent more years living with this loving and lovely woman than I did apart from her. And as I keep running into people who knew her, I realize even more how much she was loved and admired by other people, from prime ministers to fellow artists. She certainly lived a good and kind and productive life and leaves behind an enviable legacy of children and friends.

THE ESSIAC REPORT

March 1988, Ottawa ... I received a letter today from Elaine Alexander who hosts a radio show in Vancouver. We had met when I did an interview with her. Her letter bowled me over. She said, "There is a case here of a 19-year-old man with two brain tumors who was deathly ill in November. His father called me, frantic for his son's future as he had heard my program regarding Essiac. I was able to obtain some quickly for him. He was given it right away and responded unbelievably well within a week or so."

Elaine said that the boy's parents kept in touch with her and that they had done a four-hour broadcast on her hot-line program, saying how well their son was doing. He had lost all paralysis, was eating and sleeping well, and was happy and encouraged by his progress.

Shortly after, the boy had a brain scan and the results were astounding. The second tumor was gone. The original tumor was greatly reduced; the tentacles that had reached into the brain tissue had receded completely. Their doctor was in a state of shock and didn't believe that Essiac would do a thing, and would not openly give credit to the Essiac treatment.

April 1988, Ottawa ... On my desk this morning were a stack of clippings from various newspapers outlining my ongoing battle with the government about Essiac. One article, written by John Lund of the North Bay Nugget was headed, "The Ojibwa wonder drug, can Essiac cure cancer?" And that, of course, is the question.

Mr. Lund stated in his story, "The purported cancer cure, a secret blend of herbs and passed on in 1922 by Ojibwa patients to nurse Rene Caisse – whose name spelled backwards, now graces the product – had been blended by Respirin Corporation of Willowdale, Ontario, until last December.

That's when Respirin President Dr. Matthew Dymond, former Ontario health minister and custodian of the Essiac recipe, retired. That left about one hundred patients, whose doctors had won "emergency" approval from Health and Welfare Canada to use the drug, without a supply.

The company's new president, 86-year-old David Fingard said that they would begin production again, but Dr. Hugh Wilson, who is overseeing blending of the infusion said that it is pretty much a stop-gap, that exactly how much would be produced was nobody's business. He said with anger, "If you want to block it, that's the way."

Although his facilities can make enough Essiac for a four-month supply, it is not nearly enough to meet the existing demand across Canada.

No new patients were being accepted until the company's medical board, an anonymous group of fourteen doctors and five university professors, had compiled the scientific data needed to have Essiac approved by drug regulators at Health and Welfare Canada. Well, this was good news for me. I have huge files detailing patients' pleas for Essiac. My own battle, with the government and medical officials to assure general availability of Essiac, especially in my home riding, is also well-known.

Frankly, I am frustrated at the stupidity of the medical people and the government in not endorsing something that will give cancer patients some hope and comfort. There is certainly enough documentation from patients who have used Essiac and have been helped, and in some instances cured, to warrant continuing to make it available. Nobody comes looking for Essiac in the early stages of their disease. Most have gone through the agony of the damned with radiation and chemotherapy. It's really heartrending to read the letters from people, many of them my constituents, pleading for this medication and they can't get it. One family wrote to me saying, "We don't know whether Essiac or a miracle, or both, have helped. All we know is it is not harmful and there are others who have been cured by it."

What more proof do you need than hearing from people who have been kept alive with Essiac? Perhaps you can't give Essiac full credit for remissions – it may be just the psychology of the thing. But if people have faith in a medication, it's amazing what it can do.

Many doctors and bureaucrats look down their noses as if admitting that some "damned Indian cure of roots and herbs" would work, was more than they could stomach. Dr. Agnes Klein, whose section oversees approvals of anti-cancer drugs for Health and Welfare says, they don't know what Essiac can do. One early 1980s study asked 150 physicians receiving Essiac for their patients to report their findings. "They reported for more than half of them, or eighty-six patients in all. Seventy-two said that they saw no benefit, or couldn't evaluate them, or their patient had died. Of the remainder, four had improved, five needed fewer pain killers and four remained stable." Health and Welfare concluded, "Essiac did not alter the progression of cancer in these cases and did not show any specific benefit, beyond a possible placebo effect in some cases."

"It's never, ever been scientifically proven as being of benefit," said Marilyn Wefsky of the Ontario Cancer Treatment and Research Foundation.

In 1938, the Kirby Law was passed by the federal government by a two-vote margin, limiting distribution of non-approved cancer remedies. This stopped Rene Caisse from producing Essiac, for which she charged no money to cancer victims. Her fight to continue her healing treatments against the obstinate refusal of the medical community to grant Essiac legitimacy has given fuel to a cynical mistrust of the Canadian cancer treatment machinery.

Although Rene Caisse has been dead for almost a decade, the controversy of what to do with her panacea-like recipe has been avoided by members of the medical profession and politicians. And now, in 1988, two women in Bracebridge are doing their level best to turn that avoidance into action by way of a petition that I am presenting to Health Minister Jake Epp. The petition states in no uncertain terms, "Legalize the sale of Essiac, allowing people the ease to obtain it over the counter. Ensure the supply of Essiac to all cancer patients requesting it."

Citing the constant refusal of the medical profession to even consider the wide distribution of Essiac, one man whose wife was a cancer victim said, "It's the almighty dollar. They don't want a treatment for cancer, they don't want to acknowledge a cure. Why shouldn't a person be able to take whatever drug they want to when they have cancer?" Now, to administer Essiac, the patient's physician must apply to the Ministry of Health and Welfare for permission to use the drug. This permission is granted only if all other treatments have failed and is usually only requested if the patient insists.

Rene Caisse of Bracebridge lived in my riding and I have been writing to the Department of National Health and Welfare since early in 1979, when Monique Begin was health minister. Medical doctors are strongly opposed to Essiac because they would hate to admit that such a simple remedy could cure, or at least lessen, the pain of cancer. Some doctors in my riding having seen and heard the results of Essiac have no problem in recommending it as an emergency treatment only. With such pressure, they are now granting automatic approval to anyone requesting treatment through their physician. Despite a petition with thousands upon thousands of names of people requesting the easy access of Essiac, nothing has happened.

The Bracebridge Examiner in February 1988 stated, "Essiac is nowhere." They suggested that the Respirin Company, which now has ceased production of Essiac, and has not gained government approval to market the product, should market it as "Rene Caisse's Herbal Tea," and sell it in Health Food stores. We wonder, they reported in their paper, why Respirin hasn't done this and we hope our local MP, Stan Darling, will continue in his efforts to have the product made available to the people of Canada. Rene Caisse went through hell initially, when presenting patients with her product. Despite agreements of its help to cancer patients, by such people as the government pathologist, the head doctor of the College of Physicians and Surgeons, Dr. Nobel, Rene Caisse would have medical policemen visit and threaten her with arrest if she continued to treat cancer patients.

"One person cannot fight that kind of opposition," she said. "I helped patients for over forty-five years, people who were cured and are still living and well, but now I must turn them away or be taken to court. If I give the medication out by self-administration, there is a seven year penitentiary sentence. It is my opinion that the Cancer Control Commission will continue to take the public's and our government's money, but will never admit there is a cure for cancer."

Rene said that she is still willing to turn over her formula to the medical association any time that they will assure her that it will be used to help suffering humanity and that it will not be shelved in favor of present-day methods of treatments only. After the hearing of her case before the Cancer Commission of Ontario, they know Essiac has merit.

In 1995, Mary McPherson, who is 80, and lives in Bracebridge, turned over the formula for Essiac, which had been entrusted to her, to the town of Bracebridge. Although it has not been available on the open market, it is available to those who know the formula. Mary McPherson has been a true believer because of the effect she saw when first her mother and then her husband were treated by Rene Caisse. Simple though it is, it has proven effective to countless cancer patients and contains burdock root, sheep sorrel herb, slippery elm bark and Turkish rhubarb root. The cost is $20 per bottle, with dosage from half an ounce a day up to a maximum of six ounces a day.

Burks Falls, August 1995 ... I have received a letter and phone call from a man in Dallas, Texas, looking for information about Essiac. This is only one of dozens such calls and letters I receive on a regular basis. Essiac has been ignored or berated by every official person I know despite absolutely no bad effects ever recorded and countless positive stories through the years.

It is a fight I have been very sorry to lose and one I hope to live to see won by the serious, patient, dedicated people who have worked through the years to have Essiac made available to everyone who needs it.

The Bracebridge Examiner has been running columns on Rene Caisse and Essiac and they are available by contacting Ted Britton at the Examiner.

WHAT WENT WRONG

Burks Falls, September 1995 ... Flying home from Fredericton, New Brunswick, this morning, I was thinking about the Natural Law Party's public seminars which I attended at the Lord Beaverbrook Hotel. I was certainly impressed with the quality of the party's leadership and the seminars which presented speakers from England, Ireland, and the United States.

I was asked recently what I thought went wrong with the PC Party in Brian Mulroney's time and it seemed to me that the "downfall," as one person put it recently, started a long time ago. Perhaps in 1984.

When Mulroney was first elected, he won 208 seats, the greatest majority in the history of Canadian politics. There were certainly high hopes for his government and leadership.

In 1984, he inherited a lot of unemployment – it was the beginning of a deep, worldwide recession and what Canadian citizens wanted were jobs, especially new jobs. They wanted them made available immediately and in great numbers. This was not happening and it didn't do any good to point out to the Canadians that ours wasn't the only country in the world feeling the recession. The new prime minister was being blamed for every job that was lost and for any jobs that were not created.

From the start, the media in all forms, news, broadcast, print, whatever, were anti-Mulroney. They hated his guts and I don't know why. He had portrayed himself as a self-assured prime minister who knew what was right for his country and that was that! He didn't have too much time for a negative press. That created friction which just grew and grew through the years. He rarely received credit for any of the good things he did.

In 1984, people voted for Mulroney as prime minister in overwhelming numbers because they wanted a change. If it wasn't Prime Minister John

Turner who they were sick of, it was the previous sixteen years with Pierre Trudeau. Turner had only been in office for about six weeks. The people decided they would make damned sure that a Liberal government would not be returned and this acted against Turner. Turner, in my opinion, was a very highly principled and decent politician who couldn't be blamed for the ills of his country. He was elected leader in June and the election was held in September.

I first remember Mulroney addressing groups of people at the 1976 convention. He was pretty young then, and I supported Joe Clark who I thought had more experience. In 1983, I supported John Crosbie at the nomination convention and only supported Mulroney on the last ballot. I voted for him instead of Clark because I felt Clark could not win.

After Mulroney's election, the honeymoon lasted a year or so. When the recession continued, Mulroney was blamed for all the ills of the country. Unemployment continued, but it was the same scenario all around the world. But our party just couldn't get that message across to the Canadian citizens. Both Mulroney and his government were certainly trying very hard indeed to do everything they could for Canada.

As the years went on, the biased press saw to it that Mulroney became more and more unpopular. They did a hatchet job on Mulroney that he couldn't overcome. The press also did a hatchet job on Joe Clark. When Trudeau was in power, they bowed and scraped to him, no matter what awful things he said about them. They certainly didn't think much of Trudeau but never ridiculed him the way they did Clark and Mulroney. Don't ask me why. Politics is a very unfair game as I found down through the years. When Joe Clark lost his luggage on a trip overseas, the press made the greatest thing in the world about a poor, little, immature politician, and yet Trudeau could have lost his luggage a dozen times and the press wouldn't have said anything.

There is no question in my mind, the press themselves did Mulroney in. This was disheartening to me because I grew to have a great deal of affection for him, and to respect him. The PC Caucus is one of the most fractious and hard to control of any of the political parties. Mulroney had perfect control over the caucus, which I think is a tremendous achievement. He gave some inspiring addresses there and I used to say that he should have these speeches recorded and made available to the public, with a few bleeps here and there. Mulroney swore like a trooper but he sure got his message across. He usually got a standing ovation from his unruly caucus.

In the political field, not many people are that successful. The fact that he ruled the country for nine years proves that he had tremendous ability.

Canada never had a higher standing internationally than when Brian Mulroney was the prime minister. In countries world wide, he was honored as a senior, successful statesman, who contributed a great deal to his country, as well as on the international scene. But in Canada it was another story. No one was ever lower in the polls than Mulroney and it was said that when the PC held their next convention, they could hold it in a telephone booth!

When I wrote to Prime Minister Mulroney in 1993 and stated in no uncertain terms that if some of his unpopular legislation was not changed or modified, the PC Party would be toast in the next election, his reaction was, the legislation our government has brought in is in the best interest of Canada, and that's that!

All prime ministers have governed in the same way. However, one of the few who does not adhere to those lines is our present prime minister, Jean Chretien. Look what he's promised!

He promised to get rid of the hated GST, and we are half way through his term of office, and nothing has happened. He promised to get rid of the free trade agreement, and nothing has been done there either. He promised to get rid of NAFTA, and all three things are still in place. Chretien swears he is still "going to change the GST," but he still must get the $16 to $18 billion from somewhere and it must be from a tax like that.

I don't know what would have happened if Mr. Mulroney had made the same kinds of promises that Chretien made to the people of Canada, but initially, they just didn't like his style. To the press and some of the voters, Mulroney seemed too perfect, too sure of himself. Chretien looks like the average and ordinary guy from Shawinigan. But what has he done, these last two years?

These are the things that make politics so frustrating.

I know that years from now, when history is being recounted, Mulroney will be proven to be a much better prime minister than some of the others. University professors who have done studies about this, based on actual facts have proved that the Mulroney government has produced a great deal of good legislation.

Another problem was Mila Mulroney. She is so beautiful and talented. The press and the voters were not ready to accept her as their "queen," or another Jackie Kennedy. There was a great deal of envy and jealousy.

I thought that Mulroney would continue on to the next election, and run against Chretien, but when he announced his retirement I just about fell over. However, I don't think he would have won the election if he had stayed on and run. So many people said to me, "Stan, you should have stayed on in 1993 and run," but I know I made the right decision to not run again.

But it makes me mad when I think that the press and the negative attitude and the jealousy of so many people brought down the government. And, of course, the fact that the economy hadn't rebounded enough to suit the voters. Well, it hadn't rebounded anywhere in the world. In the eyes of the Canadians, the whole rest of the world was enjoying the greatest prosperity ever. And Canada was the one sink hole. Well, that was wrong.

In my estimation, Prime Minister Mulroney had the courage of his convictions. He decided early into his term of office that he could either be a good guy, and do nothing much, or he could bring in legislation which would in the long run, put Canada's economy in good shape. I've heard that he was responsible for every ill Canada ever had, including the recession, unemployment, the free trade tangle, and the unpopular GST. Jobs were lost because of the GST legislation, but many more jobs were created because of it.

Our trade with the U.S. in 1993 was $200 billion a year in two-way trade. Canada had a surplus. Many industries have enlarged their capacities because of the free trade agreements. NAFTA will provide Canada with a market of about 350 million people, the greatest market in the world.

The Canadian Tire chain of stores across Canada said that 90 per cent or more of the goods they sold last year were cheaper than when the "hidden" manufacturers' sales tax was in effect. That's a fact that does not seem to have sunk in to Canadian minds.

When I retired from my Parry Sound/Muskoka riding, there were some good people in the race for my seat. Terry Clark of Huntsville was one and others were Don Smith, a publisher of local newspapers, and Dave Heatherington, a municipal councillor in Bracebridge. Then John Stuthers of Dunchurch, George Steveron, the reeve of Humphrey Township and Jim Cullem of Novar. In the long-run, Terry Clark, who had been the mayor of Huntsville, won the nomination and he asked for my help. I said that he was probably better off on his own, that I might be blamed for the unpopular things done by the Mulroney government. I felt that Terry might be tied in with me as I had supported Mulroney. However, Terry still wanted my help and I attended a great many events throughout the riding and supported him, financially and politically as best I could. He had many friends helping him, more than I ever had, in past elections. I did pretty well everything on my own, with the help of my campaign managers, and official agent Dr. Bill Gerhart.

Terry had a lot of competition from Liberal Andy Mitchell, a former bank manager, and Jim Newman, Reform Party, a real estate broker and the NDP candidate Shrily Davy. In my wildest dreams, I never figured that Terry would finish any worse than second place but when the final figures came in on election night, I was worried that he wouldn't even get the required 15 per cent of votes. However, in the long run, he did qualify and had his $1,000 deposit returned and some of his election expenditures paid for as well.

Ottawa, June 1993 ... Some party faithfuls were having lunch in the dining room today and I told them in no uncertain terms that the PC Party was on very dangerous grounds because we had alienated so many single interest groups. As a result, I said, jokingly, "In all probability, the only people we will have supporting us in the future will be close friends and family members." Well, this was the outcome, unfortunately.

I can think of many single interest groups who have only one thought in mind: their particular interest. I think of sportsmen and members of the National Rifle Association, and other gun clubs. There is no doubt in my mind that probably 90 per cent of them, or more, voted against our party because of Bill C-17.

We also had to contend with the unpopular abortion issue, and again a great many were against the government because it was not strict enough. On the other side, we lost votes because the bill was too strict, so we couldn't win either side. There were also hundreds of fundamentalists and quite religious groups, and their views were often expressed through the news media.

No government, however clever and well-meaning, can call all the shots and be right all the time, at least if it is not to be an overly cautious government; a government that could not accomplish anything in the way of legislation or reform, or what they firmly believe they were elected into power to do for the good of their country.

I frequently get mad at people who seem to believe that governments bring in so-called unpopular legislation as a whim. I have often said to my constituents, "You voted that man or woman into power. How come you believed in him then, and you don't believe in him now?"

Canada is, thank heavens, a democracy. Every citizen in the country has the right to vote and express an opinion and yell at his politician if he wants to. Lord knows, I got yelled at often enough in the twenty-one years I was in the House.

I have taken every opportunity during the years I was representing Parry Sound/Muskoka riding, here in Canada and in countries around the world, to say that we live in the most wonderful country in the world. Canadian citizens are the most fortunate people in the world. I think, in years to come, it will be proved in no uncertain terms that Brian Mulroney was one of the best prime ministers Canada has ever known.

They were certainly wonderful years for me.

THE LAST WORD

Stan Darling is an exceptional individual who serves Canadians with intense duty and love of country. His environmental accomplishments, both nationally and internationally, are renowned. In speeches, with his colourful language and forceful delivery, he expresses his strong opinions flavored with that unique sense of humor. What a joy and honor to know Stan.

Hon. Pauline Browes, PC

Stan Darling's greatness can be measured by his frankness, candor, political courage, dedication to the public interest and a love for life.

May he live 150 years!

Hon. Charles Caccia, PC, MP

Stan once told me, not unproudly, that he was older than the Peace Tower. He never shone as a great Ottawa luminary, but he does have a lasting quality. I carry an enduring image of Stan Darling scampering through the back halls of Parliament like a gnome, me puffing along behind and the commissionaire chuckling at the spectacle. It would be fitting if the Hill's artisans could carve a gargoyle in his likeness for the Tower – spitting down rain on the statue of Mackenzie King, perhaps.

John Challis, features editor
Muskoka Publications Group

One of the unique and special privileges of my parliamentary career was to have served with Stan Darling. People are elected as Members of Parliament for a variety of reasons but few excel in being servant of the people to the degree that Stan exemplified in his years on Parliament Hill.

Stan projected a total commitment to the people of Burks Falls and Parry Sound/Muskoka. He was fearless champion of the ordinary Canadian and his first loyalty was to his constituents and constituency. His was a selfless ambition and he gained a degree of respect from Parliamentarians, in all parties, on all sides of the House, that is accorded to few. His deep dedication to his fellow man, his commitment to God and his desire to give of himself made it a quality feeling to have him as a friend. Stan set a shining example for others who desired to be outstanding members of Parliament. Stan's standard was the highest one could possibly achieve and I count myself most fortunate to be able to say he was a friend of mine.

Hon. Robert Coates, PC, QC

Stan, is what the Irish call "a Darling man" and his political diary will be daring and diverting but not diplomatic! Stan was the backbone and the soundbone of our caucus and a marvellous supporter of mine in 1983. As Mae West said, "too much of a good thing can be wonderful" and Stan is.

Warmest best wishes from John and Jane Crosbie

"I'm Stan Darling's grandson." These words have been spoken by each of us hundreds of times. The responses following that introduction have helped us understand why our grandfather is so respected. He taught us to stand up for ourselves and to always speak what we believed in.

Patrick, Stephen and Jason Darling, Burks Falls

Father started his own insurance business almost sixty years ago, a little later branching into real estate. Today his hard work and dedication are still very evident, and we can count five family members carrying on his tradition. This was also the prime reason for his success in an over fifty-year political career. Together with mother they provided us with a warn and meaningful family life and we are all very proud of him.

Peter and John Darling, Burks Falls

No one can ever say that Stan was uncertain about his position on controversial national issues. He never wavered fighting for what he believed in. Stan and I were involved in the issues of conscience and law and order i.e.: capital punishment, extradition, voluntary metric and abortion. Stan fought for his issues and as a result his admirers in Canada and throughout the world were many. I thoroughly enjoyed my association with my good friend Stan.

Bill Domm

Shy and retiring are two words that I would not use to describe Stan Darling. Stan has dedicated his entire life to public service. As Stan's provincial colleague, I have admired his well deserved reputation as the best constituency representative in government, Stan has also made his mark on the international stage, culminating in the historic acid rain accord between Canada and the United States. Stan Darling has justly earned the distinction of being a truly great Canadian. Thank you Stan for your advice, guidance and friendship over the years.

Best wishes always,
Ernie Eves

Stan joined the Burks Falls Lions Club a year after its inauguration and served as president and eventually as District Governor. He was a leader in all our club's activities, At our annual Harness Races he was the announcer in the judges stand. I vividly remember him shouting, as only Stan can shout to people crossing the track, "Get the hell off the track!"

While unavoidably absent during his years in Parliament, he is again one of the spark plugs of our club.

Harvey Fowler, Charter Member of the
Burks Falls Lions Club.

Stan and I were colleagues in the House of Commons for years and even shared an apartment, so I can say from experience that his lion-like exterior is surpassed by a pussycat tenderness that lies within this great man, he stands as a shining example of an MP who truly served the people.

Hon. Len Gustafson,
Senator

As a parliamentary colleague for over nineteen years, Stan taught me by example how to drive back and forth to my constituency each week, attend Caucus and other meetings punctually, and participate in the Wednesday morning Parliamentary Prayer Breakfasts regularly. However, I could not learn his version of the Queen's English!

Bruce Halliday, MD

I have known more than 1,000 MPs in public life and Stan Darling is unique among them – always upbeat, positive and, above all, frank. He has been a wonderful friend.

Hon. Paul T. Hellyer, PC

To know Stan Darling is to love him. As a member of parliament, the respect and affection for Stan Darling was shared on all sides of the House of Commons. With his energy, compassion, intelligence and dedication, working with Stan Darling was always a pleasure.

The Rt. Hon. Ramon John Hnatyshyn, PC, CC, CMM, CD, QC

Some people decry our legal system, believing it to produce "old fogies": party hacks who compliantly vote the way their party tells them to. Stan Darling certainly proved them wrong: fiercely independent, constantly injecting his constituents views into every debate, and always displaying more energy, and more argument, than most Members half his age. Stan was a great MP.

Hon. Allan F. Lawrence, PC, QC

If you are looking for a person to head up the Stan Darling Fan Club here in Ottawa – look no further. I am volunteering. Stan Darling epitomizes all that a Member of Parliament should be. He is a man of honor, integrity, good humor and worked tirelessly on behalf of his constituents, his country and his party. His commitment to environmental issues, particularly acid rain, quite properly put him on the international stage.

Some of you may know that Mr. Darling calls me the "dragon lady" and it goes back to the days when I was in charge of the Leader's schedule. He would plaintively ask "Do I have to genuflect to the dragon lady to get the Leader to my riding?" Once, when we encountered each other in a local department store he went on bended knee to the amazement and questioning glances of fellow shoppers!

I would respond to him, by saying, "Mr. Darling, if you need the Leader to get elected we're all in trouble!" In any event, we are in a mutual admiration society and I consider it a great honor to know Stan Darling and call him a friend.

Senator Marjory LeBreton

It is unusual get the last word on Stan and therefore I leapt at the opportunity. Friend and foe marvelled at his energy and efforts on behalf of his constituents, his country and issues such as acid rain. When he thought that the rest of us were misguided or not pulling our weight he certainly let us know in his patented "shy and retiring" manner. Make no doubt about it Stan was always full value.

Hon. Doug Lewis, FCA, QC, PC

Acerbic and witty, bombastic and lovable – with a stentorian voice that could dominate the chamber or the caucus, and a heart as expansive as the throbbing heart of Canada. Stan Darling is all of these things to me, and more.

Hon. Flora MacDonald, PC

Stan Darling epitomizes all of the finer qualities we expect from our politicians. For well over half a century he has worked tirelessly for his constituents at every level where he represented them. No problem was too small and every individual was important.

Equally important, Stan has never failed to speak out when he believed it to be important, in his unique, modest and understated fashion on issues of local, national and international significance.

Stan Darling: an outstanding Canadian and I am proud to be his friend.

Hugh Mackenzie, Huntsville

Someone has said that there are two types of people: those who enter a room and say "Here I am" and those who enter a room and say "There you are." Stan Darling is the only person I know who "explodes" into a room expressing both!

It is that dynamism that has made Stan a pleasure to know and work with over the past half century.

Norm Mason, former reeve of Burks Falls (1972-84)

When I think of Stan Darling, I think of a crusty character with a heart of gold and the tenacity of pit bull. Thanks to Stan and people like him that our Nova Scotian rivers are again clean and rich with trout and salmon.

Hon. Peter L. McCreath, PC
Hubbards, Nova Scotia

Stan was "my neighbor" throughout my time in government: his office was near mine in the West Block. As an experienced MP, he was always supportive and helpful and I frequently stopped by for a chat or for some friendly advice. I always admired (and still do!) Stan's pioneering commitment to the environment, as well as his kindliness and humor.

Hon. Barbara J. McDougall

During his very lengthy career, Stan Darling was a consummate politician and an exemplary parliamentarian who conducted himself with impeccability and the purest of intent, always the champion of the people.

He carries with him my highest regard as a true statesman and friend.

Andy Mitchell, Member of Parliament
Parry Sound/Muskoka

What better way to celebrate one's health and well being than to write a book, not just any book, a book about oneself. We have just arrived home from Windsor where we took part in the Multiple District A Ontario-Quebec, Lions Club Convention to arrive just in time to have you, my close friend, and truly a man with a lion's heart, kick off your own personal book. It really is a bonus. To top it off, I understand that the profits from sales of the book wil go to Lions' projects and therefore, back to the communitites you have served.

Stan, you represent Lionism, through and through. You are a doer, and do not sit back and wait for the seed to grow. You nurture it, weed it, water it and mother it, so that it will indeed grow more quickly. For anyone who has ever been on the nuruting end of your commitment, thay will know what I mean. We know you will not rest, nor will you let us rest until we have completed whatever it was we promised you has been completed.

I have alsways thought of you, Stan, as "A Man for All Seasons!" The politician, the reeve of all the people. Stan the Member of Parliament, never too busy to hear our proplems, and to offer a solution, the solution you offer may not have been the one we wanted to hear. But if we asked you for an answer, that's what what we received – an answer.

You are, Stan the Lion, because you truly care about people; Stan the businessman, successful because you made it happen; and Stan the family man. The only problem, Stan, is that the world is your family, and your heart is even bigger than you are. I'm reminded of the story of the man who was not too tall, as fame and fortune mark a man, but he was taller because he stooped over to help a small child. Stan, you *are* that man!

Stan, knowing you as I do, you have only just begun! Keep it up, Stan, prick our social consciences another time, and thanks Stan, for being!

Bill Moody, international director
Lions Club International

From my perspective, Stan Darling represented the ideal Member of Parliament – strong-willed, outspoken, close to his voters and highly principled. He was also warm-hearted and decent, entertaining and loyal.

Stan sat in the front row in Caucus, to my right. He was always on time, up to date on all legislation and always ready to level a blast at those MPs who were either tardy or less dedicated than he thought appropriate!

Stan loved his riding and it seemed everyone of his voters, and in spite of their political allegiance, he fought for them daily and achieved much.

His greatest national achievement was probably the Acid Rain Treaty I signed with President Bush. I believe it never would have happened without Stan Darling's leadership, prodding and consistency over many years.

Stan became a close friend and valued advisor. I will always remember him with affection and admiration – and a chuckle for many of the delightful things he said and did on behalf of his party and country.

Rt. Hon. Brian Mulroney

My forty-year friendship with Stan Darling has been based on trust, admiration and interest. He has always been interested in my business and I have been overwhelmed by what Stan has accomplished in his lifetime.

It has been a pleasure and a privilege to help Stan select the clothes that have taken him around the world on behalf of his government and I wish him many more happy travels in years to come.

Lou Myles

Few Canadians are more deserving of having their remarkable lives brought to the public's attention than you. Your lifelong service to our dear country and your rare gift of being able to identify and support the just and worthy causes have established you as a great patriot and true friend of Natural Law. We are certain that your story of uncommon dedication and achievement will be the source of great inspiration for all those who will have the good fortune to read it.

Dr. Neil Paterson
Party Leader – Natural Law Party of Canada

Stan is the bedrock upon which our House of Commons traditions have been founded. He is a true servant of the people and defender of our delicate environment.

Hon. Sinclair M. Stevens, PC, QC, LLB, BA

Stan was a great politician. He said it like it was. You never were in any doubt about his position on any issue. He also had a great sense of humor. Once, before one of my budgets, Stan asked to have his picture taken with me for use in his "householder." He watched as a number of smiling MPs had theirs taken. Then he stepped up and, just as the picture was to be taken, pulled his jacket over his head!

Hon. Michael Wilson, PC

PRINTED IN CANADA